RUSSIA, RITUAL, AND REFORM

RUSSIA, RITUAL, AND REFORM

The Liturgical Reforms of Nikon
In the 17th Century

by

Paul Meyendorff

ST VLADIMIR'S SEMINARY PRESS
CRESTWOOD, NY 10707–1699
1991

Library of Congress Cataloging-in-Publication Data

Meyendorff, Paul
    Russia, ritual, and reform: the liturgical reforms of Nikon in the 17th century / by Paul Meyendorff.
        p.   cm.
    Includes bibliographical references and index.
    ISBN0-88141-090-X
    1. Nikon, Patriarch of Moscow and of Russia, 1605-1681—Contributions in liturgical reform. 2. Russkaia pravoslavnaia tserkov'—Liturgy—History—17th century. 3. Orthodox Eastern Church—Liturgy—History—17th century. 4. Soviet Union—Church history—17th century. 5. Orthodox Eastern Church. Euchologion. 6. Orthodox Eastern Church. Sluzhebnik. I. Title
BX375.E75M48   1991
264'.01947--dc20.   91-36886
                                                                                 CIP

RUSSIA, RITUAL, AND REFORM

COPYRIGHT © 1987

by

Paul Meyendorff

ISBN 0–88141–090–X

PRINTED IN THE UNITED STATES OF AMERICA

To the memory of
Father Alexander Schmemann
(1921–1983)

Contents

Part I
The Events and Personages of the Reform

Part II
The Contents of the Reform

Acknowledgements

I wish to express my gratitude to all the people and organizations who have enabled me to complete this project. My thanks go to the graduate theology faculty and administration of the University of Notre Dame. They oversaw my training and ensured that I was given adequate support to accomplish the work. I am also grateful to have been awarded a Zahm Research Travel Grant in 1983-1984, which helped to finance research at the Library of the Pontifical Oriental Institute in Rome. My thanks also go to the Vatican's Secretariat for Promoting Christian Unity, which generously subsidized my two extended stays in Rome, as well as to the administration of the Pontifical Russian College, who provided me with comfortable quarters and a warm welcome during these sojourns. Particular thanks are also due to Professor Boris L'vovich Fonkich of the Moscow University, who provided invaluable assistance in locating materials not accessible in the West.

I wish also to express my infinite thanks to Professor Robert F. Taft, S.J., of the Pontifical Oriental Institute and the University of Notre Dame. Father Taft accepted to oversee this project, provided much-needed input and assistance, and spent many hours poring through my drafts and revisions. He never lacked for a word of encouragement, was always ready to assist in locating references, and even provided access to his personal notes and manuscripts of forthcoming publications. I am fortunate to have had him as my teacher and honored to have him as a friend.

Finally, I owe a great debt also to Father Alexander Schmemann, former Dean and Professor of Liturgy at St Vladimir's Orthodox Theological Seminary. He provided great encouragement at the initial phase of my studies, and it was he who first suggested undertaking a study of the Nikonian reform. To him this work is dedicated. May his memory be eternal!

Abbreviations

AN	Akademiia Nauk
BAS	Byzantine Liturgy of St Basil
BMST	Biblioteka Moskovskoi Sinodal'noi Tipografii
BT	*Bogoslovskie Trudy*
BV	*Bogoslovskii Vestnik*
Byz	*Byzantion*
ChOIDR	*Chteniia v Imperatorskom Obshchestve Istorii i Drevnostei Rossiiskikh*
ChOLDP	*Chtenie v Obshchestve Liubitelei Dukhovnago Prosveshcheniia*
CHR	Byzantine Liturgy of St John Chrysostom
DACL	*Dictionnaire d'Archéologie Chrétienne et de Liturgie*
DOP	*Dumbarton Oaks Papers*
EL	*Ephemerides Liturgicae*
GBL	Gosudarstvennaia Biblioteka SSSR imeni V. I. Lenina (Moscow)
GPB	Gosudarstvennaia Publichnaia Biblioteka imeni Saltykova-Shchedrina (Leningrad)
JAS	Liturgy of St James
KhCht	*Khristiianskoe Chtenie*
KS	*Kievskaia Starina*
OCA	*Orientalia Christiana Analecta*
OCP	*Orientalia Christiana Periodica*
PG	Migne, *Patrologia Graeca*
PO	*Patrologia Orientalis*
POC	*Proche-Orient Chrétien*
PRES	Byzantine Liturgy of the Presanctified
Prib	*Pribavleniia k Izdaniiu Tvorenii Sviatykh Ottsev*
PrOb	*Pravoslavnoe Obozrenie*
PrSob	*Pravoslavnyi Sobesednik*
RBS	*Russkii Biograficheskii Slovar'*
REB	*Revue des Études Byzantines*
SVTQ	*St Vladimir's Theological Quarterly*
TKDA	*Trudy Kievskoi Dukhovnoi Akademii*
TODRL	*Trudy Otdela Drevnerusskoi Literatury Instituta Russkoi Literatury (Pushkinskago Doma) Akademii Nauk SSSR*
TsGADA	Tsentral'nyi Gosudarstvennyi Arkhiv Drevnikh Aktov (Moscow)
ZhMNP	*Zhurnal Ministerstva Narodnago Prosveshcheniia*

Chronological List of Liturgical Editions Consulted With Name of Library Where Located[1]

Greek

Doucas, *editio princeps* (Rome, 1526) (Pontifical Oriental Institute)
Euchologion (Venice, 1570) (Pontifical Oriental Institute)
*Euchologion (Venice, 1602)[2] (TsGADA, BMST #3092)
Euchologion (Venice, 1638) (=GOAR)

Slavic

*Sluzhebnik (Vilna, 1583) (GBP)
Sluzhebnik (Moscow, 1602) (GBP)
Sluzhebnik (Striatin, 1604) (Pontifical Oriental Institute)
*Sluzhebnik (Kiev, 1620) (GBP)
Sluzhebnik (Kiev, 1629) (Pontifical Oriental Institute)
Sluzhebnik (Kiev, 1639) (Pontifical Oriental Institute)
Sluzhebnik (Moscow, 1646) (Pontifical Oriental Institute)
Trebnik (Kiev, 1646) (Pontifical Oriental Institute)
Sluzhebnik (Moscow, 1652) (Pontifical Oriental Institute)
Sluzhebnik (Moscow, 1655) (=Nikon's first edition) (GBL)
Sluzhebnik (Moscow, 1656) (=Nikon's second edition) (GBL)
Sluzhebnik (Moscow, May 5, 1657) (=Nikon's third edition) (GBL)
Sluzhebnik (Moscow, Dec. 10, 1657) (=Nikon's fourth edition) (GBL)
Sluzhebnik (Moscow, May 15, 1658) (=Nikon's fifth edition) (GBL)
Sluzhebnik (Moscow, July 1, 1658) (=Nikon's sixth edition) (GBL)
Sluzhebnik (Moscow, 1667) (GBL)

---

1   In the following entries, * means that the edition, not accessible to me, is cited from secondary sources. All other editions were read in the original or in microform.
2   This is the copy actually used by the Nikonian editors.

Selected Bibliography

(Works cited in abbreviated form are marked with an asterisk)

AKTY ARKHEOGRAFICHESKOI EKSPEDITSII = Akty, sobrannye v bibliotekakh i arkhivakh rossiiskoi imperii Arkheograficheskoi Ekspeditsii Imperatorskoi Akademii Nauk (1294-1700), 4 vols. (St Petersburg, 1836).

Akty Moskovskago gosudarstva izd. Imperatorskoi Akademieiu Nauk, 1571-1664, 3 vols. (St Petersburg, 1890-1901).

AKTY IUZHNOI I ZAPADNOI ROSSII = Akty, otnosiashchiesia k istorii iuzhnoi i zapadnoi Rossii, sobrannye i izdannye Arkheograficheskoiu Kommissieiu, 15 vols. (St Petersburg, 1863-1892).

ALMAZOV = Almazov, A., Tainaia ispoved' v pravoslavnoi vostochnoi tserkvi, 3 vols. (Odessa, 1894).

"Arsenii Grek pri patriarkhe Nikone," *PrSob* 1858(3) 328-353.

Avvacum, La vie de l'archiprêtre Avvacum écrite par lui-même, traduit avec des notes par P. Pascal (Paris, 1939).

Avvakum, The Life Written by Himself (Ann Arbor: Michigan Slavic Publications, 1979).

Avvakum, Zhitie i dr. ego sochineniia s komment. N.K. Gudziia (Moscow, 1955).

Bartenev, P., Sobranie pisem tsaria Alekseia Mikhailovicha (Moscow, 1856).

Belokurov, S., Adam Olearii o greko-latinskoi shkole Arseniia greka v Moskve v XVII st. (Moscow, 1888).

BELOKUROV, ARSENII SUKHANOV = Belokurov, S., Arsenii Sukhanov, ChOIDR 1891(1) pt. 3, i-iv, 1-328; 1891(2) pt. 4, 329-440, I-CLX; 1894(2) pt. 1, i-lxxxvi, 1-283.

Belokurov, S., ed., Deianie Moskovskago Tserkovnago sobora 1649 goda, ChOIDR 1894(4) pt. 3, 29-52.

Belokurov, S., Opisi moskovskago pechatnago dvora v 1649 g., ChOIDR 1887(4) pt. 4, 1-32.

Belokurov, S., ed. Silvestr Medvedeva izvestie istinnoe pravoslavnym i pokazanie svetloe o novopravlenii knizhnom i prochem, ChOIDR 1885(4) pt. 2, i-xli, 1-87.

Belokurov, S., "Sobranie patr. Nikonom knig s vostoka," KhCht 1882(2) 444-494.

Berkh, V., Tsarstvovanie tsaria Alekseia Mikhailovicha (St Petersburg, 1831).

Bornert, René, Les Commentaires byzantins de la divine liturgie du viie au xve siècle (=Archives de l'Orient chrétien, 9) (Paris: Institut français d'études byzantines, 1966).

15

*BRIGHTMAN = Brightman, F.E. *Liturgies Eastern and Western* (Oxford: Clarendon Press, 1896).

Cherniavskii, M., "The Old Believers and the New Religion," *Slavic Review* 25 (1966) 1-39.

*CHERNIAVSKII, *OB IZMENENIIAKH* = [Cherniavskii], Varlaam, *Ob izmeneniiakh v chine liturgii Ioanna Zlatoustago, Vasiliia Velikago i Grigoriia Dvoeslova, ukazannykh v pomorskikh otvetakh i meche dukhovnom* (Kishinev, 1860).

*DEIANIE 1649 = See Belokurov, S., ed. *Deianie Moskovskago Tserkovnago sobora 1649 goda.*

*DEIANIE 1654 = Subbotin, N.I., ed., *Deianie moskovskago sobora byvshago v tsarskikh palatakh v leto ot sozdaniia mira 7162, ot voploshcheniia zhe Bozhiia Slova 1654* (Moscow, 1873).

**DEIANIIA 1666-1667* = Subbotin, N.I., ed. *Deianiia moskovskago sobora 1666-1667 gg.* (Moscow, 18932) (rep: Westmead, England: Gregg Intl., 1969).

*DELO = *Delo o patriarkhe Nikone* (St Petersburg, 1897) (rep: Westmead, England: Gregg Intl., 1972).

Dmitrievskii, A.A., *Bogosluzhenie v russkoi tserkvi za pervye piat' vekov, PrSob* 1882(1) 138-166, 252-296; 1882(2) 346-373; 1882(3) 149-167, 372-394; 1883(2) 345-374; 1883(3) 198-229, 470-485.

*DMITRIEVSKII, *BOGOSLUZHENIE V XVI VEKE* = Dmitrievskii, A.A., *Bogosluzhenie v russkoi tserkvi v XVI veke* (Kazan, 1884).

*DMITRIEVSKII, *OPISANIE* = Dmitrievskii, A.A., *Opisanie liturgicheskikh rukopisei khraniashchikhsia v bibliotekakh pravoslavnago vostoka,* vol. 1, *Typika* (Kiev, 1895), vol. 2, *Euchologia* (Kiev, 1901), vol. 3, *Typika* (Petrograd, 1917).

Dmitrievskii, A.A., "Otzyv o sochinenii I. Mansvetova 'Tserkovnyi ustav (tipikon), ego obrazovanie i sud'ba v grecheskoi i russkoi tserkvakh'," *KhCht* 1888(3) 480-576.

*DMITRIEVSKII, *OTZYV ORLOVA* = Dmitrievskii, A.A., "Otzyv o sochinenii M.I. Orlova 'Liturgiia sv. Vasiliia Velikago'," *Sbornik otchetov o premiiakh i nagradakh v Imp. Akademii Nauk za 1909,* IV (St Petersburg, 1911), pp. 176-347.

Dopolnenie k Aktam Istoricheskim, vols. 3-4 (St Petersburg, 1848-1857).

*Doucas, *editio princeps* = Doucas, D., Αἱ θεῖαι λειτουργεῖαι τοῦ ἁγίου Ἰωάννου τοῦ Χρυσοστόμου, Βασιλείου τοῦ Μεγάλου, καὶ ἡ τῶν Προηγιασμένων (Rome, 1526).

Drevniaia rossiiskaia vivliofika, 20 vols., 2nd edition (St Petersburg, 1788-1791).

Drower, E.S., *Water into Wine, a Study of Ritual Idiom in the Middle East* (London: John Murray, 1956).

Duchesne, E., ed., *Le Stoglav ou les cent chapitres* (=Bibliothèque de l'Institut français de Petrograd, V) (Paris, 1920).

*FELMY = Felmy, K.C., *Die Deutung der göttlichen Liturgie in der russischen Theologie* (= Arbeiten z. Kirchengeschichte 54) (Berlin, New York: De Gruyter, 1984).

*FILARET, *OPYT SLICHENIIA* = [Hieromonk] Filaret, *Opyt slicheniia tserkovnykh chinoposledovanii po izlozheniiu tserkovno-bogosluzhebnykh knig moskovskoi pechati, izdannykh pervymi piat'iu rossiiskimi patriarkhami* (Moscow, 1875).

*FLOROVSKII = Florovskii, G., *Puti russkogo bogosloviia* (Paris: YMCA Press, 1981^2).

*FONKICH = Fonkich, B.L., *Grechesko-russkie kulturnye sviazi v XV-XVIIvv.* (Moscow: "Nauka," 1977).

Fuhrmann, Joseph T., *Tsar Alexis: His Reign and His Russia* (Gulf Breeze, FL: Academic Intl. Press, 1981).

Galavaris, G., *Bread and the Liturgy, the Symbolism of Early Christian and Byzantine Bread Stamps* (Madison, Milwaukee, and London: Univ. of Wisconsin Press, 1970). (Cf. review by R. Taft in *OCP* 40 (1974) 209-210.)

Gezen, A., *Istoriia slavianskago perevoda simvolov very* (St Petersburg: AN, 1884).

*GIBBENET = Gibbenet, N., *Istoricheskoe issledovanie dela patriarkha Nikona,* 2 vols. (St Petersburg, 1881-1884).

*GOAR = Goar, J., *Euchologion sive Rituale Graecorum,* 2nd edition (Venice, 1730).

*GOLUBINSKII = Golubinskii, E.E., *K nashei polemike s staroobriadtsami,* ChOIDR 1905(3) pt. 3, i-vi, 1-260.

Gorchakov, M. *Monastyrskii Prikaz (1649-1725g.)* (St Petersburg, 1868).

Gorchakov, M. *O zemel'nykh vladeniiakh vserossiiskikh mitropolitov, patriarkhov, i sv. sinoda* (988-1738gg.) (St Petersburg, 1871).

*GORSKII-NEVOSTRUEV = Gorskii, A., and Nevostruev, K., eds., *Opisanie slavian-skikh rukopisei Moskovskoi Sinodal'noi Biblioteki,* 2 vols. (Moscow, 1855-1917).

[Gumilevskii], Filaret, *Obzor dukhovnoi literatury* (St Petersburg, 1884^3).

*HUCULAK = Huculak, L.D., *The Divine Liturgy of St John Chrysostom in the Kievan Metropolitan Province during the Period of Union with Rome (1596-1805)* (unpublished doctoral dissertation at the Pontifical Oriental Institute, Rome, 1985).

*IZZO = Izzo, J., *The Antimension in the Liturgical and Canonical Tradition of the Byzantine and Latin Churches* (Rome: Pont. Athenaeum Antonianum, 1975).

Kapterev, N.F., "Bor'ba protopopa Ioanna Neronova s patriarkhom Nikonom," *BV* 1909(1) 196-233.

*KAPTEREV, *ISPRAVLENIE KNIG* = Kapterev, N.F., "Ispravlenie tserkovno-bogosluzhebnykh knig pri patriarkhe Nikone," *BV* 1908(3) 538-559; 1909(1) 24-44.

*KAPTEREV, *KHARAKTER OTNOSHENII* = Kapterev, N.F., *Kharakter otnoshenii Rossii k pravoslavnomu vostoku v XVI i XVII stoletiiakh* (Sergiev Posad, 1914^2) (=*Slavistic Printings and Reprintings* 107) (The Hague, Paris: Mouton, 1968).

Kapterev, N.F., "Kritika tserkovnoi reformy Nikona v literaturnykh proizvedeniiakh eia pervykh protivnikov," *BV* 1909(3) 1-23, 65-212.

*KAPTEREV, *NIKON I ALEKSEI* = Kapterev, N.F., *Patriarkh Nikon i tsar' Aleksei Mikhailovich*, 2 vols. (Sergiev Posad, 1909-1912).

*KAPTEREV, *NIKON I EGO PROTOVNIKI* = Kapterev, N.F., *Patriarkh Nikon i ego protivniki* (Sergiev Posad, 1913²).

Kapterev, N.F., "O greko-latinskikh shkolakh v Moskve v XVII v. do otkrytiia Slaviano-greko-latinskoi Akademii," *Prib* 44 (1889) 588-671.

Kapterev, N.F., "O sochinenii protiv raskola iverskago arkhimandrita greka Dionisiia, napisannom do sobora 1667 goda," *PrOb* 1888(2), appendix, 1-31.

*KAPTEREV, *OSTAVLENIE* = Kapterev, N.F., "Ostavlenie Nikonom patriarshei kafedry," *BV* 1909(2) 353-390.

Kapterev, N.F., *Patriarkh Nikon i ego protivniki* (Sergiev, Posad, 1913²).

Kapterev, N.F., *Patriarkh Nikon i tsar' Aleksei Mikhailovich*, 2 vols. (Sergiev Posad, 1909-1912).

*KAPTEREV, *PERVYIA DEISTVIIA NIKONA* = Kapterev, N.F., "Pervyia tserkovno-reformatorskie deistviia patriarkha Nikona," *BV* 1908(2) 176-220.

*KAPTEREV, *PRIEZD PATRIARKHA PAISIIA* = "Priezd v Moskvu ierusalimskago patriarkha Paisiia v 1649 godu," *Prib* 47 (1891) 178-237.

Kapterev, N.F., "Protopop Avvakum, kak protivnik tserkovnoi reformy patriarkha Nikona," *BV* 1909(1) 384-408, 509-539; 1909(2) 1-31.

Kapterev, N.F., "Sledstvennoe delo ob Arsenii greke i ssylka ego v Solovetskii monastyr'," *ChOLDP* 1881(7) 70-96.

*KAPTEREV, *SNOSHENIIA* = Kapterev, N.F., *Snosheniia ierusalimskikh patriarkhov s russkim pravitel'stvom s poloviny XVI do kontsa XVIII stoletiia* (=*Pravoslavnyi Palestinskii Sbornik* 43, vol. 15) (St Petersburg, 1895).

*KAPTEREV, *TSAR' I SOBORY* = Kapterev, N.F., "Tsar' i tserkovnye moskovskie sobory XVI i XVII stoletii," *BV* 1906(3) 326-360, 467-502, 631-682.

*KAPTEREV, *TSERKOVNO-OBRIADOVYIA REFORMY* = Kapterev, N.F., "Tserkovno-obriadovyia reformy Nikona," *BV* 1908(2) 341-381; 1908(3) 218-252.

*KAPTEREV, *TSERKOVNO-REFORMATSIONNOE DVIZHENIE* = Kapterev, N.F., "Tserkovno-reformatsionnoe dvizhenie vo vremia patriarshestva Iosifa i ego glavnye predstaviteli," *BV* 1908(1) 309-338, 456-505.

Karataev, I., *Opisanie slaviano-russkikh knig 1491-1730*, 2 vols. (St Petersburg, 1878-1883).

*KARTASHEV = Kartashev, A.V., *Ocherki po istorii russkoi tserkvi*, vol. 2 (Paris: YMCA Press, 1959).

Kazanskii, P., "Ispravlenie tserkovno-bogosluzhebnykh knig pri patriarkhe Filarete," *ChOIDR* 1848(3) pt. 1, no. 8, 1-26.

*KHARLAMPOVICH = Kharlampovich, K.P., *Malorossiiskoe vliianie na velikorusskuiu tserkovnuiu zhizn'* (Kazan, 1914) (= Slavistic Printings and Reprintings 119, The Hague, Paris: Mouton, 1968).

Kiselev, N.P., "O moskovskom knigopechatanii XVII veka," *Kniga. Issledovaniia i materialy*, 2 (Moscow, 1960) 123-186.

*KLIUCHEVSKII = Kliuchevskii, V.O., *A Course in Russian History: the Seventeenth Century* (Chicago: Quadrangle Books, 1968).

Kolosov, V., "Starets Arsenii grek," *ZhMNP* 1881(9) 77-93.

Kostomarov, N., *Russkaia istoriia v zhizneopisaniiakh ee glavneishikh deiatelei*, vol. 2 (St Petersburg, 1911).

Krajcar, J., "Early-Printed Slavonic Books in the Library of the Pontifical Oriental Institute," *OCP* 34 (1968) 105-128.

*KRASNOSEL'TSEV, *MATERIALY* = Krasnosel'tsev, *Materialy dlia istorii chino-posledovaniia liturgii sviatago Ioanna Zlatoustago* (Kazan, 1889).

Lascaris, M., "Arsène Suchanov et les manuscrits de l'Athos. Un nouveau document (10 Juin 1654)," *Byz* 28(1959) 543-545.

*LAURENT = Laurent, V., "Le rituel de la proscomidie et le métropolite de Crète Elie," *REB* 16(1958) 116-142.

Lebedev, L., "Patriarkh Nikon, Ocherk zhizni i deiatel'nosti," *BT* 23(1982) 154-199; 24(1983) 139-170.

*LEGRAND, *XVe ET XVIe SIÈCLES* = Legrand, E., *Bibliographie hellénique, ou description raisonnée des ouvrages publiés en grec par les grecs au XVe et XVIe siècles*, 4 vols. (Paris, 1885-1906) (rep: Bruxelles: Culture et civilization, 1963).

*LEGRAND, *XVIIe SIÈCLE* = Legrand, E., *Bibiliographie héllenique, ou description raisonnée des ouvrages publiés par des grecs au XVIIe siècle*, 5 vols. (Paris, 1894-1903) (rep: Bruxelles: Culture et civilization, 1963).

Lupinin, Nickolas, *Religious Revolt in the XVIIth Century: the Schism of the Russian Church* (Princeton: Kingston Press, 1984).

*MAKARII, *ISTORIIA* = Makarii, [Metropolitan of Moscow], *Istoriia russkoi tserkvi*, vol. 10 (St Petersburg, 1902²), vol. 11 (St Petersburg, 1903²), vol. 12 (St Petersburg, 1883).

*MAKARII, *PATRIARKH NIKON* = Makarii, [Metropolitan of Moscow], *Patriarkh Nikon v dele ispravlenii knig i obriadov* (Moscow, 1881).

*MANDALÀ = Mandalà, M., *La Protesi della liturgia nel rito bizantino-greco* (Grottaferrata, 1935).

*MANSVETOV, *KAK PRAVILIS'* = Mansvetov, I.D., "Kak u nas pravilis' tserkovnyia knigi," *Prib* 32(1883) 514-574.

*MATEOS, *CÉLÉBRATION* = Mateos, J., *La célébration de la parole dans la liturgie byzantine* (= *OCA* 191) (Rome: Pont. Inst. Orientalium, 1971).

*MATERIALY = Subbotin, N.I., ed., *Materialy po istorii raskola za pervoe vremia ego sushchestvovaniia,* 9 vols. (Moscow, 1875-1895).

Medvedev, Silvester, *Izvestie istinnoe...* [See Belokurov, S., ed., *Silvestr Medvedeva.*] Medvedev, Silvester, *Oglavlenie knig, kto ikh slozhil, ChOIDR* 1846(3) pt. 4, 1-82.

Milovidov, A.I., *Opisanie slaviano-russkikh staropechatnykh knig Vilenskoi publichnoi biblioteki* (Vilna, 1908).

Murav'ev, A.N., *Snosheniia Rossii s Vostokom po delam tserkovnym,* 2 vols. (St Petersburg, 1858-1860).

Muretov, S., *Istoricheskii obzor chinoposledovaniia proskomidii do "Ustava liturgii" konstantinopol'skago patriarkha Filofeiia* (Moscow, 1895).

Muretov, S., *Posledovanie proskomidii, velikago vkhoda i prichashcheniia v slaviano-russkikh sluzhebnikakh XII-XIV vv., ChOIDR* 1897(2) pt. 1, i-iv. 1-44.

Nikolaevskii, P.F., "Iz istorii snoshenii Rossii s Vostokom," *KhCht* 1882(1) 245-267, 732-775.

Nikolaevskii, P.F., "Novye dannye dlia istorii gramoty konstantinopol'skago patriarkha Paisiia I k moskovskomu patriarkhu Nikonu," *KhCht* 1881(2) 792-807.

*NIKOLAEVSKII, PECHATNYI DVOR = Nikolaevskii, P.F., "Moskovskii Pechatnyi Dvor pri patriarkhe Nikone," *KhCht* 1890(1) 114-141; 1890(2) 434-467; 1891(1) 147-186; 1891(2) 151-186.

*NIKOLAEVSKII, ROSSIIA I VOSTOK [See Nikolaevskii, P.F., "Iz istorii..."]

"Opisanie nakhodiashchikhsia v Imperatorskoi publichnoi biblioteki staropechatnykh knig (1564-1640gg.)," *KhCht* 1857(2) 99-172, 245-326.

*ORLOV = Orlov, M.I., *Liturgiia sviatago Vasiliia Velikago* (St Petersburg, 1909).

*PAISIOS OF CONSTANTINOPLE = Paisios, [Patriarch of Constantinople], "Gramota Konstantinopol'skago patriarkha Paisiia I k moskovskomu patriarkhu Nikonu," *KhCht* 1881(1) 303-353, 539-595.

*PALMER = Palmer, W., *The Tsar and the Patriarch,* 6 vols. (London, 1871-1876).

*PASCAL, AVVAKUM = Pascal, P., *Avvacum et les débuts du raskol* (Paris: Mouton, 1963[2]).

*PAUL OF ALEPPO = Murkos, G., trans., *Puteshestvie antiokhiiskago patriarkha Makariia v Rossiiu v polovine XVII veka, opisannoe ego synom, arkhidiakonom Pavlom Aleppskim, ChOIDR* 1896(4) pt. 2, i-x, 1-256; 1897(4) pt. 3, i-vi, 1-202; 1898(3) pt. 3, i-iv, 1-208; 1899(4) pt. 2, i-x, 1-195; 1900(2) pt. 3, i-v, 1-245.

Paul of Aleppo, *The Travels of Macarius, Patriarch of Antioch,* 2 vols., trans. by F.C. Belfour (London, 1829-1836).

Paul of Aleppo, *Voyage en Russie du patr. Macaire,* trans. into French by B. Radu (= *PO* 22, part 2; 24, pt. 4) (Paris, 1930).

Petrov, S.O., Biriuk, Ia. D., and Zolotar', T.P., *Slavianskie knigi kirillovskoi pechati XV-XVIII vv.* (Kiev, 1958).

*PETROVSKII, *RÉDACTION SLAVE* = Petrovskii, A., "Histoire de la rédaction slave de la liturgie de S. Jean Chrysostome," CHRYSOSTOMIKA, *Studi e ricerche intorno a S. Giovanni Crisostomo a cura del comitato per il XVo Centenario della sua morte* (Rome, 1908), pp. 859-928.

Petukhov, E.V., *Russkaia literatura. Istoricheskii obzor glavneishikh literaturnykh iavlenii drevniago i novago perioda. Drevnii period* (Iuriev, 1911).

Pevnitskii, V. "Epifanii Slavinetskii, odin iz glavnykh deiatelei russkoi dukhovnoi literatury v XVII v.," *TKDA* 1861(2) 405-438; (3) 135-182.

Pis'ma russkikh gosudarei (Moscow, 1848).

*RAES, *DIALOGUE* = Raes, A., "Le Dialogue après la Grande Entrée," *OCP* 18(1952) 38-51.

Raes, A., "Les livres liturgiques grecs publiés à Venise," *Mélanges Eugène Tisserant,* vol. 3 (=*Studi e testi* 233) (Vatican, 1964), pp. 209-222.

Rhalles, G.A., and Potles, M., eds., Σύνταγμα τῶν θείων καὶ ἱερῶν κανόνων τῶν τε ἁγίων καὶ πανευφήμων ἀποστόλων καὶ τῶν ἱερῶν οἰκουμενικῶν καὶ τοπικῶν συνόδων, καὶ τῶν κατὰ μέρος ἁγίων πατέρων ἔκδοθεν, σὺν πλείσταις ἄλλαις τὴν ἐκκλησιαστικὴν κατάστασιν διεπούσαις διατάξεσι, μετὰ τῶν ἀρχαίων ἐξηγητῶν, καὶ διαφόρων ἀναγνωσμάτων, 5 vols. (Athens, 1852-1859) (rep: Athens: K.M. Grigoris, 1966).

Rodosskii, A., *Opisanie staropechatnykh i tserkovno-slavianskikh knig, khrania-shchikhsia v biblioteke S.-Peterburgskoi akademii,* 2 vols. (St Petersburg, 1891-1898).

*ROTAR = Rotar, I., "Epifanii Slavinetskii, literaturnyi deiatel' XVII veka," *KS* 71 (1900) 1-38, 189-217, 347-400.

Rozhdestvenskii, N.V., ed., *Makarii patr. Antiokhiiskii v Rossii v 1654-1656 gg., Dokumenty Posol'skago prikaza, ChOIDR* 1906(4) pt. 1, i-vi, 1-120.

Russkaia Istoricheskaia Biblioteka, 39 vols. (St Petersburg/Leningrad, 1875-1927).

Sharov, P., "Bol'shoi Moskovskii Sobor 1666-67 gg.," *TKDA* 1895(1) 23-85, 176-222, 517-553; 1985(2) 171-222.

*SHUSHERIN = Shusherin, I., *Izvestie o rozhdenii i vospitanii i o zhitii sviateishago Nikona, patriarkha moskovskago i vseia Rossii* (Moscow, 1871).

*SILVESTER MEDVEDEV [see Belokurov, S., ed., *Silvestr Medvedeva...*]

*SILVESTER MEDVEDEV, *OGLAVLENIE KNIG* [see Medvedev, Silvester, *Oglavlenie...*]

Sklobovskii, D. Ia., "Patriarkh Nikon po novym istoricheskim ukazaniiam," *PrOb* 1883(2) 421-485, 627-692.

Skrizhal' (Moscow, 1656).

Smotritskii, Meletii, *Grammatika* (Moscow, 1648).

*SOBOLEVSKII = Sobolevskii, A.I., *Perevodnaia literatura Moskovskoi Rusi XVI-XVII vekov. Bibliograficheskie materialy* (St Petersburg, 1903).

SOBRANIE GRAMOT = Sobranie gosudarstvennykh gramot i dogovorov, 5 vols. (Moscow, 1813-1894).

*SOLOV'EV = Solov'ev, S.M., *Istoriia Rossii s drevneishikh vremen*, 6 vols. (St Petersburg, 1896²).

Solovey, M.M., *The Byzantine Divine Liturgy* (Washington: CUA Press, 1970).

Sopikov, V.S., *Opyt rossiiskoi bibliografii* (St Petersburg, 1904) (rep: London: Holland Press, 1962).

*STOGLAV = Kozhanchikov, D.E., ed., *Stoglav* (St Petersburg, 1863) (= *Rarity Reprints* 17, Letchworth, England: Bradda Books, Ltd., 1971).

*STROEV, OPISANIE KNIG TOLSTOVA = Stroev, P.M., *Opisanie staropechatnykh knig slavianskikh i rossiiskikh khraniashchikhsia v biblioteke grafa F.A. Tolstova* (Moscow, 1829).

*STROEV, OPISANIE KNIG TOLSTOVA I TSARSKAGO = Stroev, P.M., *Opisanie staropechatnykh knig slavianskikh, sluzhashchie dopolneniem k opisaniam bibliotek grafa F.A. Tolstova i kuptsa I.N. Tsarskago* (Moscow, 1841).

Subbotin, N.I., ed., *Deianie Moskovskago Sobora byvshago...* [see *DEIANIE 1654*].

Subbotin, N.I., ed., *Deianiia moskovskago sobora 1666-1667...* [see *DEIANIIA 1666-1667*].

Subbotin, N.I., ed., *Materialy...* [see *MATERIALY*].

Sukhanov, Arsenii, "Materialy dlia istorii russkoi tserkvi: a) Stateinyi spisok; b) Prenie s grekami o vere," edited by S. Belokurov, *KhCht* 1883(2) 670-738.

*SWAINSON = Swainson, C.A., *The Greek Liturgies, Chiefly from Original Authorities* (Cambridge: University Press, 1884).

*TAFT, GREAT ENTRANCE = Taft, Robert F., *The Great Entrance* (= *OCA* 200) (Rome: Pont. Inst. Orientalium, 1978²).

*TAFT, PONTIFICAL LITURGY = Taft, Robert F., "The Pontifical Liturgy of the Great Church according to a Twelfth Century Diataxis in *Codex Br. Mus. Add. 34060,*" *OCP* 45(1979) 279-307; 46(1980) 89-124.

Taft, Robert F., "Textual Problems in the Diaconal Admonition before the Anaphora in the Byzantine Tradition," *OCP* 49(1983) 340-365.

Tomadakis, N.B., "Ἡ ἐν'Ιταλία ἔκδοσις ἑλληνικῶν ἐκκλησιαστικῶν βιβλίων," *La Chiesa Greca in Italia dall'VIII al XVI secolo* (= *Italia Sacra* 21) (Padua: Editrice Antenore, 1972), 685-721.

*TREMPELAS = Trempelas, P.N., Αἱ τρεῖς λειτουργίαι κατὰ τοὺς ἐν Αθήναις κώδικας (= *Texte und Forschungen zur byzantinisch-neugriechischen Philologie*, 15) (Athens, 1935).

Undol'skii, V.M., *Ocherk slaviano-russkoi bibliografii 1491-1864* (Moscow, 1871).

Undol'skii, V.M., "Uchenye trudy Epifaniia Slavinetskago," *ChOIDR* 1846(8) pt. 4, 69-72.

*USPENSKII = Uspenskii, N.D., "Kolliziia dvukh bogoslovii v ispravlenii russkikh bogosluzhebnykh knig v XVII veke," *BT* 13(1975) 148-171. English translation in N. Uspensky, *Evening Worship in the Orthodox Church* (Crestwood, NY: St Vladimir's Seminary Press, 1985), pp. 191-240.

Uspenskii, P., trans., "Deianie konstantinopol'skago sobora 1593 goda, kotorym utverzhdeno patriarshestvo v Rossii," *TKDA* 1865(3) 237-248.

Winkler, G., "Die Interzessionen der Chrysostomusanaphora in ihrer geschichtlichen Entwicklung," *OCP* 36(1970) 301-336; 37(1971) 333-383.

*ZAPISKI = *Zapiski otdeleniia russkoi i slavianskoi arkheologii imperatorskago russkago Arkheologicheskago Obshchestva*, 13 vols. (St Petersburg, 1851-1918).

*ZERNOVA = Zernova, A.S., *Knigi kirillovskoi pechati izdannye v Moskve v XVI-XVII vekakh* (Moscow, 1958).

Zizanii, Lavrentii, *Grammatika Slovenska* (Vilna, 1596) (rep: *Specimina Philologiae Slavicae*, Bd. 1, Frankfurt, 1972).

*ZYZYKIN = Zyzykin, M.V., *Patriarkh Nikon. Ego gosudarstvennye i kanonicheskie idei*, 3 vols. (Warsaw, 1931-1939).

A Note on Style

In referring to names and places, we have generally used a transliterated form of the original: thus "Arsenios" the Greek, and "Epifanii Slavinetskii." This has the advantage of making immediately apparent the national origin of each figure. In those cases where an acceptable standard English form exists, we have used it: thus "Tsar Alexis" (rather than "Aleksei"), "Moscow" (rather than "Moskva"), etc.

We follow the Library of Congress system of transliteration, without diacritical marks, for both Russian (Slavonic) and Greek. For Old Slavonic, again following current Library of Congress procedures, we first transpose it into modern Russian orthography, then transliterate it.

In the first part of this study, we cite foreign language texts in English translation. Only in a few cases, where we must deal with problems of translation and interpretation, do we cite these texts in the original. In the second part, where we are analyzing liturgical texts, we translate all rubrics from Slavonic to English, but keep the original language for texts of the liturgical formulary itself. Because the rubrics undergo substantial, rather than merely stylistic, changes, we lose nothing by citing them in translation. In translating rubrics, we attempt to render a literal, rather than a literate, translation. This at times makes the English read rather awkwardly, but it also exemplifies how Nikon's own translators made a literal translation of Greek texts. The formulary, however, generally underwent only stylistic changes, and we are thus required to cite it in the original language, though in transliterated form for the Slavonic. Greek sources we always cite in the original. This is necessary to show how exactly the Nikonian texts follow the Greek.

Introduction

Few subjects arouse as much passion among Christians today as the issue of liturgical change or reform. In recent years, we have witnessed the turmoil produced by liturgical reforms within the Roman Catholic and Anglican Episcopal Churches. Among the Orthodox, sharp discussions and even schisms are sparked by such relatively minor issues as the liturgical calendar (Julian vs. Gregorian) and language. Yet few today would deny that liturgy has indeed evolved and continues to evolve. Within the last century, the historical and comparative study of liturgy has demonstrated this in no uncertain terms. John Chrysostom and Basil the Great, were they alive today, would hardly recognize the external trappings of the liturgies that bear their names, though the essential structure and content have remained quite unchanged.

Until Nikon's reform in the 17th century, however, liturgical change and uniformity of practice were rarely issues of debate, despite the fact that earlier changes were occasionally far more dramatic and extensive than Nikon's. Just over two hundred years earlier, in the late 14th and early 15th centuries, the Russians under Metropolitan Cyprian abandoned the Studite in favor of the Sabbaite Typikon, all with no dissent.[1] In doing this, the Russian Church was only following the lead of the Greeks, who had taken this step about a century earlier.[2] Further, a comparative study of both Greek and Slavic liturgical manuscripts right up to the 16th century would immediately show that no two manuscripts were ever identical. Only with the invention of the printing press and the subsequent appearance of printed books was variation curtailed, though never totally. Yet this lack of uniformity caused no difficulty until differences between Greek and Russian practices became an issue in Muscovite Russia during the 16th century.

In this study, we examine the nature and extent of the historic and fateful liturgical reform which took place in Russia under Patriarch Nikon (1652-1658). This reform, which aligned Russian liturgical practice with contemporary Greek usage, served as the trigger for the Old-Believer Schism (1667) and set off a debate within the Russian Church which continues to this day. The schism, by far the most dramatic and cataclysmic event in the life of the Russian Orthodox Church, has been the subject of intensive study, not only in Russia but also in the West. Numerous studies of the events and many biographies of the chief protagonists, Nikon and Avvakum, have been published.[3] But the attention of scholars has been focused on the broader results, the Old-Believer Schism, and little effort has so far been made to study the liturgical reforms in themselves, despite the availability of primary materials. There is, we shall see, a good reason for this.

1. State of the Question

i. Origins

Because of the paucity of scholarly material on the subject of the liturgical reform, it is difficult, strictly speaking, to formulate the "state of the question." The issue has up to the present been a pawn in the polemics between supporters of the Old-Believers, on the one hand, and the representatives of the established Church of Russia, on the other. The Old-Believers have sought to discredit the reforms by showing the following:

1) that the correctors, Arsenios the Greek in particular, were heretics;

2) that the new books were inconsistent, even among themselves;

3) that Nikon was destroying a perfectly Orthodox, and therefore unchangeable, tradition by introducing heretical innovations based on "corrupt" sources.

Because the Old-Believers believed that externals in themselves expressed the content of the faith, they saw any change as heretical. While they accepted the need for church reform to improve the moral life of both clergy and lay people, the Old-Believers rejected any possibility of change in the liturgical ordo. They explained differences between Greek and Russian books as caused by Greek innovations, resulting from their betrayal of Orthodoxy at the Council of Florence (1438-1439). God's condemnation of the Greeks was proved by the fall of Constantinople to the Turks shortly thereafter (1453). The defenders of the reform, representing the official position of the Russian Church, argued the diametrically opposite point of view. The Greeks, they said, were fully Orthodox; it was the Russians who had introduced innovations during the period when the two churches were isolated from each other, particularly after the Russians had proclaimed their ecclesiastical independence in the mid-15th century. The reform of the liturgical books, they affirmed, was based on primitive Greek and Slavonic sources which, they were convinced, were in total agreement with one another. Of course, neither side had any conception of liturgical development, and could therefore explain differences only as errors made by one side or the other.

ii. Later Debate

The discussion continued on this level for more than two centuries, and the majority of historians to this day accept the notion that Nikon's reform was a correction made necessary by Russian aberrations brought about by two centuries of near-isolation from the Greeks. Moreover, many today still accept the notion that these "corrections" were based on old Greek and Slavonic manuscripts, as is claimed in the introduction of each edition of the Nikonian *Sluzhebnik* (Euchology). Many historians of Russia accept such statements, or declarations of synods, at face value. A modern Russian history textbook, for instance, affirms: "Over a long period of time, errors in translation from the Greek and other mistakes had crept into some Muscovite religious texts and rituals...But in the face of general ignorance, inertia, and opposition, little was done until Nikon became patriarch."[4] A recent study of the Old-Believer Schism affirms that ancient Greek and Slavic texts were used as the basis for the reform.[5]

With the rise of both historical and liturgical scholarship in the latter half of the 19th century, a different theory was introduced. Scholars, such as Kapterev, began to suggest that in fact the reforms were based not on the old Slavonic and Greek texts, but on Greek books printed in Venice, and on the so-called "Lithuanian" books being printed in areas under Polish, and therefore Latin, influence. Scholars also discovered that the new Greek books agreed with neither the Old Greek nor Slavonic manuscripts. Further, it became apparent that many of the Russian "innovations," in fact, reflected more primitive practices than those found in contemporary Greek books.

These scholars were immediately subjected to virulent attacks for undermining the Church's official position, since many of their findings supported Old-Believer claims. The advent of the Russian Revolution in 1917 effectively halted this field of research in Russia, and it has never fully resumed.

One significant result of the flowering of historical scholarship in the last century, however, was the publication of a massive quantity of primary sources—acts of church councils, writings by the various figures involved in the reforms and attendant controversies, as well as official documents, petitions, and letters of all kinds. This provides a wealth of information which has remained untapped by liturgical scholars.

2. Previous Work

No comprehensive liturgical study of the reform of Nikon has yet been attempted. This is due largely to the sensitive nature of the topic, for polemics against the Old-Believers continue to our day. A significant amount of background work has been done, however, particularly by A. Dmitrievskii and A. Petrovskii, who have studied Russian liturgical practice before the 17th century.[6] Concerning Nikon's reform specifically, Kapterev's is the most comprehensive study,[7] but it contains no analysis of the liturgical texts themselves. I. Mansvetov has described the workings of the Moscow Printing Office, where the correctors worked, and gives a chronological list of all the editors from 1620-1700.[8] S. Belokurov's very interesting account of the work of Silvester Medvedev, who served as corrector from 1678-1688, points to the 1602 Venice *Euchologion* as the primary source for the 1655 Moscow *Sluzhebnik*, Nikon's first edition.[9] This analysis is extended somewhat by Dmitrievskii, who, within the context of a book review of Orlov's critical edition of BAS, compares several texts from Nikon's edition with this Greek source.[10] But this is hardly a comprehensive work, and Dmitrievskii himself indicates the need for a liturgical study of the available material.[11]

Since the Russian revolution, very little work has been done in the field, and historians have simply continued to repeat the accepted notion of the reform as a return to the early sources, as a correction. Recently, B.L. Fonkich has published a study of Greek influence in Russia in the 15-17th centuries. In this work, he describes the collection of Greek books and manuscripts brought back to Russia by Arsenii Sukhanov.[12] His study provides precious information on the books and manuscripts available to the Nikonian editors. But, again, no properly liturgical study of the reform has yet been attempted.

3. Importance of the Topic

An objective, historical study of Nikon's reform is therefore necessary, first of all, to set the record straight. For various historical reasons, this has not and could not be done before. The work is important because it will also bring to light the sources and indicate the background for today's Slavic liturgical practice—for the books printed under Nikon remain essentially unchanged to the present day. At a time when there is increasing talk within the Orthodox Church about the need for liturgical reform, it becomes vital to possess knowledge about the history and development of the present rites, as well as about past efforts at reform.

In point of fact, little has ever been written about any liturgical reform in any of the Orthodox Churches, such as Peter Moghila's efforts in Kiev in the first half of the 17th century,[13] or even the more radical reform in Greece at the end of the 19th century. Thus not only these reforms, but the very idea of liturgical reform, requires study. Nikon's reform, by far the most notorious, is a good place to start.

4. Outline of Study

Our study consists of two parts: the first presents the events of the reform and describes the personages involved; the second is an analysis of the reform itself.

i. Events and Personages in the Reform

In the first chapter, we discuss the events of the reform. After outlining the "official" version of the events, presented in the introduction to Nikon's *Sluzhebnik* (Euchology),[14] we review the chief episodes in the reform. Relevant councils, particularly those of 1654, 1655, 1666, and 1667 are discussed; the major actions taken by Nikon, on his own, are presented; the correspondence carried on between Moscow and Constantinople are analyzed. In short, this chapter contains a chronological account of the reform, concluding with the 1667 Moscow Council, which formally deposed Nikon but confirmed the liturgical reform in no uncertain terms.

In the second chapter, we present brief biographical sketches of the four chief figures involved in the reform: Nikon, Tsar Alexis, Arsenios the Greek, and Epifanii Slavinetskii. Each of these, in his own way, played a vital role. For each, we present his background and education, then discuss his role in and attitude to the liturgical reform. A proper understanding of these individuals will shed light both on the events of the reform and on the reaction to it by its opponents, the future Old-Believers.

ii. The Contents of the Reform

The second part, comprising the third and fourth chapters, consists of an analysis of the actual changes made in the liturgical books. This is done through a detailed comparison of the Nikonian *Sluzhebnik* with previous Muscovite books, and then through an analysis of the change. We deal chiefly with CHR, and to a much lesser extent BAS, for two reasons: because this is where the majority of changes were made, and because this suffices to indicate the nature and direction of the reform. Our comparison of the texts demonstrates that the reform, while claiming to be a return to primitive Russian and Greek practice, was in fact based on the Greek *Euchologion* of 1602, published in Venice, as well as on 17th century "Lithuanian" books printed in Striatin and Kiev.

Our analysis of the reform will indicate that the actual changes were minimal. In the texts of prayers and litanies, most of the changes were stylistic, grammatical, or orthographical, and rarely altered the meaning. Many of the changes were rubrical, but these, to the modern reader, will appear trivial, though they engendered sharp debate. The most significant changes were made in the secondary rites, such as in the prayers recited by the celebrants before entering the church, in the rites of deposition after the Great Entrance and in the concluding rites of the liturgy.

We shall see further, that the reform was of little significance theologically. While a few isolated latinized rubrics did make their way into the Nikonian texts, they were unimportant. Moreover, these were adopted not from the latinized editions of Peter Moghila in Kiev, as is sometimes thought, but from Greek books printed by Orthodox Greeks in Venice. The period of strong Latin influence in Moscow was to come some two decades after the publication of the first Nikonian *Sluzhebnik.* The reform had no connection with the polemics between Orthodox and Roman Catholics, but was rather a reaction to domestic Muscovite issues, involving various interpretations of the Moscow-Third Rome ideology prevalent in Russia.

The end-result of the reform was the standardization of the liturgical books and their conformity to Greek editions, both being goals of the reform. Yet the price of this success was high. A large segment of the Russian Church, led by Avvakum, who earlier had himself been a member of the reforming party in the Church, went into schism. The opponents of the reform considered this a betrayal of the Russian past. Identifying rubrics with dogma, and the Russian Church as the only true Orthodox Church, they saw the changes as heretical innovations, particularly as they were well aware that contemporary, "heretical" Greek books were used as models. The reform, or "correction of books," as it was called, was not accompanied by any program of education, as had earlier been the case in Kiev under Peter Moghila. Nikon never did see fit to explain the changes, beyond declaring that they were necessary because the earlier books were full of errors. The Nikonian books were imposed forcibly, and resistance was dealt with harshly.

To its credit, the Russian Church appears to have realized its tactical error and tried to repair the damage. As early as 1656, Nikon made peace with Neronov, one of the leading opponents of the reform, and permitted him to remain in Moscow and even to use the old books at the Cathedral of the Dormition. After Nikon left the patriarchal throne in 1658, Tsar Alexis made repeated attempts to pacify the future Old-Believers, insisting only that they cease condemning the new books, but willing to allow the continued use of the old. This was the only demand made of the Old-Believers at the 1666 Moscow Council. Only after all these attempts to restore peace had failed did the 1667 Council, with Greek bishops present, condemn the old books and revoke the 1551 "Stoglav (Hundred Chapters)"[15] Council. The Stoglav had rejected the new Greek practices, which were finding their way into Russia, and dogmatized Russian usage.

With this fateful decision, the die was cast, and the Church divided. The schism continues to our day, though the polemics have diminished in recent decades, and serious efforts have been made to heal the split. More recent Orthodox attempts at liturgical reforms, particularly the change to the "new" (Gregorian) calendar, have produced similar tragic results. Perhaps an objective scholarly examination of these experiences will provide us with a better understanding of a socio-cultural and religious process so frought with danger. At a time when there is increased discussion about the need for liturgical reform within Orthodoxy, the lessons of history must be taken into account.

NOTES

1. See the studies of I. D. Mansvetov, *Mitropolit Kiprian v ego liturgicheskoi deiatel'nosti* (Moscow, 1882); and "O trudakh mitropolita Kipriana po chasti bogosluzheniia," *Prib* 29 (1882) 152-205, 413-495; as well as A. A. Dmitrievskii, *Bogosluzhenie v russkoi tserkvi za pervye piat' vekov, PrSob* 1882 (1) 138-166, 252-296; 1882 (2) 346-373; 1882 (3) 149-167, 372-394; 1883 (2) 345-374; 1883 (3) 198-229, 470-485.

2. See the classic summary of Byzantine liturgical evolution by M. Arranz, "Les grandes étapes de la liturgie byzantine: Palestine-Byzance-Russie: Essai d'aperçu historique," in *Liturgie de l'église particulière, et liturgie de l'église universelle* (Conferences s. Serge 1975) (=*EL*, Subsidia 7) (Rome, 1976) 43-72.

3. The chief study in the West on Nikon, containing translations of numerous primary sources, is by PALMER. In Russian, there are numerous works, many containing extensive primary materials. These include *DELO*; GIBBENET; KAPTEREV, *NIKON I EGO PROTIVNIKI*; KAPTEREV, *NIKON I ALEKSEI*; ZYZYKIN. On Avvakum, the classical Western work is by PASCAL, *AVVAKUM*. A complete collection of Avvakum's writings is published in *Sochineniia* (=Russkaia Istoricheskaia Biblioteka, vol. 39) (Leningrad, 1927). Cf. also *Zhitie i drugie ego sochineniia s kommentarie N.K. Gudziia* (Moscow, 1955).

4. N.V. Riasanovsky, *A History of Russia* (New York: Oxford University Press, 1963), p. 219.

5. N. Lupinin, *Religious Revolt in the XVIIth Century: the Schism of the Russian Church* (Princeton: Kingston Press, 1984), pp. 130ff.

6. A. Dmitrievskii, "Bogosluzhenie v russkoi tsekvi za pervye piat' vekov," *PrSob* 1882(1) 138-166, 252-296; 1882(2) 346-373; 1882(3) 149-167, 372-394; 1883(2) 345-374; 1883(3) 198-229, 470-485; DMITRIEVSKII, *BOGOSLUZHENIE V XVI VEKE*; PETROVSKII, *RÉDACTION SLAVE*.

7. KAPTEREV, *NIKON I ALEKSEI*.

8. MANSVETOV, *KAK PRAVILIS'*.

9. Cf. SILVESTER MEDVEDEV.

10. DMITRIEVSKII, *OTZYV ORLOVA*, pp. 191-192, and *passim.*

11. *Ibid.*, pp. 259-260.

12. Cf. FONKICH.

13. See my article, "The Liturgical Reforms of Peter Moghila: A New Look," *SVTQ* 29(1985), 101-114.

14. (Moscow, 1655).

15. So-called because its Acts consist of one hundred chapters. Cf. *STOGLAV*, and E. Duchesne, ed., *Le Stoglav ou les cent chapitres* (=Bibliothèque de l'Institut Français de Petrograd, V) (Paris, 1920).

Part I

The Events and Personages
of the Reform

1

The Events of the Reform

1. The Official Account

The account of the events of the reform heretofore generally accepted is the one presented in the introduction to the first edition of Nikon's *Sluzhebnik* in 1655. This account, we shall see, does not exactly correspond to the facts, but is interesting because it presents the official explanation and justification for the reforms.

Immediately after his consecration as patriarch, Nikon "secluded himself from everyone and immersed himself in examining the holy writings: entering the library, he spent many days looking through them with great effort."[1] Here, we are told, Nikon discovered the conciliar letter sent to Moscow[2] in 1593 by Patriarch Jeremias of Constantinople, recognizing the establishment of the patriarchate in Moscow. This letter, published by Nikon in his *Kormchaia Kniga*[3] and in the introduction to the *Zhezl Pravleniia*,[4] indicates that the Patriarch of Moscow is to agree in everything with the ecumenical patriarchs, "because the Orthodox Church has reached its fulness not only in dogma…but also in its liturgical practice…," and thus the patriarch must "eliminate any innovation in order to preserve the church, seeing that innovations always serve as causes for religious dissension and division…" Thus the Russian Church must "follow the liturgical practice of the holy fathers and preserve unharmed that which it learned from them, without any addition or subtraction." This passage from the Introduction to the 1655 *Sluzhebnik* paraphrases the 1593 letter from the Patriarch of Constantinople.[6]

Nikon studies the Russian books, compares them with the Greek, and discovers that the Russian books are full of innovations. He finds that the Slavonic text of the Creed of Nicea-Constantinople does not agree with the Greek, and that there are many changes in the liturgy, as printed in the new Moscow editions.[7] He therefore asks his spiritual son, the tsar, to convene a council, which meets in 1654 at the tsar's palace.[8] At the council, Nikon asks the assembled clergy and representatives of the tsar:

> Should we follow the new, printed Muscovite books, which contain many innovations caused by the ignorance of copyists and translators, which do not agree with the ancient Greek and Slavonic books, and which contain errors? Or should we follow the ancient Greek and Slavonic books, which both contain the same liturgical ordo and rubrics?

The tsar replied that "it is proper and right to correct them according to ancient manuscripts and Greek books." Then the entire council said: "We too affirm the same, that we follow what the Greek and our own ancient books and ordos indicate." Then the tsar, the patriarch, and the council ordered that the ancient books be collected from throughout Russia and brought to Moscow. They also sent letters to the Eastern patriarchs asking for advice.[9]

A conciliar letter was received from Patriarch Paisios of Constantinople the following year, indicating that the Russians were to follow what was written in the ancient Greek and Slavic books. The letter encourages Nikon to correct all the errors in the Muscovite books, so that they agree in every detail with the practice of the Great Church. Not having sufficient old Greek and Slavonic books for this task, the tsar and the patriarch sent the elder Arsenii Sukhanov to Mt. Athos and other holy places to collect books. Arsenii brought back five hundred books, some over a thousand years old.[10]

The tsar and Nikon then studied these various books and called a new council in 1655, this time attended also by Patriarch Makarios of Antioch and Metropolitan Gabriel of Serbia. This council reviewed Paisios' conciliar letter and accepted it. Then it studied the ancient books, both Greek and Russian, and found that they did indeed agree in everything, whereas the new Muscovite books were full of disagreements and errors. The council thus ordered that a new *Sluzhebnik,* based on ancient Greek and Slavic books, be printed, and that other liturgical books be similarly corrected.[11]

Such, then, is the official version of the reform of the liturgical books in Russia, challenged only by the Old Believers until the rise of historical scholarship in the 19th century, when the chronology, if not the content, of the events began to be challenged—at first by no less a figure than Metropolitan Makarii of Moscow. Makarii points out that Patriarch Paisios' answer did not arrive until after the 1655 Council and thus could not have been read or discussed there. In addition, Arsenii Sukhanov had departed on his journey to the East months before the 1654 Council. Further, the 1655 Council did not compare Greek and Slavic texts, this having been done in advance by Arsenios the Greek and Epifanii Slavinetskii, the chief correctors.[12] But Makarii did not challenge the necessity for the reform or its content.

2. The First Steps: Prostrations and Sign of the Cross

Nikon began his reform not with the textual correction of books, but with changes in concrete ritual practice. Thus the new edition of the Psalter, published in Moscow on Feb. 11, 1653, was printed without two articles contained in previous editions: the first instructed that sixteen full prostrations be done with the Lenten Prayer of St Ephrem; the second taught the two-fingered sign of the Cross.[13] This immediately caused dissension among the correctors and three of them left their posts: the elder Savvatii, a corrector since 1635;[14] Ivan Nasedka, former dean of the Cathedral of the Dormition, corrector since 1641, and now known under his monastic name Joseph; and Sila Grigoriev, who had held his post only since 1652.[15] All of these were partisans of the "provincial" circle of zealots, who strongly maintained the superiority of the Russian practice over the Greek. Savvatii was also a close friend of Neronov, one of Nikon's first opponents. The former correctors were removed from Moscow, probably incarcerated in distant monasteries,[16] and Nikon replaced them with his own people, including Arsenios the Greek. Later that year, Nikon also took over direct control of the Printing Office from the tsar.[17]

Just two weeks later, on Feb. 21, 1653, immediately prior to the beginning of Lent, Nikon issued his famous "Pamiat'," or "Memorandum," or "Instruction," a circular letter ordering the new practices. Avvakum quotes the text of this decree: "According to the tradition of the holy apostles and holy fathers it is not proper to make full prostrations in church, but only to bow from the waist, and to make the sign of the Cross with three fingers."[18] This quote is not fully accurate, as Nikon was not forbidding full prostrations in church, but only instructing that the Prayer of St Ephrem be accompanied by only four full prostrations and twelve waist-deep bows. In any case, Nikon did not offer any explanation for this sudden change.

To the circle of zealots, led by Neronov, these changes were an assault on Russian faith. The use of two fingers to make the sign of the Cross had been decreed by the Stoglav Council in 1551, with corresponding anathemas against any other practice.[19] The teaching about the number of prostrations at the Prayer of St Ephrem had been printed in editions of the Psalter, published under Patriarch Joseph. The changes were thus in direct contradiction to Russian practice. The additional fact that Nikon first sent his decree to the Kazan Cathedral, Neronov's church, located on Red Square, indicated that this was an open declaration of war.[20] It marked the final break between the patriarch and his former friends, a fact which Avvakum and his companions realized.[21]

Since becoming patriarch, Nikon had indeed broken relations with the "provincial zealots," one of whom he had formerly been. First, he clearly did not want to share his power with anyone. Second, Nikon had seen how the zealots had mistreated Joseph, his predecessor.[22] The zealots, on the other hand, clearly expected to have an even larger voice in the running of church affairs when they supported Nikon for patriarch. Avvakum and his friends were therefore clearly upset when Nikon not only stopped conferring with them, but even refused to admit them to his private residence. They were not ready to give up without a fight, and Nikon's decree on the prostrations and sign of the Cross gave them their opportunity to counter-attack. The following is Avvakum's description of these events from the time of Patriarch Joseph's death:

> Then Nikon, our friend, brought the relics of Metropolitan Philip back from the Solovki Monastery. But before his arrival, Stefan, the tsar's confessor, and the brethren, myself with them, prayed to God and fasted for a week about the patriarch, so that God might grant a pastor for the salvation of our souls. Together with Metropolitan Kornilii of Kazan, we wrote and signed a petition and gave it to the tsar and tsarina, asking that his confessor Stefan be made patriarch. Stefan refused and pointed to Metropolitan Nikon. The tsar listened to him and sent a letter to meet Nikon: "To the Most Holy Metropolitan of Novgorod and Velikie Luki and all Russia, greetings, etc." When Nikon arrived, he behaved with us like a fox—all bows and greetings. He knew that he was to be patriarch and did not want any problems on the way. Much could be said about this treachery! As soon as he became patriarch, he would not even let his

friends into his reception hall! Then he belched forth his venom! For Great Lent, he sent a "Pamiat'" to Ivan Neronov at the Kazan Cathedral. Neronov was my spiritual father: I was living at his church with him, and when he was absent, I took charge of his church...

In the "Pamiat'" Nikon wrote: "The year and the date. According to the tradition of the holy apostles and holy fathers, it is not proper to make full prostrations in church, but only to bow from the waist, and to make the sign of the Cross with three fingers."

We assembled and thought to ourselves—we saw that winter was approaching; our hearts froze and our legs began to shake. Neronov left the cathedral in my charge and secluded himself at the Chudov Monastery, where he prayed in a cell for a week. During his prayer, a voice from an icon spoke to him: "The time of suffering has come! You must suffer without weakening!" Weeping, he told this to me, as well as to Archbishop Paul of Kolomna, whom Nikon afterwards burned at the stake near Novgorod. He later told this to Daniel, archpriest of Kostroma, and then to all the brethren. Daniel and I wrote down excerpts from various books about the sign of the Cross and the prostrations and gave these to the tsar—much was written there. But the tsar hid them, I know not where: I think he gave them to Nikon.[23]

Avvakum then goes on to describe the fate of those who dared to oppose Nikon's decree.

Realizing the danger to his plans caused by these zealots, Nikon decided to remove them. By the end of 1653, most of his opponents are gone. In July, the archpriest Loggin of Murom is tried by Nikon on charges, brought by the Voevoda of Murom, that Loggin profaned icons of Christ and Mary; he is defrocked and exiled.[24] Neronov comes to Loggin's defense[25] and ends up demoted and sent in chains to the Spasokammenyi Monastery.[26] Avvakum, who escapes defrocking only through the tsar's intervention, is exiled shortly after to Tobolsk, in Siberia.[27]

Even from exile, however, Nikon's opponents continued actively to oppose him, to send petitions and letters to the tsar, the tsar's family, and other leading figures.[28] Many of their efforts were directed at the tsar's confessor, Stefan Vonifatiev: they were under the mistaken impression that Stefan had been placed at a distance by Nikon, as they had been. They did not know of Stefan's close friendship with Nikon right up until Stefan's death on Nov. 11, 1656, and tried to convince him to come out openly on their side.[29]

Nikon's opponents frequently criticized him for betraying the tradition of the Church. They pointed to the recently canonized Russian saints, such as the confessor, Metropolitan Philip, whose relics Nikon himself had brought back to Moscow. These saints had evidently been pleasing to God: if they had crossed themselves with three fingers and failed to do enough prostrations, God would clearly not have granted them the power to work miracles. But Nikon's opponents failed to convince the tsar and the patriarch, and soon turned to apocalyptic language. Already at the beginning of 1654, before any of Nikon's new books are printed, Neronov states that the time of the Antichrist has arrived. They ask the tsar to convene a full council to resolve all the issues.[30]

His initial attempts at reform having engendered such sharp opposition, Nikon decides to pursue a different tack. In issuing his "Pamiat'," he had acted alone, on his own authority. Not having been patriarch very long, he did not enjoy great spiritual prestige. Moreover, his edict had been in direct contradiction to the Stoglav Council, and thus of dubious canonical validity. A new council, as even his opponents demanded, was the obvious solution, particularly since he was certain of the tsar's support. In any case, Nikon's "Pamiat'" did not have the desired effect. An eyewitness recounts that, during Lent in 1655, the Russians were all still doing full prostrations,[31] and the battle over the sign of the Cross was to continue for years to come.

3. The Council of 1654

Nikon therefore requested the tsar to call a council. In Russia, only the tsar had the authority to convene such an assembly and, without his approval, the decisions of a council could not receive the force of law. For the tsar was the unique source of all law, both civil and religious.[32] This view was universally accepted[33] and was even proclaimed at some councils.[34]

The council assembled at the tsar's palace in March or April 1654,[35] with the tsar and his functionaries in attendance. The ecclesiastical authorities were represented by Nikon, five metropolitans, four archbishops, one bishop, eleven archimandrites and abbots, and thirteen archpriests—thirty-four in all.[36]

Nikon opened the proceedings with a long speech in which, for the first time, the objectives of his reform are openly stated—to bring the liturgical practices of the Russian Church into agreement with those of the Greek Churches. In the introductory section of the speech, Nikon states the basic premise, held by all in Russia at the time, that the tradition of the Church, both dogmatic and liturgical, must be preserved unharmed, and therefore unchanged:

> Since, therefore, the Orthodox Church has obtained perfection, not only in the good sense and piety of its dogmas, but also in the holy ecclesiastical things and liturgical ordo, it is proper for us also to root out innovation from all aspects of church life, since innovations are always the cause of ecclesiastical conflict and division. Rather, we must follow the rules of the holy fathers, which we learned correctly, without any addition or diminution, accepting them in accordance with Canon 1 of the Seventh Ecumenical Council: "We reverently accept and keep the holy canons of the holy apostles and the six ecumenical councils, as well as of the local councils, and also those of our holy fathers, for they are all inspired by the one Holy Spirit. Those whom they have anathematized, we also anathematize; those whom they depose, we also depose; those whom they excommunicate, we also excommunicate; those whom they punish, we also punish."[37]

This is but a paraphrase of the introductory section of the Acts of the 1593 Council held in Constantinople to confirm the establishment of the patriarchate in Moscow,[38] which Nikon goes on to read in their entirety. He is therefore carefully laying the groundwork for his proposed reform, showing it to be a return to the ancient tradition handed down by the councils and the Fathers of the Church.

The acts of the 1593 Council say nothing whatever about liturgical uniformity, or even about the liturgy at all. The opening section, upon which Nikon places so much emphasis, is but an affirmation of the continuity of the tradition of the Church. Most councils, ecumenical or local, begin by affirming the actions of all previous councils and their intention to continue in this tradition, without essentially altering it. This is the context of the Acts of the 1593 Council, in which the following words appear:

> ...ἐπειδὴ, τοινῦν τὸ τέλειον εἴληφεν ἡ τῶν Ὀρθοδόξων Ἐκκλησία, οὐ μόνον κατὰ τὰ τῆς θεογνωσίας καὶ εὐσεβείας δόγματα, ἀλλὰ καὶ κατὰ τὴν ἱερὰν τῶν ἐκκλησιαστικῶν πραγμάτων κατάστασιν, δίκαιον ἐστὶ καὶ ἡμᾶς πάντα νεωτερισμὸν τῶν τῆς Ἐκκλησίας περιβόλων περιορίζειν...[39]

That the text here is referring specifically to liturgical matters is highly unlikely, particularly given the fact that no Greek council up to that time had ever legislated liturgical rubrics, much less required liturgical uniformity. This will certainly be evident in the letter sent by Patriarch Paisios of Constantinople to Nikon in 1655.

The Slavonic translation of the above text by Epifanii Slavinetskii, Nikon's chief advisor on the matter of the book reform, indicates that the Muscovites understood it in a somewhat different way:

> ...Ponezhe ubo sovershenie priiat' pravoslavnykh tserkv', ne tokmo po blagorazumiia i blagochestie dogmatom, no i po sviashchennomu tserkovnykh veshchei oustavu, pravedno est' i nam vsiakuiu tserkovnykh ograzhdenii novinu potrebliati...[40]

It is clear that the Russians understood this to refer specifically to the liturgy; and the choice of the word *ustav* for the Greek κατάστασις clearly indicates this, for the word *ustav,* in Russian, is synonymous with *typikon,* i.e. *ordo.* Further, the Russians at this time equated the liturgical ordo with dogma. Lacking any conception of the historical development of the liturgy, they identified any variation from the "true order" with error and even heresy. In this, Nikon was no different from his opponents. Simply put, the issue was that either the Greek or the Russian practice was wrong,[41] and on this issue the battle lines were drawn.

Having completed his reading of the translation of the 1593 Acts, which also contained a "pure" version of the Creed of Nicea-Constantinople,[42] Nikon told the assembled council:

> For this reason, I must inform you about certain innovations in the liturgical rites printed in the Muscovite service books. A priest when serving alone, is to recite the prayersepiscopal prayers[43] for himself: by these prayers, many human passions of bishops and priests are forgiven. These prayers are now appointed for the priest, so that the priest recites them for himself. But in the Greek service books, and in our old ones, which are written as many as one hundred, two hundred, and three hundred years ago and even more, these prayers are not found. There are many differences in practice. The Greek books and our old translations do not have a dismissal [aloud] for the whole church.[44] I ask for your decision in these matters: should we follow our new, printed books, or the Greek and our old books, which together indicate one single order and rule?
>
> And the augmented ektene at the holy liturgy contains many petitions, whereas in the Greek and in our old books there are few.[45]

Then the tsar, all the assembled bishops and clergy, and the entire council answered that "It is proper and right to correct the books in accordance with the old [Slavonic] manuscripts and the Greek books."[46] Nikon then brought up a number of other Russian practices which he wanted corrected:

i) the custom of leaving the Royal Doors open from the beginning of the liturgy to the Great Entrance;

ii) the custom of beginning the liturgy only at the 7th or 8th hour (1:00 or 2:00 p.m.) on some Sundays;

iii) the practice of not placing relics under the altar table at the consecration of a church;

iv) the custom of allowing untonsured persons, and even twice- or thrice-married men, to read or sing from the ambo;

v) the number of prostrations during Lent;[47]

vi) the custom of placing the antimension under the eiliton rather than over it, at the liturgy.

In each case, the council ruled that the Muscovite books must henceforth be corrected in accordance with the old Slavonic manuscripts and the Greek books.[48] All the bishops signed the Acts, but Paul, Bishop of Kolomna, added an objection to the decision about lenten prostrations.[49]

This council marked an abrupt shift in the Muscovite approach to the "correction" of the liturgical books. Greek models had already been used for many years, and Russians readily admitted that their books contained errors caused by the ignorance of translators and copyists. This correction had begun long before Nikon's patriarchate. Now, however, Nikon calls the differences in liturgical practice Russian innovations, thus implying that the entire Russian faith is tainted. Adding insult to injury, he further states that it is the Greek books which are pure. This is a direct challenge to the prevalent Russian notion that Moscow is the Third Rome. But faced with the combined forces of the patriarch and the tsar, the members of the council could only agree. Only Bishop Paul of Kolomna dared to speak up—and paid the price. He was imprisoned, deposed and disappeared soon after.[50]

Nikon did not bring up several other significant issues at this council.[51] The first was the sign of the Cross: the Russians used two fingers, the Greeks three. The second was the number of alleluias: at this time, the

Greeks were consistently using three alleluias to conclude psalmody in the office and the Cherubicon at the liturgy, while the Russians generally sang only two. The third issue concerned the addition of the word *istinnago* to the eighth article of the Creed in the Slavonic text—although in this case, a corrected text was included in the Acts of the council, as we have seen. The first two issues had been legislated by the Stoglav Council of 1551[52] and may for this reason have been too delicate to raise. According to Kapterev, Nikon was aware that this council, composed only of Russians, would not have directly overruled the Stoglav.[53] Undoubtedly, Nikon's opponents would have had a much stronger hand had they been able to appeal directly to the Stoglav for support.

Willingly or not, the 1654 Council accepted the proposed "correction" of the Russian books according to the Greek books. Yet what the council authorized was not the use of the contemporary Greek editions, but that of ancient Greek and Slavonic manuscripts. Thus the account of the Council, printed in the introduction to the 1655 *Sluzhebnik,* repeatedly states that the new Moscow books are to be corrected according to the "ancient Greek and Slavonic books."[54] This introduction further states that Arsenii Sukhanov brought back many Greek liturgical books, some over a thousand years old, which were used for the correction.[55] The purpose of this introduction was to show that the corrected books were a return to ancient practice shared by Greeks and Russians alike. For while the Russians could perhaps be convinced that their books contained some innovations, they were not up to admitting the superiority of modern Greek editions over the Russian ones.

The 1654 Council was interpreted by Nikon, and by the subsequent defenders of his reform, as a clear mandate for the "correction" of the liturgical books. Its decisions were signed by all the bishops, by the leading representatives of the Russian Church, and were confirmed by the tsar. Nikon understood the council as having given him the authority to bring Russian practice in line with contemporary Greek practice and to correct Russian innovations. Thus he took the decision of the Council "to correct the books in accordance with the old [Russian] manuscripts and the Greek books" to mean that the new Greek printed editions could be used. These editions were printed chiefly in Venice, as the Greeks under Turkish occupation had no access to printing presses. Like his Russian contemporaries, Nikon had no notion of liturgical evolution; so once he accepted the orthodoxy of Greek practice, he assumed that the ancient Greek manuscripts would agree totally with the modern Greek editions. And since he did not know Greek he could not judge for himself.[56] Once it was discovered that Nikon had had the Russian books reformed in accordance with modern Greek editions, the apologists for the reform went to great lengths to show that this council had actually authorized the use of Greek books—printed books, as opposed to manuscripts.[57]

Shortly after the council, on June 12, 1654, Nikon writes to Patriarch Paisios of Constantinople. In his letter, he asks a series of questions about various, often minute, rubrical details, including the same questions he posed to the 1654 Council. He adds accusations against Neronov and Bishop Paul of Kolomna.[58] While the original text of this letter is not extant, its contents can be reconstructed from an extant rough draft of this document, as well as from the answer of Constantinople, which arrived on May 15, 1655, and from comments made by Nikon's opponents.[59] In the rough draft of the letter, which has been published, Nikon states that he has discovered differences between Russian and Greek books, caused by the ignorance of translators and copyists, and asks that Paisios convene a council of Eastern patriarchs and bishops to examine the matter and send a reply. "Thus the all-holy name of our Lord and God Jesus Christ, glorified in the Trinity, may be glorified by the Eastern Orthodox Church in one voice, in one mind, and in one ordo [*edinochiniem*]."[60] He then goes on to list the liturgical differences he has found. Nikon was seeking outside support for his reform, undoubtedly because of the strong opposition his reform was provoking.[61] But this letter is also significant because it places the Eastern patriarchs in the position of arbiters over Russian church life.[62]

4. Patriarch Makarios of Antioch in Moscow

On Feb. 2, 1655, Makarios arrived in Moscow.[63] Like all the Eastern clergy and monks who came to Russia at this period, he was seeking money from the tsar. Like them, he also brought political news from the Turkish empire.[64] In Moscow, he joined the Serbian Metropolitan Gabriel, who had been in Russia since May 1, 1654, had stayed in Moscow during the plague in the latter half of 1654, and had been permitted to administer the Church while the tsar and Nikon were away.[65] Like Makarios, Gabriel participated in the debates about the reform, in councils, and in church services. On Feb. 12, 1655, the two foreigners were presented first to the tsar, then to Nikon.[66] The same day, Nikon and the two foreign bishops dined at the tsar's table.[67] Nikon was to put these visitors, particularly Makarios, to great use in pushing his reforms.

Nikon repeatedly asked his guest to instruct him about differences in practice: "If you find anything to criticize in the order of our services, tell us about it, so that we may do what is proper."[68] Makarios, eager to please him in everything, happily obliged.[69] As Paul of Aleppo states, Nikon nearly always followed Makarios' advice,[70] implicitly trusting him. Nikon constantly wanted to know the Greek way of doing things, as the following example indicates:

> Nikon repeatedly asked our teacher to write down for him the rite of consecration [ἐγκαίνια] of a church and the entire order of this service, in accordance with the practice of the Greeks...Because of this we found ourselves in great difficulty, because the rite of consecration of a church is not found in printed Greek euchologies, nor in Arabic ones, nor any others, but is completely absent from them, as our teacher did not find it after arduous searches....Having searched for a long time, we found it by inspiration from above, in one of the books from the Holy Mountain, an ancient Greek composition on this subject, and our father the patriarch translated it with great effort from Greek to Arabic. As soon as he finished it, Patriarch Nikon, of his own accord, came to him towards evening on Pentecost Monday and asked him to bless the church and to perform the entire service in Greek...The archdeacon of the Moscow Patriarch attended the service with several scribes to write down the entire service.[71]

During this period, Nikon manifested a very strong love of all things Greek. This attraction was not, as Florovskii wryly points out, a return to Greek patristic roots, but rather a passion for Greek ceremony, its richness and visible splendor.[72] When the former Patriarch of Constantinople, Athanasios Patellarios, visited Moscow in April 1653, Nikon asked him to compose an essay describing how the hierarchal liturgy is celebrated in the East.[73] Nikon built several monasteries patterned after Greek models and gave them Greek names. He invited Greek iconographers and silversmiths to Moscow. He liked Greek music and food. He introduced Greek ambos in some churches and began to carry a Greek episcopal staff.[74] On December 21, 1655, he began to wear a Greek kamilavka, or klobuk—a humorous episode described by Paul of Aleppo:

Patriarch Nikon, having great love for Greek kamilavkas and klobuks, made himself a new white klobuk, which looked like that of the Greek monks, except that a Cherubim was embroidered in gold and precious stones above the eyes. The klobuks of Muscovite monks, of bishops, and of the patriarch are very ugly: they are all knitted out of wool, do not have kamilavkas, but are sewn to the skufias without a round frame, but with fur trim. The klobuks of monks are very large, covering their eyes and ears and falling on their shoulders. From under them, you can barely distinguish their faces...[75]

The occasion was the celebration of the feast of St Peter, first Metropolitan of Moscow: this feast, Paul observes, was celebrated even more solemnly than Christmas. The tsar and his family were in attendance and the services were conducted by Nikon, Makarios and Gabriel, together with three other bishops, ten archimandrites wearing miters, twelve priests, twenty deacons, and more than twenty acolytes and subdeacons.

No better occasion than this could possibly present itself to Nikon. Knowing the tsar's love for him, and taking advantage of the presence of our teacher, one of the ecumenical patriarchs, Nikon first discussed with Makarios and then secretly handed him the above-mentioned klobuk, which, as is usual, had a kamilavka. Nikon asked Makarios to intercede with the tsar, so that the tsar would put it on him, i.e. Nikon, because he greatly feared that the lay people would say to him: "You have abolished our ancient custom and the attire of our first, holy bishops." This is exactly what happened afterward: when he put on the new klobuk, the people began to grumble strongly against him, though secretly from fear of the tsar. Our teacher, approaching the tsar, spoke to him thus: "There are four of us patriarchs in the world, and our attire is all the same. With our permission, this brother of ours is appointed Patriarch of Moscow, of rank equal to the Pope of Rome, who is distinguished from us by his white attire. If it please Your Royal Highness, I would like to place this kamilavka and klobuk, which I have made for him anew, on Nikon, so that he may appear just like us." The tsar, because of his great love for Patriarch Nikon, was very happy and answered our teacher: "*Batiushka, dobro!*" i.e., "It is good!" The tsar took them from our teacher, kissed them, ordered Nikon to remove his old klobuk and kamilavka, and placed the new ones on him. When he placed them on the patriarch, Nikon's face began to glow. This Greek dress looked very good on him, but the old one, as we have said, disfigured him, as it was a skufia and not a kamilavka, and had a small, short, and tight klobuk. The patriarch was very happy, but the assisting bishops, heads of monasteries, priests and lay people, seeing this, began to grumble strongly against Nikon, saying: "See how he is changing the attire of bishops, which they have received through the inspiration of the Holy Spirit at the time when we became Christians through St Peter. How will the earth not begin to shake under him? For, although he has up to now dressed in the Muscovite way, he has become a Greek."[76]

Subsequently, however, the new style became very popular and, as Paul sarcastically comments, a monk from the Holy Mountain could have made a killing if he were to arrive with a large supply of Greek kamilavkas and klobuks. Paul concludes this account by boasting that this "good custom" was first introduced by his father the patriarch.[77] This episode clearly exemplifies the condescending attitude of the Easterners towards the Muscovites. It also shows the petty nature of many of the "reforms," and typifies as well a people's attachment to their own practices.

On only one occasion did Nikon not follow Makarios' recommendations, "rejecting his authority on the subject," as Paul of Aleppo comments.[78] The issue involved the practice of blessing water twice at Epiphany, at the church on the eve of the feast and at the river after the feast-day liturgy—this was the practice both in Russia and in the East. Nikon, however, had discovered in some Athonite work a saying by Patriarch Photios of Constantinople that the blessing should be done only once.[79] On Dec. 16, 1655, Nikon convened a "small" council, attended only by two metropolitans, one archbishop, and one bishop, which agreed with him.[80] A decree ordering this new practice was sent out in the name of the tsar, of Nikon, and of the council.[81] On Jan. 5, 1656, the eve of Epiphany, Nikon, with the tsar and Patriarch Makarios in attendance, blessed the water at the river in a ceremony described by Paul in all its pomp and glory.[82]

The story does not end there. Paul writes that Makarios had tried to dissuade Nikon from changing the rite, and that Nikon did not listen.

> The tsar, meanwhile, thought that Nikon performed the rite precisely on the advice of our father the Patriarch. But now, when the news reached him that this was not true, he argued with Nikon and cursed him, calling him "*Muzhik, bl...n syn,*"[83] that is, "Stupid peasant." The patriarch said to him: "I am your spiritual father, why do you insult me?" To this the tsar replied: "You are not my father, but the holy Patriarch of Antioch is truly my father, and I will now order him brought back here right away."[84]

This argument, Paul tells us, took place in church, on the evening of Great Friday. Later, the 1667 Council overturned Nikon's decision and approved the Greek and former Slavic practice.[85]

On March 4, 1655, the Sunday of Orthodoxy,[86] Nikon and Makarios celebrated together at the Cathedral of the Dormition, in the presence of the tsar. After the long service, which included a recitation of the Synodicon, listing all the Greek and Russian saints, all the Orthodox emperors of Byzantium and rulers of Moscow, concluding with anathemas against all heresies, Nikon ascended the ambo and began to read and explain patristic texts about the veneration of icons. During his sermon, Nikon ordered that a number of icons painted in "Frankish" and Polish styles be brought to him. These were icons which Nikon had ordered seized from the houses of Moscow residents, including high government officials, during the summer of 1654, while the tsar was away at war. Nikon had had the eyes gouged out of these "Western" icons and ordered them paraded throughout Moscow by heralds, who announced that such icons were forbidden. These actions provoked shock among the populace, which was devoted to icons: the subsequent solar eclipse on Aug. 2, 1654, and the epidemic in Moscow that same year were blamed on Nikon's scandalous and heretical action.[87] Paul of Aleppo describes the events at the cathedral:

> A good occasion presented itself to the patriarch [Nikon] on this day, as the tsar was present. He spoke at length, saying that such iconography as on these icons was not permissible. Then he appealed to the witness of our father the patriarch, and to demonstrate the illegality of the new iconography, he indicated that it was similar to that of the Franks. The patriarchs anathematized and excommunicated both those who make such images and those who keep them in their houses. Nikon took these images in his right hand, one after the other, showed them to the people, and smashed them against the metal tiles of the floor, so that they broke into bits, and then ordered them burned…

The tsar intervened, asking that they be buried instead, and this was done.[88] This condemnation of the new icons upset everyone. The defenders of the old ways could not tell the difference between the old icons and the new, so Nikon's actions appeared to them as blasphemy. The upper classes, increasingly westernized, were needlessly alienated.[89] Yet these considerations had no effect on Nikon. But this was not yet the end:

> Then Nikon began to speak about the sign of the Cross, for Russians don't cross themselves as we do, with three fingers, but hold their fingers like the bishop when he blesses. Then Nikon again referred to the authority of our father the patriarch. Our teacher had already talked to Nikon about this, that such a sign of the Cross is not permissible; and now he said the following to all the people through an interpreter: "In Antioch, and nowhere else, were believers in Christ first called Christians. From there the practices spread. Neither in Alexandria, nor in Constantinople, nor in Jerusalem, nor on Sinai, nor on Athos, nor even

in ,Wallachia and Moldavia, nor in the land of the Cossacks, does anyone cross himself in this way, but with all three fingers held together."[90]

Thus Nikon used the presence of Makarios to push his reform. The latter, in Moscow to collect money, was obliging in everything, doing and saying whatever Nikon and the tsar wished, and more than happy to serve as the authority.

5. *The 1655 Council and the New Sluzhebnik*

Not waiting for the reply from Constantinople, Nikon called a new council during the fifth week of Lent (March 25-31, 1655). We have two accounts of this sobor, one from the foreword to the 1655 *Sluzhebnik*, the other from the eyewitness description of Paul of Aleppo. Nikon's purpose in calling this council was to gain conciliar approval for his reforms, not just from Russian bishops and clergy, but also from the Eastern patriarchs.[91] The council was thus attended by Makarios and Gabriel, as well as by Russian authorities. The tsar, however, was absent, having left Moscow on March 1.[92]

As we saw at the beginning of this chapter, the foreword to the 1655 *Sluzhebnik* gives the "official" description of the events leading up to the council[93] and of the council itself.[94] According to this account, not only did Paisios' reply come before the council, but Arsenii Sukhanov was sent to the East to collect books after this reply. The books he brought back were then examined and compared at the present council to the Russian books. This is inaccurate in a number of respects. First, the council lasted a week at most, as Paul of Aleppo states.[95] The members of the council would not have had the time for a thorough examination and comparison of the texts. Second, had they in fact been able to conduct such a study, they would have learned that none of the "ancient" books agree even among themselves, much less with the printed Muscovite editions. Third, having left already in October 1653, Sukhanov returned to Moscow only on Feb. 22, 1655, bringing with him 498 Greek books and manuscripts from Mt. Athos. One month would hardly be sufficient to study all these books! Finally, Sukhanov's collection contained almost no liturgical books, as the research of S. Belokurov,[96] and recently of B. Fonkich,[97] has pointed out. Thus the "official" account gives a deliberately fabricated version of the events, intended to justify the reforms in the face of growing opposition.

Paul of Aleppo's eyewitness account gives a somewhat different view. Nikon, he tells us, assembled the council at the suggestion of Patriarch Makarios in order to address the problem of certain innovations and errors in matters of faith. Paul then lists these "errors":

i) the Russians do not celebrate the eucharist on antimensia, which have representations on them and contain relics, but on plain white cloths;

ii) at the *proskomide*, they remove not nine ranks (particles), but only four;[98]

iii) the text of the Nicene Creed contains several errors;

iv) Russians venerate icons only once or twice a year;

v) they do not distribute antidoron at the end of the eucharistic liturgy;

vi) they place their fingers differently for the sign of the Cross;

vii) Russians rebaptize Roman Catholics;

viii) other unspecified practices.

Following Makarios' advice, Paul continues, Nikon had had the *Sluzhebnik* translated from the Greek, so that it agreed fully with "authentic" Greek practice in its rubrics and explanations, so that "even a child could understand them." At one of the sessions, Paul tells us, Nikon declared: "I am a Russian, the son of a Russian, but my conviction and my faith are Greek." Some of the bishops reacted to all this with approval; but others, "who had a dull mind," secretly objected, saying to themselves that "we will not change our books and customs, which we accepted in ancient times." But remembering the fate of Bishop Paul of Kolomna, they kept their objections to themselves. Following the council, several thousand copies of the new *Sluzhebnik* were printed and distributed throughout the country. Nikon further ordered that 15,000 new antimensia, with representations and inscriptions, be printed. He blessed these with relics of saints and similarly ordered them distributed. The practice of rebaptizing Latins was abolished, and "many other errors were corrected."[99]

Thus this council, without a great deal of discussion, simply approved the new *Sluzhebnik*, which had been prepared in advance by Nikon's chief correctors, Arsenios the Greek in particular. The decisions concerning rubrical issues raised at this council were incorporated, and the new book was quickly printed, together with the lengthy introduction discussed in the first section of this chapter. The introduction is dated Aug. 31, 1655, and the book was released on Sept. 20. Just four days after its release, on Sept. 24, Nikon orders that eighty quaternia be reprinted, and on Oct. 26, he commands that ninety-five more quaternia be reprinted. This final version was released on Jan. 5, 1656.[100] So there are three variant recensions of the 1655 *Sluzhebnik*, all containing the same introduction and with the same pagination.[101]

Because of these constant revisions, as well as further editions in 1656, 1657, and 1658, none of Nikon's *Sluzhebniks* agree even among themselves. This inconsistency was noted by the earliest opponents of the reform. Thus priest Nikita Dobrynin (also known as Nikita Pustosviat) writes in a petition to Tsar Alexis: "Six editions of Nikon's *Sluzhebnik* were forcibly distributed, and no single one agrees with another."[102] Deacon Fedor, in a 1666 petition submitted to the tsar made when he was being defrocked, says the same.[103] This inconsistency was, for the Old-Believers, in itself evidence that the Nikonian books were full of errors.

The early opponents were also aware that the new books were modeled on Venetian Greek editions.[104] Thus Deacon Fedor writes in the same 1666 petition: "The modern books, which Patriarch Nikon had purchased in Greece, are Greek. These books are published in the realm of the apostate Pope of Rome in three cities—Rome, Paris, and Venice—in Greek, but not according to the ancient piety."[105] Elsewhere he says:

> From these newly-printed Greek books Nikon published the new books in Moscow: that is why they don't agree with our old books. Arsenios the Greek, the enemy of God, taught him, Nikon, to buy those heretical books, which he then translated into our Slavonic tongue; and thus was created a great upheaval in all the churches of the entire Russian land.[106]

Nikita Dobrynin, a priest at the cathedral in Suzdal, says the same thing in his petition.[107]

Questions are raised by some bishops as well. Bishop Alexander of Viatka asks a question at the 1666 Council regarding the new books: "The new *Trebnik* does not agree with either the Kievan, or the previous Moscow editions. From where does truth come if we must use Greek books published in Venice? We must not accept customs and rules from Greeks living unwillingly among the Latins."[108] The best evidence comes from Silvester Medvedev, who was a corrector working in the Printing Office from 1679 to 1689: "They did not want to agree with the ancient Greek and Russian books, by which our saints have achieved salvation, but they liked the Greek books, newly-printed in foreign lands, and followed them."[109] But these new books, he insists, were spoiled, and the 1654 Council had ordered that the ancient Greek and Slavonic books be followed.[110]

There is, of course, an obvious reason why modern Greek books were followed. First, the primary goal of the liturgical reform was to bring Russian practice in line with contemporary Greek usage. This Greek practice was expressed in the Venetian editions, the only ones available. Second, the use of ancient manuscripts, both Greek and Russian, was complicated by the simple fact that no two manuscripts were identical. And, in any case, the absence of critical tools, not to mention a total ignorance of liturgical evolution, made a "return to antiquity" impossible. Under the circumstances, the choice to use the modern Greek editions was inevitable.[111]

The 1655 Council and the subsequent publication of Nikon's *Sluzhebnik* thus represent a milestone in the reform. The program received sanction from the universal church, in the person of Patriarch Makarios. Nikon formally declared his adherence to the Greek model. The council is used as justification for the printing of the *Sluzhebnik*, which, because it contains the most commonly used services, is by far the most important single product of the reform.

6. The Reply from Constantinople

On May 15, 1655, six weeks after the 1655 Council, a Greek merchant, whom Russian sources call Manuil Konstantinov, delivered two letters to Nikon. The first was the official reply to the list of questions that Nikon had submitted after the 1654 Council.[112] This letter contained an explanation of the liturgy and answers to Nikon's questions. It was composed by Meletios Syrigos,[113] the leading Greek theologian of the day, and signed by Patriarch Paisios, together with 24 metropolitans, one archbishop, three bishops, and a number of officials from the Great Church.[114] Nikon published a Slavonic translation of this letter, with some alterations, in the *Skrizhal'*,[115] and in the second part of both editions of the 1658 *Sluzhebnik*.[116] Accompanying this conciliar letter was a personal epistle from Paisios to Nikon. The original text is lost, but excerpts from it are printed in the foreword to the 1655 *Sluzhebnik*.[117]

The conciliar reply, in answer to the questions sent to Constantinople in 1654, is a remarkable document. Though initially interpreted by Nikon as a blanket mandate for his reform, it is in fact a well-balanced statement cautioning Nikon not to act rashly and instructing him that total unity is necessary only in matters of faith—in essentials. The letter opens with an introductory passage praising Nikon for his zeal and efforts in pastoring his flock, and particularly for his wisdom in turning to Constantinople for advice. It encourages Nikon to turn to Constantinople in the future, "so that we shall always be as one, both in one faith and in one baptism, always saying one and the same thing with one mouth and one heart, so as not to disagree with each other in anything."[118] But then the letter goes on to define what this total agreement means:

> You complain strongly regarding disagreements in certain practices which exist in local churches, and you wonder whether these various practices damage our faith. We praise this notion, for whoever is afraid of falling into minor sins protects himself also from falling into large sins. But we correct this thought, for, with regard to heretics, we do in fact have a commandment from the apostle to avoid them as perverted after the first and second admonitions (Tit 3:11), just as schismatics who, although they agree with the Orthodox in the most important dogmas, still have certain peculiar beliefs foreign to those accepted by the entire Church. But if it happens that a certain church differs from another in certain practices which are not important and essential to faith, or which have nothing to do with the chief articles of faith, but only in insignificant practices, such as for example the time for celebrating the liturgy, or which fingers a priest uses to give the blessing, and the like, then this should not cause any division, as long as one and the same faith is preserved. This is because our church did not receive the entire present *typikon* from the beginning, but little by little.[119]

The liturgy, Paisios writes, developed over time, but the faith remained unchanged. We did not always have antiphons or troparia, canons, kontakia...[120] "So we must not think even now that our Orthodox faith is spoiled if someone has liturgical practices which differ somewhat from another in non-essentials . . . as long as they agree in the essentials with the catholic Church."[121] The introductory section concludes with an offer to send Nikon an "Orthodox Confession of Faith," so that Nikon himself may judge what is essential to faith.[122] The intention to temper Nikon is evident in this letter.

Following this introduction, the letter answers Nikon's rubrical questions one by one. These questions strike the modern reader as petty and irrelevant, and the occasionally sarcastic tone of the replies shows that it struck the Greeks in Constantinople in much the same way. The reply to the question concerning the proper time for celebrating the eucharistic liturgy is not devoid of humor:

> As to the time for the liturgy, which is the second question, and about which you also ask in the eleventh, to this we answer that you do well in beginning it at the third hour, according to the canons, and completing it before the seventh or ninth hour of the day. For the longer one occupies oneself in praising the Lord, the greater the benefit and merit, just as for the heavenly angels who ceaselessly sing praises to the Lord. But we must add that these times are not set once and for all, so that we cannot celebrate the liturgy at any hour other than the third; for on the holy and great day of Easter, and of the Nativity of Christ, and of the Theophany, the liturgy begins during the night; and on Holy Thursday and Holy Saturday, we have received the tradition of celebrating the liturgy in the evening because of certain mysteries connected with those days, about which we shall not speak here; and in the Monastery of the Non-Sleepers, they celebrated it at almost every hour.[123] That is why we also write that if the third hour passes, or another earlier hour, because of some pressing need, the liturgy must not be omitted. This is what we do in our churches, for the grace of the Spirit is not limited by one or another moment in time.[124]

In answering Nikon's questions, the letter repeatedly attempts to temper his zeal. Thus the answer to the seventh question, where Nikon asked about what to do with those who opposed the reform, Paisios writes:

> Concerning the polemics which you carry on about the order of divine services, regarding which you write in the seventh question, we beg Your Beatitude in the name of our Lord Jesus Christ to put an end to them in your sagacity. "For the servant of the Lord must not be quarrelsome" (2 Tim 2:24), especially about those things which do not belong among the chief and essential articles of the faith. And convince them to accept that order which we described, the order held by the entire Eastern Church without any change, just as it has come down to us from the beginning through tradition. We are proud of the fact that while other churches, after they separated themselves from us, have accepted and daily accept many innovations and newly-devised dogmas, we, with the help of the Holy Spirit, have changed nothing from the time that the Seventh Council assembled and confirmed our order. As a result of this, just as our old books,

located in various libraries, agree with the text of the liturgies of Chrysostom and Basil, so our new books manifest not the smallest difference. But it may be that yours do not agree with ours in essential matters, and not only in those things which the Typikon leaves to the discretion of the bishop: in that case, write to us about them, and we shall discuss it in a synod.[125]

Nikon's questions are thus dismissed as trivial. This passage, however, is interesting in that it shows that the Greeks themselves seem to believe that their own liturgy has remained unchanged for the nine centuries since the last ecumenical council. Further, this passage could easily be used to justify Nikon's reform on the basis of the newly-printed Greek books, which are now affirmed as pure by Greek conciliar decree.

Together with answers to specific rubrical questions, Paisios includes the then current Byzantine interpretation of the liturgy. This explanation, based entirely on a "life-of-Christ" symbolism, is used as the basis for answering certain details, such as the proper time for opening and closing the doors of the sanctuary. Every single action in the liturgy is given a specific, symbolic meaning which connects it to an event in Christ's life: thus the exclamation "The doors, the doors...," which immediately precedes the Creed, is seen as the opening of the doors of the tomb, and the waving of the aer over the paten and chalice during the Creed represents the earthquake which accompanied the resurrection.[126] In short, Paisios attempts to instill a somewhat broader, theological perspective, to pass from the external detail to the underlying meaning. Nowhere is this more evident than in the answer to Nikon's question about how priests and bishops are to fold their fingers for blessing:

The Church blesses all who represent the name of the Messiah, or, which is the same, the name of Jesus Christ—that is, representing the letters iota and sigma, which is the abbreviation for Jesus, and the chi and sigma, which similarly stands for Christ. But which fingers are used to represent these four letters is irrelevant, as long as he who blesses and the one blessed have in mind that this blessing comes down from Jesus Christ through the hand of the priest, and that Jesus Christ himself gives the grace of blessing at the request of the one who seeks it with faith. But it is better to do it as Christ is represented blessing on icons, for that way of holding the fingers most clearly expresses the name of Jesus Christ. The large, that is the first [thumb], and the fourth fingers joined together represent Jesus; and the two [index and third] extended, one of them slightly bent, represent X, and the last, small finger, C—together standing for Christ. But it will also mean the same thing if he holds the last two fingers bent in the shape of the two sigmas, and the first three fingers upright, representing iota and chi—and this doesn't make any difference.[127]

Significantly, Nikon excludes the last few sentences, which allow an alternate form, from the translation published in the *Skrizhal'*. Moreover, the Slavonic translation reverses the symbolism of the fingers, so that "the second and third fingers, held together, represent Jesus, and the first and fourth, joined together, represent Jesus, and the first and fourth, joined together, represent X, and the last, small finger, C, together forming XC."[128]

The personal letter from Paisios to Nikon, which accompanied the conciliar epistle, is no longer extant. The brief excerpts from it, printed in the foreword to the 1655 *Sluzhebnik*, consist of strong praise of Nikon and of his reform program, urging total agreement in practice with the Great Church. Differences in the text of the Creed, not mentioned by Nikon in his 1654 letter, are even brought up, and the foreword mentions that a correct text of the Creed was appended to Paisios' letter.[129] The tone of the passages is radically different from that of the conciliar letter, specifically in the insistence on total agreement in every detail. This can be explained either by the fact that these excerpts are simple fabrications or, more likely, that the citations are selective and quoted out of context.

Because the letters arrived after the 1655 Moscow Council, which had approved the first edition of Nikon's *Sluzhebnik*, they could not be used in the preparation of this edition. The Constantinopolitan practices described, however, were incorporated into the 1656 edition.[130] But the letters did not succeed in tempering the reform, and Nikon continued his hard line.

7. The Battle Continues

Following the ratification of the new *Sluzhebnik* by the 1655 Council, Nikon continued to push the reform. Not personally involved in the actual "correction" of the books, he busied himself chiefly with ritual, rather than textual, details. It is not surprising, therefore, that it was mainly over these external details that the battle lines were drawn. By far, the most inflammatory issue was the proper way to make the sign of the Cross. This came to be the symbolic issue which stood for all of Nikon's reform, and with which modern readers are most familiar. Nikon addressed this issue from the beginning, with the publication of the 1653

Psalter, and the issuing of his "Pamiat'" in February of the same year. Because it engendered such strong opposition, and because it contradicted the decision of the 1551 Stoglav Council, Nikon did not push the issue for the time being, and it was not even raised at the 1654 and 1655 Councils. However, Nikon felt that he had gained the upper hand. His opponents were on the defensive, his reforms had received the sanction not only of the Russian bishops, but of the Eastern patriarchs, represented by Makarios of Antioch. Now he felt strong enough to address the subject once more.

An appropriate occasion presented itself on Tuesday, Feb. 12, 1656, the feast of the Saints Meletios of Antioch and Alexis of Moscow. As this was also the name day of the tsar, a large crowd gathered for the vigil service at the Chudov Monastery. The tsar was present, with his entire retinue, together with Nikon, Makarios of Antioch, and many clergy and notables.[131] At the synaxarion,[132] Nikon ordered that the story about Meletios of Antioch be read. This legend had been quoted in the Acts of the Stoglav Council to justify the use of two fingers for the sign of the Cross:

> Meletios, Bishop of Sebaste, is illustrious for his life and for his words. Because of disorders by those under his authority, he renounced his episcopacy and kept his silence. Then the heretics, thinking that Meletios shared their ideas, asked the emperor to make him patriarch, which he did. Later, at a council held on the issue of the one essence [of the Trinity], the Arians expressed a contrary opinion, and Meletios gave a visible proof of the divine teaching. The people asked him to show them God's teaching right away, so Meletios raised three fingers in the name of the Father, the Son, and the Holy Spirit: there was no sign.[133] Then Meletios, holding two fingers together, with his three other fingers bent down, blessed the people: lightning came forth from him like fire. He then pronounced these praise-worthy words: "We understand three but speak only of one."[134]

The Acts then strongly emphasize that the use of two fingers is the only proper way, as demonstrated by this spurious text.

When the reading from the synaxarion was completed, Nikon asked Makarios to explain how this passage was to be understood. Makarios answered:

> All Orthodox people, hear! I am the successor and heir of the throne of St Meletios. I know for certain that when St Meletios showed his first three fingers spread apart, there was no sign. And when he put the three together, he showed

the sign with them. And if anyone does not make the sign of the Cross on his face with these three fingers, but takes the last two with the large finger, having two large fingers outstretched, and makes the sign of the Cross in this way, imitates the Armenians, for that is how the Armenians make the sign of the Cross.[135]

Thus, for the first time, the traditional Russian custom is condemned as a heresy. The same spurious text which was used to support one side is now appropriated by the other.

Having engaged in battle, Nikon soon escalated it. On the Sunday of Orthodoxy,[136] Feb. 24, 1656, Nikon, the tsar, Patriarch Makarios of Antioch, and Metropolitans Gabriel of Serbia and Gregory of Nicea were all assembled at the Cathedral of the Dormition. During the anathemas, Makarios stood before the crowd, put the three large fingers of his hand together "in the image of the most holy and undivided Trinity, and said: 'Every Orthodox Christian must make the sign of the Cross on his face with these three first fingers: and if anyone does it based on the writing of Theodoret and on false tradition, let him be anathema!'"[137] The anathemas were then repeated by Gabriel and Gregory.[138] Nikon further obtained written condemnations of the two-fingered sign of the Cross from all these foreign bishops.[139]

On April 23, a new council was called in Moscow. Its purpose was twofold: first, Nikon wanted to affirm the three-fingered sign of the Cross by conciliar decree; second, he wanted sanction for the publication of the *Skrizhal'*. Once again, the presence of foreign bishops in Moscow served his purpose. In his speech to the assembled council, Nikon explains the reasons for his request. The two-fingered sign of the Cross, he states, does not adequately express the mysteries of the Trinity and the Incarnation. He appeals to the synodal letter of Paisios, claiming that it condemns the use of only two fingers,[140] as well as to Makarios' statements of Feb. 12, to the anathemas of Feb. 24, and to the subsequent written statements by the foreign hierarchs. He then asks the sobor to add its own decision.[141] Nikon then asked the council for approval of the *Skrizhal'*. This was a book he had received from Paisios of Constantinople in 1653, which had then been translated into Slavonic by Arsenios the Greek.[142] Written by the Greek hieromonk John Nathaniel and published in Venice in 1574,[143] the *Skrizhal'* was a commentary on the liturgy based mainly on Cabasilas, but with excerpts also from other mystagogies, chiefly those of Symeon of

Thessalonika and Germanus of Constantinople.[144] To John Nathaniel's work, Nikon added a number of shorter articles, dealing mostly with the text of the Creed and the sign of the Cross, as well as an edited version of Paisios' 1655 reply. The book was printed already in October 1655, but it was released only after this council formally approved it. After the council, an introduction entitled "*Slovo otveshchatelnoe*" was added, explaining the reform and containing the decision of the council.[145]

The significance of this council lies chiefly in its formal condemnation of those who rejected the three-fingered sign of the Cross—and, by extension, those who rejected the Greek model—as heretics. For those who make the sign of the Cross by folding their thumb together with their two small fingers "are demonstrating the inequality of the Holy Trinity, which is Arianism,"[146] or "Nestorianism."[147] By branding his opponents as heretics, Nikon was making schism unavoidable.[148]

On May 16, 1656, the Sunday following Ascension, the council met in another session, this time to try Ivan Neronov, now the monk Gregory.[149] After being imprisoned in a monastery in 1653, Neronov had escaped, been tonsured a monk, and continued his active opposition to the reform. He found support everywhere, due to his great popularity, and thus managed to evade Nikon's henchmen for a long time, even spending a few weeks in Moscow with the tsar's confessor, Stefan Vonifatiev, in the latter's cell and with the knowledge of the tsar.[150] Neronov was accused of slandering the tsar, Nikon, and the Eastern patriarchs, and of condemning the old books [!], because he asserted that the modern Greek books did not agree with the old,[151] as well as of being tonsured a monk without permission. The council condemns him for insubordination. Patriarch Makarios himself pronounced the verdict at the cathedral. The event is described by Paul of Aleppo:

> Our father, the Patriarch, said the following to all the people through an interpreter: he called him [Neronov] a second Arius, for just as the latter was archpriest in Alexandria, so the former was archpriest in Moscow. He anathematized him, cursed and excommunicated him, as well as anyone who follows his words. The singers and priests sang "Anathema" three times.[152]

Thus, once again, Makarios served Nikon well.

In October 1656, another council in Moscow, composed only of Russian bishops, approved for publication a corrected *Trebnik* (Ritual) and set up new episcopal sees in Smolensk and Viatka.[153] The most significant change in the *Trebnik* was the abandonment of the Russian practice of rebaptizing all converts to Orthodoxy, including Latins and Uniates, and even those Orthodox who had been baptized by sprinkling rather than full immersion. A Moscow Council on May 11, 1656, attended by Makarios of Antioch, had opted for the current Greek practice of accepting the validity of Latin baptism.[154] Interestingly, the publication of the *Trebnik* did not cause the same uproar as did that of the *Sluzhebnik*. This can be explained by the fact that the common people reacted chiefly to changes in the most commonly used, and therefore best known, practices. This is why changes in the sign of the Cross, in the number of prostrations, and in the text of the Creed, aroused such furor and became symbols for the entire reform. Nikon's own role in the reform largely involved settling these issues, and he did not personally concern himself with the actual correction of the books.[155] This helps to explain his future behavior with respect to the reform.

8. Can Schism Be Avoided?

After the end of 1656, Nikon's position on the reforms began to soften. We see no more dramatic trials or condemnations, no more councils are held. In fact, Nikon seems simply to lose interest in this task and to busy himself with other matters, such as his ambitious construction program. The reasons for this change of attitude are unclear, but there are several plausible explanations. The first possibility is that Nikon changed his attitude toward the old Russian books,[156] finally comprehending the content of the 1655 letter from Paisios. Though Nikon never expressed this publicly, there is, we shall see, some basis for accepting this view. The second explanation is that Nikon, once he lost the strong support of the tsar, lost his desire to push the reform.[157] In either case, Nikon's change of attitude is evident.

The first intimation of this different approach came at the beginning of 1657. On Jan. 4, Neronov, carrying a copy of the *Skrizhal'*, came to the patriarchal palace to see Nikon. He met with the patriarch and told him that he did not want to live under the condemnation of the Eastern patriarchs. If only he were restored to communion, he would accept the three-fingered sign of the Cross. At the same time, however, Neronov launched into a tirade against the new liturgical books, complaining that they were being corrected by Greeks and South-Russians, whose faith was corrupt. Nikon said nothing, and then ordered that Neronov be provided with food and lodging.[158] A few days later, at the insistence of the tsar, who had just returned to Moscow from an unsuccessful war with Sweden, Nikon restored Neronov into communion with the Church. Neronov, however, continued to abuse Nikon publicly. Despite these attacks, Nikon not only gave Neronov his blessing, but allowed him to continue using the old liturgical books, saying: "Both are good. It doesn't matter, use whichever books you wish."[159] Thus one of the most visible opponents of the book reform was permitted to use the old books at the Cathedral of the Dormition, the central cathedral of the Russian Church!

Such tolerant behavior is hardly characteristic of Nikon. Only the personal intercession of the tsar could have preserved Neronov from the fate shared by all who dared to oppose Nikon publicly. This, however, indicates that Nikon could no longer count on the tsar's unconditional support, which was the basis for his own, formerly unlimited, power. Indeed, from this point on, Nikon ceased pushing his reform. A year later, on Jan. 21, 1658, while attending vigil at the Cathedral of the Dormition, Nikon ordered the psalmist and singers to sing the triple alleluia after the psalmody. Neronov, who was present, began once again to berate him and insisted that the choirs sing the double alleluia, as in the old books. The choir followed Neronov's instruction, and Nikon, once again, did nothing.[160]

The once close relations between patriarch and tsar gradually cooled, and Alexis began avoiding Nikon.[161] In mid-1658, the situation was brought to a head. On July 10, following an incident between one of Nikon's functionaries and a representative of the tsar, Nikon resigned from the patriarchate. At the Cathedral of the Dormition, after celebrating the liturgy, Nikon removed his vestments, put on a simple monastic robe, and left.[162] He was undoubtedly hoping that the tsar himself would come to him to ask forgiveness and to renew the promise made when Nikon first became patriarch. But this did not happen. For over eight years, the Russian Church remained without a patriarch, and the tsar was the *de facto* head of the Church. However, in Nikon's absence, the reform of the liturgical books continued unabated. The correctors kept on working at the Pechatnyi Dvor, and new editions of various books were published,[163] though no new editions of the *Sluzhebnik* appeared after 1658. Most of the bishops of the Russian Church, all appointed by the tsar because of their support of the reforms, continued to oversee their implementation. Opposition to the reforms was not as heavily repressed, however, and this allowed the Old-Believers to expand their base of support.[164] In 1658, the famous Solovki Monastery in the Diocese of Novgorod, where many Greeks formerly had been sent for the "correction" of their faith, formally rejected the new books.[165] The situation grew increasingly chaotic, and heated polemics continued between proponents of the two sides. Part of this problem was merely logistical: the Moscow typography was unable to produce a sufficient number of books for all the churches and monasteries in Russia. In addition, the new books were very expensive.[166] Thus, right up to the 1666 Council, the old books were used even at the Convent of the Ascension in the Kremlin.[167] Compounding the issue was the simple fact that many of the lower clergy, particularly those in the provinces, were barely literate and had great difficulty in using the new books: often, they simply justified themselves by rejecting the new books as heretical.[168]

The continuation of the reform thus depended on the will of the tsar. Nikon, having abandoned his throne, no longer took any interest in it. In his frequent correspondence with Alexis, he never mentions the reform, a fact about which even the tsar complains.[169] But the tsar's resolve remained firm. Deacon Fedor, one of the early Old-Believer polemicists, describes a scene which took place at the ordination of Archbishop Simon of Vologda, on Oct. 23, 1664. During the service, on hearing Simon use the old text of the Creed, the tsar halted the consecration and sent him away in anger. Only after Simon fell at the tsar's feet and swore to use the new books did Alexis agree to proceed.[170]

The tsar did make repeated efforts to convince and convert the opponents of the liturgical reform. Thus, in early 1664, he ordered that Avvakum be brought to Moscow. Avvakum was treated very well here, and engaged in long discussions with Rtishchev and the tsar.[171] The tsar sought to reconcile him with the Church and was willing to allow him to use the old books, just as he had done with Neronov earlier.[172] Avvakum refused.[173] The tsar's desire to restore church peace was not fulfilled.

Because the tsar did not wish to use excessive force, as well as for practical reasons, a significant amount of flexibility was tolerated. Thus, in Oct. 1664, Pitirim, Metropolitan of Novgorod and *locum tenens* of the patriarchal throne, ordained thirteen monks from the Solovki according to the old books.[174]

9. The Councils of 1666-1667

His efforts to restore peace by negotiation having failed, the tsar decided to take a different approach. On August 29, 1664, Avvakum was again banished,[175] and the persecution against the Old-Believers increased. At the same time, Alexis began preparing for a council which would settle the issues once and for all. In addition to the liturgical reform and the question of what to do with those who continued to oppose it, the problem of selecting a successor to Nikon remained. Though the 1660 Council in Moscow had formally declared the see vacant, the tsar did not dare to select a replacement while Nikon remained not only alive and active, but also adamant in his declarations that only the ecumenical patriarchs could depose him.[176] For this purpose, already in December 1662, the tsar had invited the four Greek patriarchs to Moscow to resolve the Nikon affair.[177] The patriarchs did not come but sent a written answer, which reached Moscow in May 1664. This answer recommended that Nikon be formally deposed and a successor chosen.[178] However, some Greeks in Moscow, who favored Nikon, spread rumors that this letter was a forgery composed by Paisios Ligarides, or that the Greek patriarchs had been heavily bribed. These accusations caused sufficient confusion that the recommended action could not be taken.[179] In September 1664, the tsar again sent emissaries to the patriarchs requesting their assistance at a council,[180] and this time two of them, Paisios of Alexandria and Makarios of Antioch, agreed to come. Not waiting for their arrival, the tsar decided to assemble a council to deal with other matters.

i. The Council of 1666

The council was convoked on April 29, 1666, to address the issue of the correction of books and rubrics, and to deal with the opponents of the reform. Only Russian bishops were invited, although a number of foreign bishops were present in Moscow, including Paisios Ligarides of Gaza, who was to play such a visible role at the 1667 Council.

Prior to the opening of the council, in February, the tsar assembled all the bishops and heads of important monasteries and asked them for written declarations, in answer to certain questions concerning the reform:

a) "How are we to consider the most holy Greek patriarchs—of Constantinople, Alexandria, Antioch, and Jerusalem? Are they Orthodox?"

b) "How are we to consider the Greek printed books and ancient manuscripts which the most holy Greek patriarchs use, and according to which they praise God and celebrate the rites?"

c) "How are we now to consider the council held in the God-protected, glorious, sovereign, great city of Moscow…and subscribed to by all the clergy…in the year 1654?"[181]

The answers to these leading questions were obvious and clearly indicated the tsar's desires. Subsequently, the text of the questions and of the responses was added to the Acts of the Council, which were composed by Simeon of Polotsk.[182]

On Sunday, April 29, the tsar opened the council in his palace with a speech to the assembled bishops, higher clergy, and government officials. The reply on the part of the bishops was made by Metropolitan Pitirim of Novgorod.[183] In the version of his speech printed in the Acts,[184] Alexis painted a dim picture of the disorders in the Russian Church, caused by the opponents to the reform, and instructed the members of the council to resolve the problem. He concluded his speech, bade them to sit, and then read the "Chrysobull," the conciliar letter of the 1593 Council in Constantinople establishing the Moscow Patriarchate.[185] Pitirim's answer contained praise for the tsar's great concern for the welfare of the Church and a pledge that the council would uphold the canon of faith expressed in the "Chrysobull."[186] Following Pitirim's response, the tsar kissed the text of the Creed, which was part of the "Chrysobull," and then all the members of the council, clergy and boyars, did the same.[187] Thus the tsar again made plain that he wanted the liturgical reforms upheld, for this reading of the Acts of the 1593 Council was but a reenactment of the 1654 Council.

In its ensuing sessions, held at the patriarchal palace, the council proceeded to try all the leading opponents of the reform. The first was Bishop Alexander of Viatka, who had come to Moscow with a dossier of materials against the revised text of the Creed, as well as against the new *Sluzhebniks* and *Trebniks*.[188] After several discussions, Alexander recanted his opposition and signed a declaration in which he accepted all the reforms. He wrote out the new text of the Creed, in full, and signed it. This declaration, more complete than those required from his fellow bishops, Simeon included with all the other declarations, even though it was made several months later.[189] From the fourth session, Alexander is listed among the bishops attending the council. Alexander was to set the pattern for a number of others who were put to trial and repented.

Some of the chief leaders of the opposition, including Avvakum, were brought to Moscow before the council. Here, efforts were made once again to get them to accept the new books as Orthodox, and they were treated with relative gentleness.[190] All that was demanded of them was that they stop condemning the Eastern patriarchs and accept the new books—not that they reject the old books.[191] Those who refused, including the most visible leaders such as Avvakum, Lazar', and Deacon Fedor, were brought before the council, which ordered them defrocked and anathematized.[192] The judgement was based on their refusal to obey the bishops, and on their slander of the Eastern patriarchs and of the new books. All were sentenced to imprisonment in various monasteries.

In its last session on July 2, the Council addressed issues of church order, correcting various abuses. Services must be conducted respectfully and "*edinoglasno*" (only one part at a time).[193] Churches must be kept clean, free of accumulations of dust and cobwebs, liturgical vestments and cloths clean and in repair, liturgical vessels washed. Proper registries of baptism, deaths, and weddings are to be kept. Priests are urged to visit the sick and teach the laity. Begging by the poor during services is forbidden. Clergy, both black (monastic) and white (married), are to remain in their assigned places, leaving only with episcopal permission. Services are to be conducted in accordance with the corrected Nikonian books, which "have been published by order of the tsar," with "the blessing of Nikon and the entire council," in "accordance with the advice of the holy Greek patriarchs," and which are based on "Greek and ancient Slavonic books."[194] Thus the council now addressed many issues which had been on the program of the reformers well before Nikon's patriarchate. When the circle of reformers had supported Nikon's election, this was what they had wanted him to do. But Nikon had neglected all this and focused exclusively on the reform of books and rubrics.[195]

Significantly, the council never mentioned the old books, never condemned them as wrong or heretical. Nor was any mention made of the 1551 Stoglav Council. Thus, in speaking of the new form of the Jesus Prayer ("Lord Jesus Christ, our God, have mercy on us") the Acts specify that the previous version ("Lord Jesus Christ, *Son of God,* have mercy on us") is also acceptable; but they condemn those who reject the new form as Arian heretics.[196] Similarly, while the council mandates the use of three fingers for the sign of the Cross, the previous practice is never condemned.[197]

Finally, the council attempted to counter the arguments of the Old-Believers. On May 7, 1666, Simeon of Polotsk was commissioned to compose a refutation of the writings of Nikita and Lazar'.[198] This work, entitled *Zhezl Pravlenia,* was completed on July 13, was immediately printed, and was released after approval by the 1667 Council.[199]

ii. The Council of 1667[200]

The 1666 Council had dealt with the Old-Believers, with Nikon's reforms, with correcting various problems in church order, but not with the other chief issue facing the Russian Church—Nikon and his succession. On November 2, 1666, Patriarchs Paisios and Makarios arrived in Moscow,[201] and preparations were immediately made to begin the new council. It began on November 7, with thirty bishops in attendance, of whom fourteen were foreigners.

The first item on the agenda, the Nikon affair, took about a month. On December 12, Nikon was condemned for leaving his position; he was defrocked and sent under guard to the distant Ferapontov Monastery.[202] Nikon's condemnation did not come without some debate, and several Russian bishops at first refused to sign the edict, because it explicitly affirmed the total precedence of civil over religious authority. There followed a sharp debate, lasting through January 1667, in which the Greeks, led by Metropolitan Paisios Ligarides of Gaza, affirmed the authority of the tsar over the Russian bishops, who sought to preserve ecclesiastical authority. Two Russian bishops, Metropolitan Paul of Krutitsa and Archbishop Hilarion of Riazan', were placed under arrest by order of the angered tsar: they were released only after they repented and agreed to sign. The tsar then ordered the records of the debate removed from the Acts.[203] This first part of the 1667 Council concluded with the election and enthronement of a new patriarch, Joasaph II, on January 31, 1667.[204]

During the next months, the council turned its attention to Nikon's liturgical reforms, which it reaffirmed. The reason for retreading ground already covered by the 1666 Council was the presence of two foreign patriarchs, whose approval could help to consolidate the reform. Thus, by the Russians' own choice, the Oriental bishops were made official judges over all Russian life—a position they were more than happy to fill.[205] But these Greek bishops knew no Russian and had to rely on other, Russian-speaking Greeks to advise them. Thus Paisios Ligarides was their adviser in the matter of Nikon; and the Archimandrite Dionysios, from the Iviron Monastery on Mt. Athos, was the expert on the Old-Believers and on liturgical matters.[206] It was through the eyes of these Greek consultors that the patriarchs saw the Russian Church, and on the basis of whose judgments they made decisions.

Dionysios had come to Russia in 1655, returning to Mt. Athos only in 1669. In 1663, he became the chief corrector at the Printing Office, replacing Arsenios the Greek.[207] Prior to the council, he composed a polemical treatise against the Old-Believers in which, point by point, he rebutted all their arguments against Nikon's reforms.[208] This work was used by the patriarchs as the basis for their decisions and answers—for this reason Dionysios was particularly disliked by the Old-Believers.[209] Dionysios' view was that liturgical peculiarities arose in Russia after the Russian metropolitans ceased to be ordained in Constantinople—i.e. after the Russian Church had gained its independence. He equated differences in practice with outright heresy. He therefore saw Nikon's reform, carried out under Greek tutelage, as the restoration of true piety and Orthodoxy in Russia.[210] This view was thus diametrically opposite to the conviction of many Russians that it was the Greeks who had lost the true faith after Florence and the fall of Constantinople.

The 1667 Council, therefore, did not simply confirm the 1666 decision about Nikon's reform, but did so in the light of Dionysios' perceptions. Thus, in its May 13, 1667 decision, this council condemned previous practice.[211] The two-fingered sign of the Cross, for example, was branded as Arian, Nestorian, Apollinarian...It was seen as a Trinitarian heresy, because the three folded fingers (representing, for the Old-Believers, the Trinity) are uneven in size.[212] The Old-Believer version of the Jesus Prayer ("Lord Jesus Christ, Son of God, have mercy on us") was branded as an Arian heresy.[213] The double alleluia was labeled a Latin heresy.[214] The decisions of the Stoglav council on these matters were specifically overturned, on the grounds that they were made by Russians alone, without the consent of the ecumenical patriarchs.[215] The Old-Believers were not only anathematized, but were handed over to the secular authorities for punishment.[216]

In nearly every case, the Council mandated the adoption of current Greek practice. The December 1655 decision by Nikon to bless water only once at Epiphany was overturned.[217] The Oriental bishops demanded agreement on even the smallest details, prefacing most orders with: "As is done from ancient times in all the holy churches in Eastern countries, and in Kiev, and everywhere, except the Muscovite Kingdom..." They required clergy to wear Greek-style vestments, under penalty of being defrocked.[218] Because of a special request by the tsar, as is noted in the Acts themselves, archimandrites were permitted to celebrate as bishops, wearing miters and blessing with the dikirion and trikirion,[219] and metropolitans were allowed to wear white klobuks.[220]

The 1667 Council was therefore the final seal on the liturgical reforms set into motion by the tsar and carried out by Nikon. Thus, in approving the publication of the 1667 *Sluzhebnik*, the council declares: "Let them print it thus in the future, and let no one dare add, remove, or change anything from now on. And even if an angel should say anything different, do not believe him."[221] In going far beyond the 1666 Council, this assembly also confirmed the schism, for the Old-Believers were now formally branded as heretics. From the liturgical standpoint, Russian practice was brought firmly into line with the Greek. While the Council claimed to be fulfilling the directives of the 1655 conciliar letter to Nikon from Constantinople,[222] it had, in fact, moved in the opposite direction.

NOTES

1. The entire foreword is published in STROEV, *OPISANIE KNIG TOLSTOVA I TSARKAGO*, pp. 147-169. We quote from this edition, p. 149.

2. *Ibid.*

3. (Moscow, 1653), ff. 21-55. The *Kormchaia Kniga* is the official collection of canon law for the Russian Church.

4. (Moscow, 1667).

5. STROEV, *OPISANIE KNIG TOLSTOVA I TSARSKAGO*, p. 150.

6. The text of the conciliar letter is published in the Acts of the 1655 Council in Slavonic, *DEIIANIE 1654*, ff. 3v-15v. The Slavonic translation in this edition is undoubtedly the work of Epifanii Slavinetskii, to whom Nikon had assigned the task—cf. KARTASHEV, p. 151. A Russian translation from an unnamed Greek Sinai ms. is published by Porfirii Uspenskii, "Deianie konstantinopol'skago sobora 1593 goda, kotorym utverzhdeno patriarshestvo v Rossii," *TKDA* 1865 (3) 237-248. An English translation is printed in PALMER, v. 5, appendix, pp. 179-191. The original Greek text of the 1593 Acts is published by G.A. Rhalles and M. Potles, Σύνταγμα τῶν θείων καὶ ἱερῶν κανόνων..., v. 5 (Athens, 1859) (Rep: Athens: K.M. Grigoris, 1966), pp. 149-155.

7. STROEV, *OPISANIE KNIG TOLSTOVA I TSARSKAGO*, pp. 151-152.

8. *Ibid.*, pp. 152ff.

9. *Ibid.*, pp. 155-157.

10. *Ibid.*, pp. 158-163.

11. *Ibid.*, pp. 163-165.

12. MAKARII, *PATRIARKH NIKON*, pp. 65-69; MAKARII, *ISTORIIA*, v. 12, pp. 176-177.

13. NIKOLAEVSKII, *PECHATNYI DVOR, KhCht* 1891(2) 160; KARTASHEV, p. 151.

14. MANSVETOV, *KAK PRAVILIS'*, pp. 538-539.

15. NIKOLAEVSKII, *PECHATNYI DVOR, KhCht* 1891(2) 161.

16. *Ibid.*, pp. 162-163.

17. V.I. Rumiantsev, *Drevniia Zdaniia Pechatnago Dvora* (Moscow, 1869), p. 33, quotes from the accounting ledger of the Printing Office.

18. *MATERIALY* V, p. 18.

19. Ch. 31. *STOGLAV*, pp. 103-106. A French translation and commentary is published by E. Duchesne, *Le Stoglav, ou les cent chapitres* (=Bibliothèque française de Petrograd, V) (Paris, 1920), pp. 87-90.

20. KAPTEREV, *PERVYIA DEISTVIIA NIKONA*, pp. 185-186.

21. Cf. for example *MATERIALY* V, pp. 181-189.

22. KAPTEREV, *PERVYIA DEISTVIIA NIKONA*, pp. 180-181.

23. *MATERIALY* V, pp. 17-19.

24. PASCAL, *AVVAKUM*, pp. 216-219, 225, describes the events. But Pascal has a strong anti-Nikon bias, so his observations must be taken with a grain of salt.

25. "Rospis' spornykh rechei protopopa Ivana Neronova s patriarkhom Nikonom," *MATERIALY* I, pp. 41-51. This document, composed by Neronov, was an appeal to the tsar to intervene on behalf of Loggin himself.

26. KAPTEREV, *PERVYIA DEISTVIIA NIKONA*, p. 193. The Acts of the 1656 Council, which also condemns him, state that the original condemnation in 1653 is based on Apostolic Canon 55: "If any of the clergy insult the bishop...," *MATERIALY* IV, pp. 128-129. Neronov's fate is described by PASCAL, *AVVAKUM*, pp. 220-221.

27. "The Life," *MATERIALY* V, pp. 21-22. Avvakum also describes the events in a letter to Neronov, dated Sept. 14, 1653, *MATERIALY* I, pp. 20-26. Cf. also PASCAL, *AVVAKUM*, pp. 222-227.

28. *MATERIALY* I, pp. 23-24, 37-38, 54-67, 80, etc.

29. *MATERIALY* I, pp. 25, 47, 67-68, 70-94. See also KAPTEREV, P*ERVYIA DEISTVIIA NIKONA*, pp. 197-202. After Vonifatiev died, Nikon would often go to his tomb to weep for him and to pray—"Zapiska o zhizni protopopa Ivana Neronova s 1653 po 1659 god," *MATERIALY* I, pp. 158-159. This is a contemporary account of Neronov's life.

30. Characteristic is Neronov's second petition to the tsar, dated Feb. 27, 1654, written from imprisonment at the Spasokammenyi Monastery, printed in *MATERIALY* I, pp. 51-69. In connection with the power to work miracles, see pp. 58-59. The apocalyptic element, so prevalent later among the Old-Believers, is evident already on pp. 52-53.

31. PAUL OF ALEPPO, *ChOIDR* 1898(3) pt. 3, 123.

32. KAPTEREV, *TSAR'I SOBORY*, pp. 493-494.

33. E.g. Neronov, *MATERIALY* I, pp. 53, 56; Lazar', *MATERIALY* IV, pp. 253-254; monk Avraamii, *MATERIALY* VII, p. 275.

34. E.g. in the Acts of the 1660 Moscow Council, published in *DELO*, p. 95.

35. The council must have met after the Feb. 27 petition of Neronov, which requested a sobor, *MATERIALY* I, pp 66. Neronov's letters to the tsarina and to Stefan Vonifatiev, dated May 2, 1654, mention the mistreatment of Bishop Paul of Kolomna, after the council, and complain about some of Nikon's statements made at the council, *MATERIALY* I, pp. 79, 87-88.

36. Their names are listed in the Acts of the Council, *DEIIANIE 1654*, ff. 16v-17v.

37. *Ibid.*, ff. 2v-3. The quotation from the Seventh Ecumenical Council is, of course, an epitome.

38. *Ibid.*, ff. 5-5v.

39. Rhalles, v.5, *op.cit.,* p. 150. "Because the Orthodox Church has attained its fulness, not only because of the wisdom and piety of its dogmas but also because of the holy ordering of ecclesiastical offers, it is also proper for us to exclude all novelties from the bounds of the Church."

40. *DEIIANIE 1654*, f. 5. For the English translation, see note 39 above.

41. Cf. for example GOLUBINSKII, pp. 60-62.

42. *DEIIANIE 1654*, ff. 6v-7. This edition also contains a reproduction of the Greek text of the Creed sent by Patriarch Jeremias of Constantinople. Needless to say, the Slavonic translation of Epifanii Slavinetskii corresponds exactly to that in the Nikonian books. Nikon, however, does not bring up the subject of the text of the Creed at this council.

43. The "episcopal prayers" were prayers read by the priest as he entered the church. These were taken from the rite of confession, in which they were recited by the confessor over the penitent.

44. This refers to the dismissal for the Hours, which were always read before the liturgy.

45. *DEIIANIE 1654*, ff. 16-16v.

46. *Ibid.*, f. 17v.

47. Which accompany the recitation of the Lenten Prayer of St Ephrem.

48. *DEIIANIE 1654,* ff. 17v-21.

49. *Ibid.,* f. 17. Paul was the only bishop to maintain close relations with the leaders of the future Old-Believers. His correspondence with Neronov was among the documents seized by the tsar's agents from the elder Feoktist, an Old-Believer, in 1666. Cf. *MATERIALY* I, 331. Miraculous legends about Bishop Paul rapidly spread—cf. *ChOIDR* 1905(2) pp. 41-46.

50. Avvakum states that he was burned at the stake—see the excerpt from Avvakum's *Life* quoted above.

51. KARTASHEV, p. 155.

52. The sign of the Cross—*STOGLAV,* ch. 31. The double alleluia—*STOGLAV,* ch. 42. The triple alleluia is condemned as a Latin, Trinitarian heresy, caused by the *filioque.*

53. KAPTEREV, *NIKON I ALEKSEI,* v. 1, pp. 138-139.

54. STROEV, *OPISANIE KNIG TOLSTOVA I TSARSKAGO,* pp. 155-158.

55. *Ibid.,* pp. 161-163.

56. KAPTEREV, *ISPRAVLENIE KNIG, BV* 1909(1) 34. Cf. also FLOROVSKII, pp. 63-64.

57. For example, see GOLUBINSKII, pp. 53-62. KAPTEREV, in *ISPRAVLENIE KNIG, BV* 1909(1) 25ff., however, asserts that Nikon fully believed that the ancient Greek books were being used.

58. Appendix I of *DEIIANIE 1654* contains a draft of this letter, which contains only those questions posed by Nikon at the 1654 Council.

59. Deacon Fedor writes: "Nikon then wrote false tales to the Greek patriarchs against Bishop Paul of Kolomna, the new confessor, and Archpriest Ioann Neronov of Kazan, justifying himself and slandering them, like the devil. He claims that they composed their own new prayers and liturgical services, caused dissension among the people with them, and separated themselves from the catholic church. And Patriarch Paisios of Constantinople believed his lies and sent him an answer...," "Letter from Pustozersk...," *MATERIALY* VI, p. 198.

60. *DEIIANIE 1654,* App. I, f. 3.

61. MAKARII, *ISTORIIA,* v. 12, pp. 148-149.

62. KAPTEREV, *TSERKOVNO-OBRIADOVYIA REFORMY, BV* 1908(2) 342.

63. All the official documents relating to Makarios' visit to Russia are published by N.V. Rozhdestvenskii, "Makarii patriarkh antiokhiiskii v Rossii v 1654-1656 gg., Dokumenty posol'skago prikaza," *ChOIDR* 1906(4) pt. 1, i-vi, 1-120.

64. *Ibid.,* p. 1.

65. NIKOLAEVSKII, *ROSSIIA I VOSTOK,* pp. 752-753.

66. Rozhdestvenskii, *op.cit.,* pp. 28-31.

67. All this is fully described by Paul of Aleppo, archdeacon and son of the Patriarch of Antioch. He was charged with keeping a complete account of the travels. The only complete text of his account, originally written in Arabic, is published in a Russian translation by G. Murkos—it is cited here as PAUL OF ALEPPO. A French translation by B. Radu, *Voyage du Patriarche Macaire d'Antioche,* accompanied by the Arabic text, is published in *PO* 22 (fasc. 1) and *PO* 24, (fasc. 4), but it contains only a fraction of the entire text and does not include any part of the journey to Moscow. An abbreviated and inaccurate English translation is published by F.C. Belfour, *The Travels of Macarius, Patriarch of Antioch,* 2 vols. (London, 1829-1836). Sections of the account are also published in English in vol. 2 of PALMER. Thus, for the description of Makarios' stay in Russia, the Murkos translation is by far the

most reliable: cf. S. Senyk, "Rites and Charters," *OCP* 47 (1981) 426-440. We therefore cite from this edition. The reception of Makarios by the tsar and by Nikon is described in PAUL OF ALEPPO, *ChOIDR* 1898(3) pt. 3, 14-30.

68. PAUL OF ALEPPO, *ChOIDR* 1898(4) pt. 2, 169.

69. PAUL OF ALEPPO, *ChOIDR* 1898(3) pt. 3, 50-51, 181; *ChOIDR* 1898(4) pt. 2, 169, 179-180.

70. PAUL OF ALEPPO, *ChOIDR* 1898(4) pt. 2, 169.

71. *Ibid.*, pp. 179-180.

72. FLOROVSKII, p. 64.

73. NIKOLAEVSKII, *ROSSIIA I VOSTOK*, p. 741. The text of this Pontifical formed the basis for the Pontifical approved by the 1667 Council. The text of the 1667 Pontifical is printed in *MATERIALY* II, pp. 291-336. Subbotin adds extensive notes, based on the original Greek text sent to Nikon and the first Slavonic translation, which allow a reconstruction of the version sent by Athanasios.

74. KAPTEREV, *KHARAKTER OTNOSHENII*, pp. 444-445.

75. PAUL OF ALEPPO, *ChOIDR* 1898(4) pt. 2, 107. As used here, the term *klobuk* stands for the *epikamilavka*, or veil worn over the *kamilavka*.

76. *Ibid.*, p. 108.

77. *Ibid.*, pp. 108-109.

78. *Ibid.*, p. 169.

79. *Ibid.*, p. 117.

80. MAKARII, *PATRIARKH NIKON*, pp. 91-92. A "small" sobor was one attended only by bishops who were in Moscow at the time—cf. KAPTEREV, *TSAR' I SOBORY*, pp. 341ff. The decision of this council is printed in the *Skrizhal'* (Moscow, 1656). An English translation appears in vol. 3 of PALMER, pp. 413-414.

81. The text of the decree is published in *ChOIDR* 1884(1) pt. 5, 21-22.

82. PAUL OF ALEPPO, *ChOIDR* 1898(4) pt. 2, 117.

83. Literally "Peasant, son of a whore."

84. PAUL OF ALEPPO, *ChOIDR* 1898(4) pt. 2, 169.

85. *MATERIALY* II, pp. 237-238.

86. This is the name given to the first Sunday of Lent, which commemorates the restoration of icons and the triumph of Orthodoxy at the Seventh Ecumenical Council in 787.

87. PAUL OF ALEPPO, *ChOIDR* 1898(3) pt. 3, 131-137. For Nikon's responsibility for the subsequent eclipse and plague, cf. GIBBENET, v. 2, pp. 473-475, and MAKARII, *ISTORIIA*, v. 12, pp. 207-209.

88. PAUL OF ALEPPO, *ChOIDR* 1898(3) pt. 3, 137.

89. KAPTEREV, *TSERKOVNO-OBRIADOVYIA REFORMY*, *BV* 1908(2) 346-347.

90. PAUL OF ALEPPO, *ChOIDR* 1898(3) pt. 3, 137.

91. KAPTEREV, *TSERKOVNO-OBRIADOVYIA REFORMY*, *BV* 1908(2) 348.

92. MAKARII, *ISTORIIA*, v. 12, p. 175.

93. STROEV, *OPISANIE KNIG TOLSTOVA I TSARSKAGO*, pp. 157-163.

94. *Ibid.*, pp. 163-165.

95. PAUL OF ALEPPO, *ChOIDR* 1898(3) pt. 3, 170.

96. BELOKUROV, *ARSENII SUKHANOV*.

97. FONKICH, ch. 2: "Arsenii Sukhanov i grecheskie rukopisi patriarshei biblioteki v Moskve," pp. 68-104.

98. This refers to the commemorations during the prothesis rite.

99. PAUL OF ALEPPO, *ChOIDR* 1898(3) pt. 3, 170-171.

100. DMITRIEVSKII, *OTZYV ORLOVA*, p. 254. He refers to the account ledgers of the Moscow Typography, No. 57, ff. 52-106.

101. *Ibid.*, pp. 254-55.

102. *MATERIALY* IV, p. 109. This petition, taking up 178 pages of this volume, is obviously the result of several years of work. Details of its composition are discussed by Subbotin in the introduction to this volume.

103. *MATERIALY* VI, pp. 22-23.

104. KAPTEREV, *ISPRAVLENIE KNIG, BV* 1908(3) 546-551. .

105. The entire petition is printed in *MATERIALY* VI, pp. 21-45. The quote is on p. 41.

106. Deacon Fedor, "Letter from Pustozersk...," *MATERIALY* VI, p. 158.

107. *MATERIALY* IV, pp. 15-16.

108. GORSKII-NEVOSTRUEV, v. 2:4, No. 294, f. 114.

109. SILVESTER MEDVEDEV, p. 8.

110. *Ibid.*, pp. 3-8.

111. KAPTEREV, *ISPRAVLENIE KNIG, BV* 1909(1) 24.

112. A diplomatic edition of the Greek text, together with a Russian translation, appears in PAISIOS OF CONSTANTINOPLE.

113. *Ibid.*, p. 577.

114. *Ibid.*, pp. 575-578.

115. (Moscow, 1656) pp. 639-753. An English translation of a few excerpts from the letter is published in vol. 3 of PALMER, Appendix 2, pp. 407-411, but this translation is from the *Skrizhal'* text and not from the Greek original.

116. ZERNOVA, pp. 82, 86.

117. STROEV, *OPISANIE KNIG TOLSTOVA I TSARSKAGO*, pp. 158-160. These excerpts are found translated into English in vol. 3 of PALMER, pp. 411-412.

118. PAISIOS OF CONSTANTINOPLE, p. 315.

119. *Ibid.*, pp. 316-317.

120. *Ibid.*, pp. 317-318.

121. *Ibid.*, pp. 318-319.

122. *Ibid.*, pp. 319-320.

123. This is one of the latest references to the survival of the usage of the Non-Sleepers (ἡ τῶν ἀκοιμήτων ἀκολουθία) into the post-Studite epoch of Sabbaitic dominance. For bibliographical references to this ancient Byzantine tradition, see R. Taft, "The Byzantine Office in the Prayerbook of New Skete: Evaluation of a Proposed Reform," *OCP* 48 (1982) 359.

124. PAISIOS OF CONSTANTINOPLE, pp. 539-540.

125. *Ibid.*, pp. 547-548.

126. *Ibid.*, p. 342. Several excellent studies of the Byzantine understanding of the liturgy have appeared in recent years, notably those of H. J. Schulz, *Die byzantinische Liturgie; vom Werden ihrer Symbolgestalt* (=Sophia; Quellen östlicher Theologie, Bd. 5) (Freiburg im Breisgau: Lambertus Verlag, 1964), English translation: *The Byzantine Liturgy* (New York: Pueblo, 1986); R. Bornert, *Les Commentaires byzantins de la divine liturgie du vii⁰ au xv⁰ siècle* (=Archives de l'Orient chrétien, 9) (Paris: Institut français d'études byzantines, 1966); and R. Taft, "The Liturgy of the Great Church: an Initial Synthesis of Structure and Interpretation on the Eve of Iconoclasm," *DOP* 34-35 (1980-1981) 45-75. For the transposition of this tradition onto Russian soil, see K.C. Felmy, *Die Deutung der göttlichen Liturgie in der russischen Theologie* (=Arbeiten z. Kirchengeschichte, 54) (Berlin and New York: De Gruyter, 1984). The Slavonic version of the letter printed in the *Skrizhal'* adds here the text of the Creed.

127. PAISIOS OF CONSTANTINOPLE, pp. 568-569. Question #25.

128. *SKRIZHAL'* (Moscow, 1656), pp. 740-743.

129. STROEV, *OPISANIE KNIG TOLSTOVA I TSARSKAGO*, p. 160. Nikon had this text printed in the *Skrizhal'* as part of the conciliar reply, in the context of the commentary on the liturgy—see note 126 above.

130. DMITRIEVSKII, *OTZYV ORLOVA*, p. 257.

131. MAKARII, *ISTORIIA*, v. 12, p. 188. The events are described in the "*Slovo otveshchatelnoe,*" Nikon's introduction to the *Skrizhal'*, ff. 10v-11.

132. A short account of the life of the saint of the day, or a commentary on the meaning of the feast, read at Matins. Through the efforts of the zealots of piety, who stressed preaching and instruction, it was given an important role in the service.

133. In Russian, *znamenie*. The meaning of the term is ambiguous. It can mean both a sign, or symbol, as in a "sign of the Cross," and a "miracle," or "apparition." See for example, I.I. Sreznevskii, *Materialy dlia Slovaria drevnerusskogo Iazyka*, v. 1 (St Petersburg: AN, 1893) (Reprint: Moscow, 1958).

134. *STOGLAV*, ch 31. The origin of this legend is Theodoret's *History of the Church*, II, ch. 27, describing the 361 Council of Antioch: "Third, the great Meletios arose and taught the correct theology...Then all the people cheered loudly and asked him to give a brief summary of his teaching. Showing three fingers, then folding two of them, leaving only one extended, he uttered this praiseworthy statement: 'There are three which are understood, but we speak only of one.'" (*PG* 82:1081BC). Sozomen places the incident in the context of a sermon given by Meletios in his cathedral. Hearing Meletios preach that the Son is of the same essence as the Father, the archdeacon covers the bishop's mouth with his hand, to prevent him from speaking further. Unable to speak, Meletios demonstrates his teaching by extending first three fingers, then one. Finally, freeing himself from the archdeacon's grasp, he made his famous statement. (*Ecclesiastical History*, IV, ch 28, *PG* 57:1203AB).

135. *Skrizhal'* (Moscow, 1656) f. 11 11v.

136. See note 86 above. The liturgical celebration of this day includes a rite containing a solemn reading of the Synodicon or "Anathemas," where all heresies are formally listed and rejected.

137. *Skrizhal'*, f. 12-12v. Paul of Aleppo does not mention this event, except to say that Nikon preached a great deal about the sign of the Cross, and that the services lasted a full nine hours, PAUL OF ALEPPO, *ChOIDR* 1898(4) pt. 2, p. 153.

138. *Skrizhal'*, f. 12v.

139. *Ibid.*, f. 10.

140. The letter does not in fact contain any condemnation of the Russian practice, but only an explanation of the Greek practice of using three fingers. Cf. PAISIOS OF CONSTANTINOPLE, pp. 566-567.

141. The speech is summarized in the "*Slovo otveshchatelnoe,*" Nikon's introduction to the *Skrizhal*.

142. FELMY, p. 82.

143. LEGRAND, *XV* *ET XVI* *SIÈCLES*, v. 2, #268, pp. 201-205.

144. A detailed study of the *Skrizhal'* is found in ch. 3 of FELMY, pp. 80-111.

145. Ff. 1-21. The introduction has its own pagination, independent of the rest of the volume.

146. *Skrizhal*, "*Slovo otveshchatelnoe,*" f. 15.

147. *Ibid.*, f. 16, 16v.

148. KARTASHEV, pp. 159-160. Makarii, however, dates the beginning of the formal schism to the condemnation of Neronov on May 18, 1656, MAKARII, *ISTORIIA*, v. 12, pp. 213-214.

149. The Acts of the Council are published in *MATERIALY* I, pp. 124-133.

150. *MATERIALY* I, p. 142.

151. *Ibid.*, p. 129.

152. PAUL OF ALEPPO, *ChOIDR* 1898(4) pt. 2, pp. 178-179. See also MAKARII, *ISTORIIA*, v. 12, pp. 211-213.

153. The Acts of this Council are published in *MATERIALY* I, pp. 9-14.

154. Cf. PAUL OF ALEPPO, *ChOIDR* 1898(4) pt. 2, pp. 176-177. See also MAKARII, *ISTORIIA*, v. 12, pp. 195-197.

155. Cf. for example KAPTEREV, *NIKON I ALEKSEI*, v. 1, pp. 259-269; KARTASHEV, p. 164; FLOROVSKII, p. 65.

156. KAPTEREV, *TSERKOVNO-OBRIADOVYIA REFORMY*, *BV* 1908(3) 231; KAPTEREV, *NIKON I ALEKSEI*, v. 1, p. 261; SOLOV'EV, v. 3, p. 205; MAKARII, *PATRIARKH NIKON*, pp. 113-115.

157. KAPTEREV, *NIKON I ALEKSEI*, v. 1, pp. 262-264.

158. The encounter is described in a contemporary biography of Neronov, *MATERIALY* I, pp. 147-153. Neronov himself recalls the events in a 1666 letter, *MATERIALY* I, p. 258.

159. *MATERIALY* I, pp. 154-157. See also MAKARII, *ISTORIIA*, v. 12, pp. 214-217.

160. *MATERIALY* I, pp. 162-163.

161. SHUSHERIN, p. 31; KARTASHEV, pp. 144-145; MAKARII, *ISTORIIA*, v. 12, pp. 306-310.

162. The most complete description of the events is found in MAKARII, *ISTORIIA*, v. 12, pp. 311-325. An eyewitness account by the Boyar Aleksei Nikitich Trubetskoi, who was sent by the tsar to find out why Nikon was abandoning his throne, is published in *DELO*, pp. 15-16.

163. A complete list appears in ZERNOVA, pp. 87-96.

164. PASCAL, *AVVAKUM*, pp. 299-316.

165. *MATERIALY* III, pp. 3-6. Many of the documents relating to this famous uprising are contained in this volume. The chief study is by I.Ia. Syrtsov, *Vozmushchenie Solovetskikh monakhov-staroobriadtsev v XVII veke* (Kostroma, 1888) (Reprint: Westmead, England: Gregg Intl., 1969). Cf. also *Istoriia ob ottsakh i stradal'tsakh solovetskikh* (Moscow, 1912). The revolt was brought to an end only after a seven-year siege of the monastery during 1668-1676.

166. KAPTEREV, *NIKON I ALEKSEI*, v. 1, pp. 506-507.

167. According to a 1666 petition from the abbess to the tsar, published in *PrOb* 1885(2) 66-67. See also PASCAL, *AVVAKUM,* p. 328.

168. KAPTEREV, *NIKON I ALEKSEI,* v. 1, pp. 503-506.

169. KAPTEREV, *ISPRAVLENIE KNIG, BV* 1909(1) 39-40. The tsar complains about this in a letter to Nikon, cf. GIBBENET, v. 1, p. 242.

170. "Letter to his son, Maksim," *MATERIALY* VI, pp. 229-230.

171. As Avvakum himself notes in his autobiography, *MATERIALY* V, pp. 59-60. Cf. PASCAL, *AVVAKUM,* pp. 321-325.

172. KAPTEREV, *NIKON I ALEKSEI,* v. 1, pp. 339-342.

173. *MATERIALY* V, pp. 119-132.

174. I.Ia. Syrtsov, *Vozmushchenie solovetskikh monakhov-staroobriadtsev v XVII veke* (Kostroma, 1888) (Reprint: Westmead, England: Gregg Intl., 1969) pp. 84-85.

175. PASCAL, *AVVAKUM,* p. 359.

176. The Acts of the 1660 Council are published in *DELO,* pp. 94-110.

177. MAKARII, *ISTORIIA,* v. 12, pp. 433-438; GIBBENET, v. 1, pp. 561-580.

178. *SOBRANIE GRAMOT,* v. 4, No. 27 (in Greek, with a Russian translation). Cf. also MAKARII, *ISTORIIA,* v. 12, pp. 471-475.

179. *Ibid.,* pp. 475-479.

180. *Ibid.,* pp. 479-480.

181. *MATERIALY* II, pp. 35-44. Also *DELO,* pp. 250-263.

182. *DEIANIIA 1666-1667,* pt. 1, ff. 7v-9.

183. The original text of these speeches is not extant; it is replaced in the Acts by Simeon's own compositions, as is noted in the Acts themselves (*DEIANIIA 1666-1667,* pt. 1, f. 10v), KAPTEREV, *NIKON I ALEKSEI,* v. 2, pp. 28-29. But since the tsar reviewed and approved the Acts, these speeches may still be considered as the "approved version." On the composition of these Acts, cf. also MAKARII, *ISTORIIA,* v. 12, p. 643.

184. *DEIANIIA 1666-1667,* pt. 1, ff. 10v-12v; *MATERIALY* II, pp. 68-74, *DELO,* pp. 250-263.

185. See Section 3 of this chapter.

186. *DEIANIIA 1666-1667,* pt. 1, ff. 12-13.

187. *Ibid.,* f. 13v.

188. *Ibid.,* ff. 14v-15.

189. *MATERIALY* II, pp. 39-40; *DELO,* pp. 257-258.

190. KAPTEREV, *NIKON I ALEKSEI,* v. 2, pp. 24-25. Cf. *MATERIALY* VI, pp. 235-236.

191. Cf. for example the questioning of the monk Avraamii, in *MATERIALY* VII, pp. 386-416.

192. Avvakum—*DEIANIIA 1666-1667,* pt. 1, f. 16-16v; Deacon Fedor—*ibid.,* ff. 22-23; Priest Lazar'—*ibid.,* ff. 31-32v.

193. This refers to the abuse called "*mnogoglasie*" (many voices), whereby several parts of the service were conducted simultaneously. This was a time-saving device for the Russians, who legalistically insisted that the services must be done in their entirety, according to the Typikon. Abolishing this abuse was an important element in the program of the zealots. See KAPTEREV, *NIKON I ALEKSEI,* v. 1, pp. 84-104; *DEIANIE 1649.*

194. *DEIANIIA 1666-1667,* pt. 1, ff. 33-48v.

195. KAPTEREV, *NIKON I ALEKSEI*, v. 2, pp. 43-47.

196. *DEIANIIA 1666-1667*, pt. 1, f. 42.

197. *Ibid.*

198. Nikita's composition against the *Skrizhal'* and the new books is printed in *MATERIALY* IV, pp. 1-102. Lazar's writings are found in *MATERIALY* IV, pp. 179-219.

199. Cf. the foreword to the *Zhezl Pravlenia* (ZERNOVA, p. 96). This work is a rewriting and expansion of an earlier refutation written by Paisios Ligarides. Ligarides' original work, translated into Slavonic by Simeon, is published in *MATERIALY* IX, pp. 13-265.

200. The title is something of a misnomer—this council actually began at the end of 1666. I take the liberty of using the later year, in order clearly to distinguish it from the previous council, at which only Russian bishops were present.

201. In *DELO*, pp. 271-273. The events of this journey are described in great detail in MAKARII, *ISTORIIA*, v. 12, pp. 528-535.

202. For Simeon's official account of the trial, see *MATERIALY* II, pp. 166-178. Cf. also SHUSHERIN, pp. 52-80, and MAKARII, *ISTORIIA*, v. 12, pp. 684-752. A full discussion of these debates is beyond the scope of the present work.

203. On this episode, cf. esp. N.F. Kapterev, "Suzhdenie bol'shago moskovskago sobora 1667 goda o vlasti tsarskoi i patriarshei," *BV* 1892(6) 483-516; 1892(8) 171-190; 1892(10) 46-74.

204. *Drevniaia rossiiskaia vivliofeka*, 2nd. ed. (St Petersburg, 1788-1791) vol. 6, p. 295.

205. FLOROVSKII, p. 65.

206. See for example his description of the services on Mt. Athos, published in KAPTEREV, *KHARAKTER OTNOSHENII*, App. 11, pp. 563-565.

207. MANSVETOV, *KAK PRAVILIS'*, p. 540.

208. Cf. N.F. Kapterev, "O sochinenii protiv raskola iverskogo arkhimandrita greka Dionisiia, napisannom do sobora 1667 goda," *PrOb* 1888(7) appendix, pp. 1-31.

209. *MATERIALY* VI, pp. 244-247.

210. Kapterev, "O sochinenii protiv raskola...," *op.cit.*, pp. 16-17.

211. *DEIANIIA 1666-1667*, pt. 2, ff. 3v-7v.

212. *Ibid.*, ff. 31-32.

213. *Ibid.*, f. 33-33v. The reason for this is unclear.

214. *Ibid.*, f. 30v.

215. *Ibid.*, ff. 7v-8, 90-91.

216. *Ibid.*, ff. 81-82.

217. *Ibid.*, f. 15v.

218. *Ibid.*, f. 13-13v.

219. *Ibid.*, ff. 11v-12. The dikirion and trikirion are two- and three-branched candlesticks used by bishops for blessing.

220. *Ibid.*, f. 13-13v.

221. *Ibid.*, ff. 15v-16.

222. *Ibid.*, f. 16.

2

The Personages of the Reform

To better understand the reform, it is important to know something of its chief promulgators. This chapter, then, offers a brief review of what is known about four of the chief actors, with particular regard to their role in and attitude toward the liturgical reforms. We have drawn upon available published materials, and make no pretense to exhaustiveness. The persons of Tsar Alexis and Nikon have been thoroughly studied by historians, and it would be useless to repeat all their work here. Comparatively little is known, on the other hand, about Epifanii Slavinetskii and particularly Arsenios the Greek; we base our comments on what little material exists.

Choosing these four figures allows us to provide a balanced picture of the way in which the reforms were carried out and helps us to understand the strong opposition they engendered. Alexis and Nikon were the prime movers behind the reform, without whose support the entire program could never have taken place. Epifanii and Arsenios were the two chief implementors of the book reform, translating texts, writing explanatory introductions, and overseeing their publication. Much of the opposition to the reform can be explained by the negative reactions of various strata of Russian society to the persons of Nikon and Arsenios the Greek. In short, our knowledge of these four will provide an adequate perspective from which to view the liturgical reform.

1. Nikon

Few historical figures have provoked as much passionate response as Nikon. A man of strong will and action, Nikon affected the lives of all Russians, not only in his own day, but also up to the present. Credited by some for saving the Russian Church, by correcting heretical errors in its liturgical books[1] and returning to the ancient tradition,[2] he is condemned by others as simply a lover of power,[3] whose highhandedness ultimately led to the total subjugation of the Church by Peter the Great.[4] Any description of Nikon's personal characteristics is strongly colored by the author's position regarding Nikon's policies and accomplishments. This holds true both for accounts by Nikon's contemporaries, such as Shusherin's biography,[5] and for modern studies, such as Pascal's biography of Avvakum,[6] or the more recent series of articles by Lebedev.[7] The controversy concerning the person of Nikon remains unresolved because the issues raised in his patriarchate are still with us today— issues involving relations between church and state, between ecclesiastical and civil authority; issues which are as old as Christianity itself.

i. Early life

Our only source of information about Nikon's birth and early life is Shusherin's biography. Written in a rather hagiographical style, it is replete with accounts of early predictions of Nikon's future greatness and of the incorruptibility of his body after death.[8] Yet there is little reason to doubt the authenticity of the simple biographical details provided by Shusherin, who remained with Nikon from the latter's days in Novgorod (1649) until 1666.[9]

Nikon was born into a peasant family in the village of Vel'demanov, some ninety miles from Nizhnii-Novgorod, on May 24, 1605. It was the feast of St Nikita, the Wonderworker of Pereiaslavl, for whom the child was named according to the custom of the time. His father was called Mina, so Nikon was known as Nikita Minich. Nikita's mother died when he was still a child and, Shusherin tells us, he was brought up by a stepmother who mistreated him. When Nikita was quite young, his father entrusted him into the care of a teacher, who taught him to read and write.[10] Russian education in those days consisted only of learning the rudiments of reading and writing. The textbooks were liturgical books and Scripture.[11] Soon after Nikita returned home, he ran away to the Makar'ev Zheltovodskii Monastery, in the Kostroma Province, near Nizhnii-Novgorod, where he continued his education and completed his formation.[12]

At age twenty, Nikon was called home because of his father's death. There, his relatives convinced him to stay home and marry. An educated man by Russian standards, Nikon became a psalmist and soon after was ordained a deacon and priest. He then went to Moscow, where he served as a parish priest for about ten years.[13] He had three children, all of whom died in infancy. This, Shusherin indicates, led him to seek the monastic life once more. Thus, in 1636, he placed his wife in the Alekseev Convent in Moscow and went north to a monastery on Anzer Island, on the White Sea, which was about twenty miles from the Solovki Monastery. Here he was tonsured and assumed the monastic name of Nikon. The Anzerskii "skit," under the leadership of the elder Eliazar, consisted of twelve monks, each living in an individual cell. Cells were about two miles apart and two miles from the church, which was on the center of the island. The monks assembled once weekly for the all-night vigil on Saturday night and for the Sunday eucharist. Nikon took well to the monastic life, augmenting the already burdensome monastic rule with strict fasting, daily recitation of the entire Psalter, and a thousand prostrations.[14] In his cell, Nikon frequently saw visions[15]—a phenomenon which was to remain with him in his later life.

After a few years on Anzer Island, Nikon had a falling out with Eliazar over the issue of spending a large sum of money for the erection of a stone building. Eliazar wanted to proceed cautiously, while Nikon wanted to build right away.[16] Nikon left the community and joined the Monastery of the Epiphany on Lake Kozhe, in the diocese of Novgorod. He lived alone on an island and caught fish for the monastery. When the old abbot died, Nikon was elected by the monks to replace him. Thus, in 1643, Nikon was consecrated abbot by Metropolitan Afonii of Novgorod.[17] Under his administration, the monastery grew both in numbers and wealth.[18]

We know nothing of Nikon in this early period beyond these sparse details provided by his loyal biographer. Shusherin gives no reason for Nikon's move to Moscow and does not say where Nikon was assigned.[19] Makarii indicates that tradesmen from Moscow noticed Nikon's talent and convinced him to move to the capital.[20] Solov'ev agrees with Makarii, but neither indicates his source for this information.[21] More recently, Kartashev accepts this account.[22] Certainly Nikon must have stood out somehow from other provincial parish clergy, or he would never have obtained a parish in Moscow. We get some idea of his impatient temperament from his conflict with Eliazar. His ascetical feats as a monk certainly earned him the esteem of his brothers, as indicated by his election as abbot. In general, however, there is little to distinguish him from others who made their careers in the church. His transition from the "white" (secular, married) to the "black" (monastic) clergy certainly opened up greater possibilities for advancement, but there was little in this early period to indicate that these would come his way, particularly given his provincial, peasant background.

ii. The steps to the patriarchate

In 1646, Abbot Nikon came to Moscow to collect money for his monastery. According to custom, all abbots arriving in the capital were expected to present themselves to the tsar. Nikon made a great impression on the seventeen-year-old Alexis, who had been brought up according to the traditional Russian piety. So great was the effect, that the tsar ordered him to remain in Moscow and assume the vacant position of archimandrite of the Novo-Spasskii Monastery. This was the royal family's personal monastery, where former tsars were buried, and Nikon suddenly found himself in the position of being the tsar's personal priest.[23] The friendship between the two developed quickly, and Alexis soon asked that Nikon come for Matins in the royal chapel every Friday, after which the two would spend time in conversation. Nikon's open access to the tsar also made Nikon popular among the populace, for Nikon willingly took their petitions and presented them to the tsar.[24] This same popularity, however, could only arouse the enmity of the boyars toward the peasant upstart who circumvented their authority. As archimandrite, Nikon proved himself an able administrator. The Novo-Spasskii Monastery had been nearly demolished during the Time of Troubles, and Nikon was instrumental in its rebuilding. Nikon built a cathedral, added new cells, and erected a new wall around the monastery, which was located about one mile from the tsar's palace. The reconstruction, remarkably, was completed in less than two years, and its new cathedral impressed the Muscovites for its ornateness.[25]

Nikon also became a member of the reforming party in the Church, which was led by the tsar's confessor, Stefan Vonifatiev, and the boyar Fedor Rtishchev, and was strongly supported by Alexis. For example,

Nikon, together with Vonifatiev and Neronov, refused to sign the Acts of the 1649 Council, which sanctioned the Russian practice of "*mnogoglasie.*"[26] Within the circle of reformers, Nikon in this early period clearly fit within the "provincial" group, composed of men like Avvakum and Neronov. These were people of peasant background and they shared a typically Russian xenophobia.[27] At this time, Nikon distrusted the Greeks and their books,[28] as his opponents were to remind him later.[29] This provincial group focused primarily on eliminating moral and liturgical abuses, as well as on the restoration of preaching.[30]

At the same time, the other group among the reformers, led by Vonifatiev, Rtishchev, and the tsar, had a different perspective toward the Greeks. Far more open to foreign cultural influence, they encouraged the publication of such works as the *Kirillova Kniga* (1644) and the *Kniga o Vere* (1648), which affirmed the full orthodoxy of the Greeks. Personally close to the tsar, Nikon eventually fell in with this group and changed his attitude toward the Greeks. This shift becomes apparent by 1649, when Patriarch Paisios of Jerusalem came to Moscow to collect funds to pay off the debts of the Holy Sepulchre in Jerusalem, and also to encourage the tsar to adopt a policy leading to the liberation of the Orthodox under the Turkish yoke.[31] Paisios repeatedly met and conversed at length with Nikon. While the subject of these discussions is not documented, Paisios wrote several letters to Tsar Alexis praising Nikon.[32] Subsequently, Nikon listed Paisios as one of the Eastern bishops who brought to his attention errors in Russian books and abusive practices,[33] so it is highly likely that differences between Greek and Russian practices were discussed. The discussions between Nikon and Paisios, moreover, could have taken place only with the tsar's consent, so this was quite probably an attempt to win Nikon over to the grecophile side.[34]

On March 9, 1649, Nikon was consecrated Metropolitan of Novgorod, the second highest position in the Russian hierarchy. The ordination was performed by Patriarchs Joseph of Moscow and Paisios of Jerusalem.[35] A few days after this, Paisios sent another letter to the tsar, praising him for selecting Nikon and asking permission to present Nikon with a mantia from the Holy Land.[36]

As metropolitan, Nikon again proved himself an able administrator, both in secular and religious matters. In this way, he gained great popularity and, more importantly, the respect and love of the tsar. He abolished *mnogoglasie* in Novgorod, as well as the old style of "*khomovoe*" singing.[37] He brought singers from Kiev and introduced the Western type of polyphonic music. He introduced preaching in church, to supplement the simple reading of patristic or hagiographical texts.[38] In 1651, Nikon succeeded in closing down the taverns in Novgorod in order to reduce the problem of drunkenness, even though this resulted in a significant decline in state income.[39] He fed the poor when famine broke out.[40] In 1650, Nikon played the leading role in calming a revolt in Novgorod that was provoked by an increase in the price of bread after a disastrous crop failure.[41] These accomplishments increased his stature before both tsar and people. Nikon also continued to maintain contact with the members of the reforming circle[42] and to implement their programs.

On April 15, 1652, Patriarch Joseph of Moscow died. Nikon, close friend of the tsar, and an able administrator, was an obvious candidate for the patriarchal throne. However, some of the leaders among the reformers, including Avvakum and Neronov, pushed Stefan Vonifatiev, the tsar's confessor, as their candidate. They had grown accustomed, under a weak patriarch, to having great influence in the life of the church and in the selection of bishops and important clerics; undoubtedly, they now feared a strong ruler. Stefan, who must have been aware of the tsar's preference in the matter, declined in favor of Nikon.[43] The fears of the reformers proved well-founded, as later events were to show. Nikon, at this time, was away on a journey to the Solovki Monastery, to obtain the relics of Metropolitan Philip of Moscow (1566-1569)[44] and bring them back to Moscow. On May 25, the tsar sent Nikon a letter, in which he addressed the metropolitan as "my beloved favorite" and "my own special friend," informed him of Joseph's death, and urged him to "return as quickly as possible to us, so that we may choose 'Theognost'[45] as patriarch," for "without you I will do nothing."[46] The letter made it abundantly clear that Nikon himself would be selected.

Nikon arrived in Moscow on July 6 and a Council, held on July 22, formally chose him as the new patriarch. When notified of his election, Nikon at first refused to accept. Only after the tsar, the boyars, and the bishops begged him and agreed to take an oath of obedience to him did he finally do so.[47] That Nikon could have undertaken such an unusual gesture is proof positive of his supreme confidence in the authority he enjoyed. On July 25, 1652, Nikon was consecrated Patriarch of Moscow.[48]

iii. Nikon the Patriarch

A very brief look at Nikon's character is in order at this point. Nikon was a product of his time.

> Nikon had a faith as solid, as total, as naive as that of all his contemporaries: in this, he was in no way different from an Avvakum, or a Neronov. As easily as they did, he accepted heavenly or infernal intervention in the activity of this world. He heard God speaking to him, he fought with devils. He zealously performed all the exercises of the old Russian piety...

> But he also drew attention to himself for his seriousness and devotion to his duties. He knew how to make others obey him. He knew how to administer. He loved beautiful ceremonies...

> In his exterior, he reflected the majesty of the priesthood. He exhibited uncommon activity and energy for doing good. He had the traditional education, he liked books.[49]

But Nikon was also "irritable, capricious, hot-tempered, domineering, and, above all, proud and vain."[50]

In short, once he was patriarch, Nikon became a ruthless tyrant. As indicated by the pledge of obedience he sought from tsar, bishops, and boyars, he wanted absolute authority. Having obtained it, he brooked no opposition. The following is a description provided by a foreigner who spent two years in Russia during Nikon's reign:

> Having become patriarch, he immediately exiled three archpriests to Siberia, together with their wives and children...

> After this, peace set in and everyone began to fear Nikon. He is, to the present time, a great tyrant towards bishops, archimandrites, and all the clergy, and even towards government functionaries. He accepts petitions for no one. He had the Bishop of Kolomna imprisoned and then ordained another to that see. Hearing about someone's misdeed, even just drunkenness, he immediately has him imprisoned: for his soldiers regularly search through the city, and as soon as they see a drunk priest or monk, they put him in jail, subjecting him to all sorts of humiliation. Because of this, we had the occasion to see jails overflowing with such people...

> Formerly, the boyars used to come see the patriarch without being introduced by doorkeepers; and he would come to greet them and would accompany them

as they left. But now, as we saw with our own eyes, ministers and friends of the tsar sit for a long time at the outside doors, until Nikon allows them to enter. They come in with extreme timidity and fear and, until the conclusion of their affairs, stand on their feet, while Nikon continues to sit even as they leave. The love of the tsar and tsaritsa towards him cannot be described.[51]

This last sentence is of key importance, for Nikon's personal authority was based almost entirely on his close friendship with the tsar. Once that friendship began to fade, so did Nikon's influence.

Florovskii describes Nikon as "one of those strange people who have no face, but only temperament. Instead of a face, they have an idea, or program. The whole secret to Nikon is his temperament."[52] In everything he did, the patriarch's guiding principle was the aggrandizement of the Russian Church. This expressed itself in two ways: first, Nikon wanted to achieve the primacy of the church over the state; second, he wanted to make the Russian Church the center of world Orthodoxy. Nearly all historians of the Russian Church have accepted this assumption.[53] These two points deserve some elaboration.

Nikon's position on church and state

Nikon firmly believed in the supremacy of the Church over the state, and this guided his actions throughout his patriarchate, and even earlier, while he was Metropolitan of Novgorod. In particular, he opposed the 1649 *Ulozhenie*, a set of laws which restricted the power of bishops over church-owned lands and the serfs attached to them.[54] Because of his close friendship with the tsar, Nikon, already in 1651, was exempted from its provisions.[55] Nikon's 1652 journey to the Solovki, to retrieve the relics of Metropolitan Philip, was highly significant in this regard. Philip had died a martyr's death for daring to oppose Ivan the Terrible. Nikon took with him from Moscow a letter from the young tsar, in which Alexis, addressing Philip, asks forgiveness for the sins of his forebear and begs him to return home.[56] In this way, the future patriarch sought to impress the tsar with the notion that the secular authorities must be subject to the ecclesiastical. Nikon's actions at his election reveal the same concern.

When he became patriarch, Nikon wasted no occasion to assert his authority. To the *Kormchaia Kniga* (Moscow, 1653), which had just been prepared for publication under his predecessor, Nikon added a Slavonic translation of the *Donation of Constantine*, together with an essay entitled

"The Schism of the Roman Church."[57] This was intended to show that all the prerogatives of the Roman papacy, including both civil and ecclesiastical rights, had now passed to the Russian Patriarchate, the "Third Rome."[58] Already in 1652, Nikon began to be addressed as "Great Sovereign" (*Velikii Gosudar'*), at first only by heads of monasteries, and then, by 1653, even by the tsar himself. The only previous patriarch to have used this title was Filaret (1619-1634), and then only by virtue of being father to Tsar Michael.[59] In fact, Nikon was by this time easily the most powerful man in Russia. When Alexis went off to war in mid-1654, Nikon was left in charge of the government and issued decrees, sometimes in the name of the tsar and himself, sometimes simply in his own name. The tsar returned to Moscow in February 1655, left again only a month later until December; he was absent again from May 1656 to January 1657.[60] Thus the title "Great Sovereign" reflected reality and was not merely honorific. Nikon's authority was virtually limitless, on both the ecclesiastical and secular planes. He appointed and removed bishops at will, administered the government, conducted diplomatic affairs, and saw himself as at least the equal of the tsar in every respect.[61] With the aid and support of the tsar, Nikon greatly expanded the size of the patriarchal estates. During his reign, they grew from approximately 10,000 households to 25,000,[62] easily making the patriarch the wealthiest man in Russia, after the tsar. Nikon also founded three richly-endowed monasteries.[63]

There are those who maintain that Nikon was doing nothing more than attempting to restore the traditional Byzantine notion of the "symphony" between church and state.[64] Yet Nikon's use of the *Donation of Constantine*, as well as his actions, indicate that he was aiming higher.[65] To be fair, however, one must admit that the Byzantine patriarchs themselves had been using the same text to buttress their own claims since the 11th century.[66] In addition, the "*Ulozhenie*" did indeed place severe limitations on the freedom and independence of the church, and Nikon's opposition to it is understandable.[67] Acting in such a highhanded fashion, however, Nikon provoked the opposition of both boyars and bishops. As long as he could rely on the personal support of the tsar, he could continue to push his plans. Once that support weakened, Nikon's position became untenable. It was primarily this, rather than his liturgical reform, which caused his downfall.

Nikon and "Moscow-Third Rome" [68] ideology

All Russians in this period shared the notion that Moscow was now the capital of the Orthodox world. This belief, shaped after the Council of Florence and the fall of Constantinople, was encouraged also by the numerous Greek and Eastern clerics who frequented Moscow in their search for financial and political support. The Russian tsar was now the sole Orthodox ruler. Since 1593, Moscow had its own patriarch, thus completing the pentarchy. The Patriarch of Moscow replaced the Pope of Rome, who, the Russians affirmed, had fallen into schism and heresy. Russians were not unanimous, however, in their evaluation of the orthodoxy of non-Russians. Some, like Neronov, Avvakum, and the "provincial" zealots, affirmed the complete superiority of Russian faith and practice over the Greek. Others, the tsar, Vonifatiev, and later Nikon, preferred the Greek model. The latter group considered that the adoption of Greek models would eventually lead to the establishment of a new Orthodox empire, with Russia as its center. Largely because he accepted this dream, Nikon was selected by the tsar as the new patriarch. [69]

As patriarch, Nikon constantly strove for the aggrandizement of the Russian Church, not only vis-à-vis the state, but also vis-à-vis the Greek Churches. Thus the monasteries he built were patterned after Greek models and bore Greek names. His Monastery of the Resurrection, also called "New Jerusalem," contained a cathedral which was an exact replica of the Anastasis in Jerusalem. [70] This new church contained five altars, one for each of the Eastern patriarchs, the fifth and central one for himself, as Patriarch of the Third Rome.

Nikon always focused on externals, and much that is now considered "typically Russian" in liturgical solemnity and opulence can be traced back to him. He loved the ornate ceremonial of the Greeks, its festive character, its richness, and its apparent splendor. [71] He introduced Greek ambos, episcopal staffs, monastic headgear, and music, and invited Greek iconographers and silversmiths to Moscow. [72] His love for the ornate at times took on extreme proportions: he would wear costly vestments—on Easter 1655, he wore vestments made of gold and jewels worth 30,000 rubles, which was an astounding fortune in those days. Wearing vestments weighing hundreds of pounds, he would stand through services lasting six to eight hours. He frequently had 40-75 clergy concelebrating with him. All these were symbols of his power,[73] and served his purpose to make Russia a new Byzantium, and Moscow a new Rome.[74] This is the context into which his liturgical reforms fit.

The liturgical reforms

If Nikon's program of making Moscow the capital of world Orthodoxy was to succeed, something had to be done about the confusing variety in liturgical practices. Since Nikon, like all Russians, identified liturgical rubrics and details with dogma, differences could only be explained as errors by one side or the other. Such incidents as the burning of Muscovite liturgical books on Mt. Athos only a few years earlier brought these differences in practice into stark relief. If Nikon's, and the tsar's, plans were to become reality, then standardization was the only logical choice. Nikon opted for the Greek model; his opponents, the future Old-Believers, chose the Russian one. In the latters' eyes, choosing Greek practice over Russian also meant rejecting the Russian past.

Nikon's personal role in the reform was generally limited to rubrical changes. He had little to do with the textual reforms, which he left to his appointed correctors. In this, he was consistent with his overall policy as patriarch, emphasizing external and visual trappings. Because of this limited role, he was little aware of what his correctors were actually doing, and believed, apparently right to the end, that the books were being corrected according to ancient Greek and Slavonic models. In a letter to Patriarch Dionysios of Constantinople in 1666, he writes that the reform was based on books sent by Patriarch Paisios of Constantinople and on the ancient books collected by Arsenii Sukhanov in the East.[75] But Nikon's primary goal was to unify the external ritual, and he was less concerned with the text itself.[76] This may help to explain why Nikon allowed Neronov to use the old books in 1656, and why later, after his abandonment of the patriarchate, he allowed monks at his Iverskii Monastery to reprint the old-style service books.[77]

For Nikon the liturgical reforms were, in fact, only a peripheral item in his program of aggrandizing the Russian Church. As we have seen, most of his energy was directed toward the expansion of patriarchal power. He spent a great deal of time ruling the state, in place of Alexis, and expended much effort and resources on building monasteries and increasing the patriarchal estates. Once Nikon resigned in 1658, he entirely ceased fostering the liturgical reforms, though he continued his building programs and the defense of his patriarchal prerogatives. For this reason, we give only a brief, schematic outline of further developments in his career.

iv. The fall from power

On July 10, 1658, after celebrating liturgy at the Cathedral of the Dormition, Nikon removed his vestments, put on a plain monastic robe, and announced that he would no longer be patriarch.[78] This took place a few days after an incident in which one of Nikon's emissaries was mistreated by a representative of the tsar. Nikon expected an apology from the tsar, but none was forthcoming. Subsequently, the tsar failed to appear at several church services which he traditionally attended.[79] To add insult to injury, Prince Iurii Romodanovskii was sent to inform Nikon that the tsar was angry, and that the patriarch was to cease using the title "Great Sovereign."[80] Nikon thus left the throne in the apparent hope that the tsar would beg him to return, just as he had begged him to accept the patriarchal throne some six years earlier. But this time Nikon miscalculated.

In fact, the above incident was nothing more than a final push. The basis for Nikon's power had always been his close friendship with the tsar, a friendship which cooled noticeably in the later years of Nikon's patriarchate. Alexis was no longer the impressionable, teen-age youth, whom Nikon could easily control. In a letter to Patriarch Dionysios of Constantinople, Nikon wrote that the tsar, after returning from war against Lithuania, became proud and began to meddle in church affairs.[81] After the unsuccessful war, the tsar became perceptibly cooler towards Nikon. But the patriarch could not adjust to the new situation.[82] Nikon had too much pride to accept any loss in status, such as the tsar's demand that he stop calling himself "Great Sovereign."[83] In addition, Nikon could not depend on the support of the boyars and the clergy, all of whom he had alienated by his highhandedness, ruthlessness, and dictatorial demeanor.

When Nikon was still Metropolitan of Novgorod, the boyars had already complained that "the tsar has handed us over to the metropolitans."[84] Opponents, like Neronov, bombarded the tsar with complaints about Nikon.[85] Thus both clergy and nobles joined forces to oppose Nikon, and the battleground they chose was the issue of liturgical reform.[86] As early as 1656, Alexis had had a public argument with Nikon over some liturgical changes.[87] Thus the events in July 1658 were but the culmination of a long series of developments.

Alexis did not ask Nikon to return. After years of indecision, the tsar finally convened a council of Greek and Russian bishops. On December 12, 1666, this council officially deposed Nikon, reduced him to the status of a lay monk, and ordered him imprisoned in the Ferapontov Monastery.[88] The three monasteries he built, which belonged to him personally, were confiscated. Nikon spent nearly ten years at the Ferapontov Monastery and, in 1676, was transferred to the Kirillov Monastery.[89] Tsar Alexis died in 1676; but before dying he stated that he wanted to restore Nikon to patriarchal rank. Fedor, the new tsar, asked a council in 1681 to do this, but the council refused. Fedor then wrote to the Eastern patriarchs, asking them to restore Nikon's title. Meanwhile, Nikon became gravely ill, and the tsar ordered him brought to the Monastery of the Resurrection near Moscow. On August 17, 1681, as he was being transported back to Moscow, Nikon died. By order of the tsar, Nikon was buried with the full episcopal rite. In 1682, the Eastern patriarchs ordered that Nikon be commemorated once again as patriarch.[90]

2. Tsar Alexis

Born on March 29, 1629, Alexis Mikhailovich inherited his father's throne at the age of 16. He ruled Russia from 1645 until his death on January 29, 1676—a pivotal period in Russian history. These years saw increasing influence from the West, as well as conflict with it. Alexis was personally involved in campaigns against both the Poles and the Swedes. During his reign, the bulk of Kievan Russia was united with the Muscovite Kingdom, which grew into an empire. More significantly for us, he played an integral part in the events which shook the Church at this time. A complete biographical study of this tsar is outside the scope of this work.[91] We shall limit ourselves to a brief examination of his attitude toward the liturgical reforms and of his role in them.

i. Education

Alexis went through the entire cycle of Russian "literary learning," and he was thus an educated man by the standards of his time. Kliuchevskii describes his course of study:[92]

age 6: he learned the alphabet from a textbook compiled for him at the request of his grandfather, Patriarch Filaret. This book contained the alphabet, the common abbreviations used in Slavonic, as well as the commandments and a short catechism. He was taught by the secretary of one of the government departments.

age 7: he began to read the *Horologion*,[93] five months later the Psalter, three months later the Book of Acts;

age 8: he was taught to write;

age 9: the choirmaster began to teach him the *Octoechos*[94] and, eight months later, the Holy Week chants from the *Triodion*.[95]

The use of liturgical books as primers was standard in Russia in the 16th and 17th centuries, though Latin models began to be adopted in the second half of the 17th century.[96] The tsar's tutor was Ivan Morozov, a boyar, who was very open to everything Western, and who would dress Alexis and his brothers in the German fashion.[97] Thus, while Alexis was steeped in the traditional Russian piety, he did not share the xenophobia of the majority of his countrymen.[98] Alexis' love for and knowledge of the liturgy dates to this early time in his life.

ii. Piety

Throughout his reign, the tsar distinguished himself by his very strong piety, which was typically Russian in character. This consisted of frequent attendance at long church services, strict observance of all the fasting periods, as well as generous support for the Church and aid to the poor. Foreigners, in particular, were struck by these traits, which were not common among absolute monarchs. Paul of Aleppo, a Syrian, observes:

> On each day of the year which has a commemoration of a saint in whose honor there is a church in this city—and there are enough churches named after saints and feasts for the whole year, and even more—he has the custom...of going to

their churches. He even walks to them, not wishing to ride out of love and respect for them. He stands from the beginning of the service to the end, just like any other person, and constantly prostrates himself before the icon of the saint of the day, striking his forehead against the ground with tears and weeping. This is how he acts in the presence of the people. And inside his palace, we are told, he and the empress lead a way of life higher even than the saints, with constant vigils and prayers in their churches lasting entire nights. What we have said here is but a small fraction of what we have heard about the tsar and seen with our own eyes.[99]

During periods of fasting, these efforts were redoubled, as the same witness recounts:

According to custom, the tsar and the empress fast these three days [the first three days of Lent], giving themselves over to prayerful vigil, making prostrations, and observing strict abstinence, as we have now observed. Finally, having stood through the liturgy on Wednesday,[100] the tsar broke the fast by eating some sweet compote, as is his usual custom...Then he again fasted from that night until late Saturday morning, when he stood through the liturgy, received the Holy Mysteries, ate some antidoron, and then had lunch.[101]

During Lent, the tsar spent five to six hours a day standing in church and would make 1000-1500 prostrations each day.[102]

Alexis was under the strong influence of his personal confessor, Stefan Vonifatiev, who was a leader of the circle of zealots of piety. Stefan, who was also Archpriest of the Cathedral of the Annunciation in the Kremlin, met frequently with the tsar, gave him spiritual readings, and was responsible for his spiritual formation.[103] Through Stefan, the young tsar became a strong supporter of the zealots' plans to reform religious life, to abolish abuses in morals, to raise the spiritual and intellectual level of both clergy and lay people, as well as to correct liturgical abuses. As early as February 1646, Alexis issued a decree, ordering that during the ensuing period of Lent, "Archpriests, priests, deacons, and all Orthodox Christians are to fast and live in purity and all temperance, and refrain from drunkenness, falsehood, and from every sin."[104] When, on January 16, 1648, Alexis took a bride, his wedding celebration contained none of the customary Russian excesses in eating and drinking. Guided by Stefan, Alexis forbade games and dancing, and the rites were performed "piously and soberly."[105] When a dispute arose between Vonifatiev and Patriarch Joseph (1642-1652), Nikon's predecessor, over the issue of *mnogoglasie*, the tsar sided with Stefan in pushing for the total abolition of this abuse. Stefan was also an ardent supporter of learning and was instrumental in the publication in Moscow of such works as Meletii Smotritskii's *Grammar* (1648), Abbot Nathaniel's *Kniga o vere* (1648), and Peter Moghila's *Small Catechesis* (1649).[106] This openness to foreign (South and West Russian, or Ukrainian) influence and the stress on education was characteristic of the "urban" group of zealots, which was led by Vonifatiev and Rtishchev. Through Vonifatiev, Alexis became a strong supporter of this group.

iii. Moscow-Third Rome

Together with his contemporaries in Moscow, Alexis firmly believed that Moscow was the capital of the Orthodox world, and that he himself was heir to the Byzantine emperors.[107] This seemed largely borne out by historical fact: since the collapse of the Byzantine empire, Muscovite Russia was indeed the only independent Orthodox kingdom, whose star was manifestly rising. Orthodox from throughout the world came to Moscow to seek the tsar's support. Alexis' belief that he was the new "Orthodox emperor" was reinforced by foreigners, including even patriarchs. Typical is the speech made by Patriarch Paisios of Jerusalem at his reception by the tsar on February 4, 1649:

> The most-holy Trinity—Father, Son, and Holy Spirit—one kingdom and lordship, will bless your sovereign kingdom, and may it magnify you higher than all rulers and manifest you as the victor and conqueror over all visible and invisible enemies, just as both ancient and new rulers—Kind David, King Hezekiah, and the great Emperor Constantine. May it strengthen you and multiply your years to a great age. May it grant you successfully to assume the most high throne of the great Emperor Constantine, your forefather, so that you will deliver the multitude of pious and Orthodox Christians from impious hands, from the wild beasts who devour them mercilessly. May you be the new Moses, may you free us from captivity as he freed the Sons of Israel from the hands of the pharaoh with a staff, the symbol of the righteous, life-giving Cross...[108]

Patriarch Athanasios Patellarios of Constantinople said much the same upon his arrival in Moscow in 1653.[109] When, in 1652, Nikon was made patriarch, he addressed the tsar, asking that God might expand his kingdom "from sea to sea, from the rivers to the ends of the earth, and might return those who are scattered into [his] pious kingdom, and may unite them...so that [he] might be the Christian emperor and sovereign over all, and may shine like the sun among the stars."[110]

There are a number of indications that Alexis understood this on both the religious and political planes. He repeatedly expressed the desire to unify the whole Orthodox world under his rule. At a reception on Easter in 1656, addressing a group of Greek merchants, he asks them to entreat their bishops, priests, and monks to pray for him, so that his sword might be strengthened. An eyewitness describes the scene:

> Then, spilling copious tears, he said to the officials of his government: "My heart is broken over the enslavement of those poor people who are under the power of enemies of the faith. God—may His name be glorified!—will call me to account for them at the day of judgment, because, having the possibility to free them, I neglect it…And I have taken on myself the obligation that, if it will be pleasing to God, I will sacrifice my army, my treasury, and even spill my own blood for the sake of liberating them.[111]

Domestic problems and poor relations with neighboring countries, particularly Poland and Sweden, prevented him from making any attempts to carry out this goal. But he never abandoned the idea and, in 1666, sent to Mt. Athos asking, among other things, for all available material about Greek imperial rites.[112] It is in this context that the tsar's view of the Greeks, and particularly of the liturgical reforms, is to be understood.

iv. Attitude toward the Greeks

Alexis certainly believed in the full orthodoxy of the Greeks. He shared this belief with the urban zealots of piety, and followed the line of his predecessors on the Muscovite throne. Former rulers in Moscow always held the Greeks in high regard and frequently sent money and gifts to all four Eastern patriarchs, as well as to Mt. Athos. In return, the Eastern patriarchs proved their usefulness to the tsars. In 1562, for example, the Patriarch of Constantinople had supported Ivan the Terrible by recognizing his claim to the title of tsar (caesar), and even ordered that Ivan be prayed for in all Orthodox churches.[113] Job, the first Patriarch of Moscow, was confirmed and installed by Patriarch Jeremias II of Constantinople.[114] Filaret, Alexis' grandfather, was consecrated patriarch by Theophanos of Jerusalem.[115] The patriarchs, as well as numerous other Greeks, frequently served as the tsar's agents in Turkish-dominated areas.[116] Alexis himself grew up in grecophile circles, for both his grandfather, Filaret, and father, Michael, were strongly pro-Greek, welcoming Greeks to Moscow and giving them large sums of money.[117] In 1652, Alexis ordered that the

Eastern patriarchs be commemorated, together with the Patriarch of Moscow, at the "*mnogoletie*," thus publicly proclaiming the full unity of the Russian and Greek churches. Nikon praised this decree in a letter to the tsar.[118]

Alexis' dreams of political and religious unity with the Greeks were obviously sincere, and were motivated in part also by his admiration for Greek learning. During his reign, several attempts were made to bring learned Greeks to Moscow to teach, and according to an eyewitness, the tsar repeatedly expressed the wish to learn Greek.[119] As early as 1645, a Greek archimandrite named Benedict came to Moscow from Kiev, where he had been teaching at the Academy of Peter Moghila.[120] In 1649, a number of other scholars who knew Greek were brought to Moscow, including Epifanii Slavinetskii and Arsenios the Greek. They were to play a major role in the liturgical reform. That same year, the tsar asked Paisios of Jerusalem to send educated Greeks to Moscow, a request which Paisios fulfilled in 1652 by sending Metropolitan Gabriel of Naupaktos and Arta.[121] Alexis' goal of introducing education, that was consistent with the program of the urban group of reformers, remained with him to the end of his life;[122] though once again, circumstances made its implementation difficult.

v. The liturgical reform

In order to achieve his dream of uniting all Orthodox into one empire under Moscow, Alexis believed that total unity must be achieved with the other Eastern Orthodox churches. The ongoing negotiations with Bogdan Khmelnitskii, Hetman of the Ukrainian Cossacks, which finally led to the annexation of much of Kievan Rus', added urgency to the matter.[123] The liturgical reforms of Peter Moghila (†1646) in Kiev had, in the years just past, brought South and West-Russian practice much closer to the Greek. This also helps to explain the subsequent employment of Kievan scholars and Ukrainian liturgical books in the "correction" of the Moscow books. Encouraged by his close friends, Vonifatiev and Rtishchev, the tsar decided to push through the liturgical reforms which would make this unity possible. In keeping with the Russian approach, which equated every detail of liturgical practice with dogma, the tsar and his advisors were convinced that such a reform was essential.[124] The apparent need for reform was brought into even sharper focus during the visit of Patriarch Paisios of Jerusalem in 1649,[125] and the by subsequent report of Arsenii Sukhanov that the monks on Mt. Athos had burned Russian liturgical books as heretical.[126] The tsar thus decided that liturgical unity must be achieved before his goal of creating an Orthodox empire could be realized. Further, this liturgical reform was to take precedence over all other items on the program of the zealots of piety. Significantly, this decision was made before the beginning of Nikon's patriarchate. Thus the liturgical reform of Nikon was in fact the creation of the tsar and his friends: Nikon was selected to implement it.

Once the decision to carry out the liturgical reform was made, preparations became necessary. While Paisios of Jerusalem was still in Moscow, the tsar had already asked his advice about some liturgical details.[127] In May 1649, Alexis wrote to Metropolitan Silvester Kosov of Kiev, asking him to send two scholars, Arsenii Satanovskii and Damaskin Ptitskii, to Moscow to correct the Slavonic translation of the Bible from Greek, "because they know the Divine Scripture and know the Greek tongue, and are able to translate from Greek to Slavic, and know Latin sufficiently well, for such persons are useful to our Royal Highness."[128] In response to this request, Arsenii Satanovskii and Epifanii Slavinetskii, who replaced Damaskin Ptitskii, reached Moscow on July 12, 1649. On June 10, 1649, Arsenii Sukhanov, charged with learning about Greek liturgical practice and with collecting Greek books, departed Moscow, accompanying Paisios of Jerusalem.[129] The "correction" of the books began immediately, but with a different approach. The new editions were based on contemporary Greek and South-Russian models.[130] Since the tsar firmly believed that the Greeks were fully Orthodox, he clearly assumed that they had preserved the ancient liturgical practices intact, and he saw no difficulty in using contemporary Greek books as models.

The reform was thus well under way when, in 1652, Nikon became patriarch and took personal control of the program. Nikon's acceptance of the reform was undoubtedly one of the criteria used in his selection by the tsar to replace Joseph,[131] who had resisted the reforming zeal of the tsar and Vonifatiev.[132] After Nikon began to push the reforms in his own name, Alexis strongly supported him. The 1654 Moscow Council, which officially designated Greek practice as the model for the reform, was convened by the tsar and ratified by him.[133] When zealots such as Neronov and Avvakum petitioned the tsar to stop Nikon, the tsar simply handed their petitions to the patriarch.[134] Subsequently, Alexis forbade Neronov to write to him any longer.[135] The tsar supported the liturgical reform not merely because of his close friendship with Nikon, but because it was part of his own program. True, in 1656, Alexis publicly argued with Nikon over the reform, but only after he discovered that one of Nikon's changes was not consistent with Greek practice.[136] Even after relations between the two had cooled, the tsar remained a strong partisan of the reform.

Toward the end of his patriarchate, Nikon began to lose interest in the correction of liturgical books, and once he left his throne, as we have seen, he had nothing more to do with it. If the reform had been simply his own idea, it would have collapsed at this point. Alexis, however, never changed his position. After Nikon abandoned his post, the tsar became the *de facto* patriarch and administered the Church until 1667, when Joasaph II was selected.[137] During this span of nine years, the correctors continued their work, and many new liturgical books were published.[138] Alexis promoted bishops such as Metropolitan Paul of Krutitsa, Archbishop Hilarion of Riazan, and Joachim, Moscow Archimandrite of the Chudov Monastery and later patriarch, all of whom were strong supporters of the reform.[139]

Unlike Nikon, however, Alexis was willing to discuss the issues with opponents of the reform and made repeated efforts to achieve reconciliation with them. Thus, in 1664, he ordered Avvakum brought back from exile to Moscow for talks. Avvakum himself states that he was treated well, but refused to accept the new books.[140] Only after he had failed to convert the enemies of the liturgical reform did the tsar assemble a council to deal with Avvakum and his companions. Before the council met, Alexis obtained from each delegate a pledge of support for the reform.[141] At the 1666 Council, more efforts at reconciliation were attempted, and a number of opponents were convinced; but Avvakum and his staunchest supporters refused to budge.[142] Only then did the council proceed to condemn the Old-Believers and reaffirm the decision of 1654. The 1667 Council, with numerous Eastern bishops in attendance, condemned Nikon but reaffirmed the liturgical reform in no uncertain terms.[143]

Just as the Greek bishops had been willing tools of Nikon in fostering the liturgical reform, they now became willing accomplices to the tsar in deposing Nikon and in placing the final seal on the new service books. Throughout the proceedings, Alexis was in firm control. When several Russian bishops refused to sign the edict condemning Nikon, because it affirmed the superiority of the state over the Church, the tsar had them jailed. On the matter of liturgical practice, the council mandated the use of the Nikonian editions, based on Greek usage. By special request of the tsar, however, several peculiarly Russian customs were permitted.[144]

Thus the attribution of the reforms to Nikon is not entirely accurate. It was Alexis who remained consistent throughout his reign, in desiring to align Russian practice with Greek. Nikon neither conceived nor completed the reform. Clearly, the reform would have collapsed after 1658, when Nikon left, had the tsar not continued to further it in his own name.

3. Arsenios the Greek

Of all Nikon's correctors, none caused so much consternation among opponents to the reform as the monk Arsenios. In a letter to the tsar dated February 27, 1654, the archpriest Neronov complains that the heretic Arsenios, who only five years earlier had been sent in chains to the Solovki Monastery, was now living in a cell at Patriarch Nikon's palace, translating books.[145] Confronting Nikon a few years later, Neronov complained to the patriarch about Arsenios.[146] Deacon Fedor, a leader in the opposition, wrote to the tsar in a 1666 petition:

> That Greek whom Nikon brought back from exile…the monk Arsenios, was a known heretic, and that is why he was imprisoned…But Nikon took to that heretic and, having brought him back, put him to work on the books! There, at the Solovki Monastery, his [Arsenios'] spiritual father attested to his heresy, judged him to be cut off from the church, and excommunicated him until the time of his death. They say that he was even a Jew and took an oath to the Pope of Rome. This enemy has stirred up trouble in your entire kingdom and has sown weeds into the books, and taught others to do the same.[147]

The monk Avraamii,[148] in his "Defense of the Christian Faith," written in 1669-1670, also repeatedly refers to Arsenios as a heretic.[149] In the centuries that followed, Arsenios continued to serve as the target for Old-Believer polemics.[150] For the opponents of the liturgical reform, this

Greek monk was a typical manifestation of the degeneracy of the Greeks and of the Greek Church!

i. Background and early life

Our chief information about Arsenios' life, before his arrival in Moscow, comes from his own admissions made at the inquisition which he faced soon after his arrival.[151] He was born ca. 1610[152] in the city of Trikkala, near the center of Thessaly, and presently in Northern Greece but then under Turkish rule. His father, a priest, held a high ecclesiastical position in the city. His godfather was an archbishop, so Arsenios was evidently born into the wealthy classes. He had four brothers, two of whom pursued ecclesiastical careers. He received his early education from his father; but at the age of fourteen he accompanied his brother Athanasios to Venice, where he remained to continue his studies. After a year in Venice, Arsenios was taken by his brother to Rome, to study "Homer, Aristotle, and the Seven Councils." In Rome, he stayed at the Collegium Athanasianum, or Greek College, where he undoubtedly became a Uniate to continue his studies. After five years in Rome, he went to the famous University of Padua where, for the next three years, he studied philosophy and medicine.

At the age of twenty-three, now highly educated, Arsenios returned to the East and sought out his brother Athanasios, who had become an archimandrite in Constantinople. Arsenios asked his brother to tonsure him, but Athanasios refused on the ground that Arsenios was of "Latin faith." Arsenios then formally thrice renounced the Roman faith and, after his brothers failed to convince him to marry, became a monk. A year later, Arsenios was ordained deacon, and then priest, by Bishop Callistos of Larisa, a city near his home town of Trikkala. Shortly thereafter, he became abbot of a monastery on the island of Skiathos, off the Aegean coast of Thessaly.

After six months at his monastery, he left for Constantinople, in search of a book on the Seven Councils. Once in the capital city, bored with life on a small island, he arranged to stay on as a tutor in the household of Antonios Babas, a wealthy Greek. Arsenios soon came to the attention of Patriarch Parthenios, who sought to appoint the intellectual young monk as bishop of Methoni and Koroni, in the southwest corner of the

Peloponnesus. This brought Arsenios to the attention of the Turkish Vizier, particularly because Arsenios had spent time in Venice, with which Turkey had just began a war. Suspected of being a spy, Arsenios was arrested, questioned, and thrown in jail. After two weeks in jail, where he was subjected to torture, he agreed to accept the Moslem faith and be circumcized, in order to regain his freedom.

His apostasy, even though under duress, made it impossible for him to return home. He went first to Wallachia (present-day southern Romania), to the Voevoda Matvei. After three months there, suffering from pangs of conscience, he made his confession to Metropolitan Joasaph of Ioannina, who chrismated him and reunited him to Orthodoxy. From Wallachia he made his way to Moldavia, where he lived for two years. After that he traveled to Lvov, at that time within Poland, where he learned of the Academy of Peter Moghila in Kiev. While in Poland, Arsenios may once more have become a Uniate. Needing permission from Vladislav, King of Poland, to go to Kiev, Arsenios journeyed to Warsaw to obtain it. When the king, who was suffering from kidney stones, learned of Arsenios' medical knowledge, he appointed him his personal physician. After successfully curing the king's malady, Arsenios finally obtained permission to go to Kiev, as well as a letter of recommendation from the king to Silvester Kosov, Metropolitan of Kiev.

Arsenios was not very long in Kiev when Patriarch Paisios of Jerusalem passed through on his way to Moscow to ask the tsar for money for the Holy Sepulchre. Paisios met Arsenios and took him along in the capacity of patriarchal "*didaskalos*" (teacher), thus expanding the size of his retinue and assuring himself of even more revenue.[153] On January 5, 1649, Paisios and his group reached Putivl, on the western border of Muscovite Russia, where they had to wait until permission to proceed to Moscow arrived from the capital. On January 10, they departed for Moscow, which they reached on the 27th.[154]

ii. In Moscow and exile

Arsenios the Greek was just the kind of person the Muscovite authorities were looking for at the time. He was highly educated, knew Slavonic, Greek, and Latin, and came with the recommendation of the Patriarch of Jerusalem. Quite naturally, the Russians asked Paisios to leave the Greek monk behind. The patriarch, happy to be of some use, agreed, and Arsenios thus remained in Moscow after Paisios left on June 10, 1649.[155] Arsenios was immediately put to work as a teacher, giving private lessons in Greek. The names of at least two of his students are known: Stepan Oliab'ev and Feodoseika Evtikheev. The latter was subsequently charged with taking an inventory of Arsenios' personal possessions.[156] From this inventory, we also know of the books Arsenios brought along to Russia.[157] These include a number of Greek and Latin grammars and lexica, a few classical Greek works, and several biblical and liturgical books, among which was one Greek *Euchologion*, the Venice edition of 1602.[158] This, we shall see, is the edition used as the basis for the 1655 Moscow *Sluzhebnik*.

Arsenios' future seemed secure; but, once again, fortune deserted him. Accompanying Paisios of Jerusalem, on the journey back East, was Arsenii Sukhanov, who was being sent to "describe the holy places and Greek liturgical practice."[159] On June 25, this party reached Putivl, where Arsenii Sukhanov learned of Arsenios' past from a monk named Joasaph, who was Paisios' bursar. Sukhanov, who had little love for Greeks, immediately wrote back to Moscow with a report of what he had heard:

> Arsenios is Greek by birth and was a monastic cleric; then, under circumstances I know nothing about, he became a Moslem. Then he left the Moslem faith, came to Poland, and was of the Uniate faith. And, coming from Poland, he lived in Kiev. When the Patriarch of Jerusalem came to Kiev, his *didaskalos* passed away, and the patriarch took that elder Arsenios with him to Moscow, in place of his *didaskalos*, and gave him the title of *didaskalos*. But about his city of birth, none of them know.[160]

Worried about his own credibility before the Russians, Patriarch Paisios similarly sent off a letter to the tsar, denouncing his *didaskalos*:

> Let it be known, pious tsar, about Arsenios, who has remained in your kingdom. Question him thoroughly, for he is not strong in his pious Christian faith. He was formerly a monk and a priest, then became a Moslem, then fled to the Poles and among them became a Uniate, and he has a great, evil weakness. Question him thoroughly and you will learn all…for it is necessary to eliminate also those who have any heresy and are two-faced in their faith…I did not know about his illegal state. But now I have learned of it and am writing to your kingdom so that you may preserve yourself from such persons, so that such rotten and evil people may not defile the churches of Christ.[161]

These letters caused a considerable stir when they reached Moscow. Arsenios was immediately placed under arrest and questioned about his past by the boyar Nikita Ivanovich Odoevskii and the secretary of the Boyars' Council, Mikhail Volosheninov.[162] Arsenios at first denied ever having been either Uniate or Moslem, claiming that he had feigned illness when the course of study in Rome reached the Eighth and Ninth Councils, and that he subsequently left Rome, so as not to become Roman Catholic. When asked whether he had ever received the sacraments in Rome, Arsenios said that he had received them from the Greek Orthodox metropolitan with whom he had lived, together with five or six elders. This "Metropolitan holds to the Seven Councils, but not to the Eighth or Ninth, and does not communicate with the Pope; but when the Pope orders him to attend a council, he goes to it and prays for the Pope." This answer did not satisfy his questioners, who insisted that the Greek metropolitan was known by everyone to be a Uniate, since he attended the Pope's councils. Arsenios continued to stick by his story. When asked about his conversion to the Moslem faith, Arsenios similarly denied the fact. The Russians then threatened to conduct a physical examination and, at this, the unfortunate Greek confessed, stating that his conversion had been coerced through torture and duress during his two-week imprisonment. Only then was Arsenios told that Patriarch Paisios had denounced him as having been first a Uniate, then a Moslem, then again a Uniate. Arsenios defended himself by saying that he had told the patriarch about his past, and that Paisios had pardoned him, had even given him a letter of forgiveness and blessing, and that this was the reason he had not bothered to inform the Russians about the matter. Finally, Arsenios correctly pointed out that he had remained in Moscow only at the tsar's command, and not of his own free will. The Russians again accused him of falsehood, because Paisios had stated in his letter that he knew nothing of Arsenios' past.[163]

On July 27, 1649, the tsar ordered that Arsenios, for his heresy, be sent in confinement to the Solovki Monastery, in far northern Russia, "for the correction of his Orthodox Christian faith." Instructions were sent to the abbot of the monastery that Arsenios be kept in strict confinement in perpetuity, and be given the same food and clothing as a common monk.[164] Surprisingly, his personal belongings, including his books, were returned to him.[165] Arsenios was to spend the next three years at Solovki, where he learned traditional "Russian piety."[166] Old-Believer materials originating from this monastery indicate that, in this period of incarceration, Arsenios learned how to cross himself with two fingers, admitted that the Greeks had lost the true faith, but that he refused to fast properly, or to make the required number of prostrations.[167] The veracity of these sources is certainly open to question, but Arsenios had indeed demonstrated his ability to adapt in the past!

iii. Arsenios the corrector

When Nikon became patriarch in 1652, Arsenios' fortunes improved. Nikon knew about Arsenios[168] and undoubtedly met him at Solovki early that year, when he had traveled there to obtain the relics of Metropolitan Philip. Soon after assuming the patriarchal throne, Nikon ordered that Arsenios be brought back to Moscow. Here, the Greek monk was put in charge of the "Greco-Latin" school, which existed from 1653 to 1655.[169] Shortly after Nikon began pushing the reform of the liturgical books, Arsenios was appointed, in March 1654, to the post of corrector at the Printing Office, with an annual salary of fifty rubles.[170] Nikon made no effort to clear Arsenios' name and from the very beginning the opponents to the reform brought up Arsenios' shady past in their polemics. Nikon's only response to Neronov's accusations was that Arsenii Sukhanov had lied in denouncing Arsenios.[171]

During his tenure as corrector, Arsenios translated a number of works from the Greek, and, as chief corrector, he oversaw the publication of many liturgical, patristic, and hagiographical books. Most of Arsenios' translations were made from contemporary, Venetian, printed editions. He is known to have translated the following works:[172]

a. *Skrizhal'* (1656);[173]

b. *Anthologion* (1660);[174]

c. the "Chronicle" of Pseudo-Dorotheos;[175]

d. an essay by Paisios Ligarides.[176]

Twentieth-century scholars have a generally dim view of Arsenios' translating skills. Sobolevskii, for example, states: "Arsenios the Greek, though he translated a great deal, knew Church-Slavonic poorly to the end of his life and wrote it improperly; thus he was unable to produce satisfactory translations."[177] This critical evaluation is confirmed by Perets, who studied Arsenios' translation of the life of Alexis, the Man of God. Arsenios, she demonstrates, translated the Greek word for word, nearly always preserving the exact word-order of the original. For complex Greek words, rather than using several words in Slavonic, Arsenios would create new, compound calques. The translation is therefore frequently unclear or incomprehensible.[178] Lebedeva says much the same in her examination of the original manuscript of Arsenios' translation of the "Chronicle" of Pseudo-Dorotheos.[179] Kiselev, on the other hand, calls Arsenios a "gifted philologist" and praises him for the accuracy of his translation of the *Anthologion*.[180]

Just what role Arsenios had in the translation of liturgical books is not very clear, and there are no direct indications that he himself translated any service books. Kolosov suggests that, in 1656, Arsenios prepared a new edition of the *Trebnik* (Ritual), which was published in 1658; but this attribution is not certain.[181] As chief corrector, however, he must have shared responsibility for the publication of the liturgical books. He also evidently shared the tsar's and Nikon's view that Russian practice had to be brought in line with the Greek. The Old-Believers, as we have seen, did not fail to point this out. Further, Arsenios' penchant for using contemporary, printed editions for his translation work is significant, setting the pattern for the reform of the liturgical books as well.

We know little of Arsenios' ultimate fate. After Nikon abandoned his throne in 1658, Arsenios at first remained in his position at the Printing Office. Beginning with 1660 his standing apparently fell, and he was no longer the highest-paid among the correctors. From September 1662, his name no longer appears on the list of correctors, and the Greek monk was again sent into exile to Solovki. The worsening of Arsenios' position in this period can certainly be explained in the context of the tsar's policy of appeasement towards opponents of the liturgical reform.[182] When Arsenios was exiled the second time, his collection of books was confiscated and placed in the library of the Printing Office.[183] In 1666, once the tsar decided that appeasement was doomed to fail, he ordered that Arsenios be released from his imprisonment at Solovki and allowed to reside in a monastery selected by the tsar.[184] Arsenios must have returned to Moscow, as he is known to have been in contact with Paisios Ligarides, whose essay he translated.[185] But beyond these few details, there remain no further traces of Arsenios' stay in Russia remain.

4. Epifanii Slavinetskii

The hieromonk Epifanii, though one of the chief promulgators of the reform, was certainly the least visible. He preferred to remain in the background, and sought no power or glory. A scholar by nature, he liked nothing more than to sit in his cell translating books from Greek or Latin. He had broad interests, ranging from Scripture and patristics to cosmology, anatomy, and poetry. A man of consistently high principles, he was one of the few who remained faithful to Nikon after the tide had turned against the patriarch. Though a "foreigner" in Muscovite Russia, Epifanii succeeded in gaining the respect of all, and thus even the Old-Believers do not include him as a target for their polemics, despite his leading role in the liturgical reform.

i. Background and early life

Very little is known about Epifanii before his arrival in Moscow from Kiev. He was of Ukrainian or White Russian background, possibly born in the city of Pinsk.[186] He studied at the school of the Kievan Brotherhood before its reorganization by Peter Moghila.[187] He then traveled abroad to complete his studies, attending a Latin school, most likely in Poland.[188] After returning to Kiev he was tonsured at the Monastery of the Caves, and then became a junior member of the faculty at the Moghilan Academy, instructing children in the Collegium, the lower branch of the Academy.[189] Here, in 1642, he commenced his literary career by translating the Latin lexicon of Ambrogio Calepino (Basel, 1577).[190] But the bulk of Epifanii's work was done in Moscow, where he spent the last twenty-six years of his life.

ii. Literary career in Moscow

In the later 1640's, Tsar Alexis and the circle of reformers in Moscow were laying the foundations for the development of education and for the liturgical reform. To bring these goals to fruition they needed educated men. Consequently, on May 14, 1649, the tsar wrote to Metropolitan Silvester Kosov of Kiev, asking him to send two learned monks, Arsenii

Satanovskii and Damaskin Ptitskii, to Moscow for the purpose of preparing a new translation of the Bible from the Greek.[191] Silvester immediately sent Arsenii Satanovskii and Epifanii Slavinetskii.[192] The two monks reached Moscow on July 12, escorted by the Moscow merchant, Porfirii Zerkal'nikov, with whom the tsar's request had been dispatched.[193] On July 20, the Kievans were received by Tsar Alexis,[194] and each received a gift of forty sables, worth thirty rubles, and twenty-five rubles in cash.[195] They were housed at the Posol'skii Dvor, in the Kremlin.[196]

Epifanii was immediately put to work translating texts, beginning with CHR, which he completed by August 1649.[197] The same year, he translated from the Latin a letter of Athanasius of Alexandria to Marcellinus on the Psalms[198] and, from the Greek, a Canon to St Mary of Egypt.[199] During the ensuing twenty-six years, Slavinetskii produced a large number of translations from Greek and Latin, as well as original compositions, many of which were published.[200] His literary work can be divided into several categories:

Scriptural

It was to translate the Bible that Epifanii was first called to Moscow. Other pressing needs, including the liturgical reforms and his educational duties, did not permit him to complete this task. Thus the 1663 Moscow edition of the Bible[201] was a virtual reprint of the 1581 Ostrog version. Only a few orthographical differences distinguished the two. Vowels replaced semi-vowels, which had fallen into disuse, certain archaic words were replaced, and a few corrections in translation were made.[202] In his second preface to the 1663 edition, Epifanii explained why a full new translation was not attempted: first, no ancient texts of the Greek Bible were available; second, there was a lack of people who knew Greek; third, "difficult times" impeded adequate material support for the project; fourth, the prevalent negative attitude of Russians toward Greeks made the endeavor suspect. The present, hastily-prepared edition, he stated, was ordered by the tsar because of a shortage of available Bibles, but a new translation would be made in the future.[203] A council in Moscow in 1674, did in fact commission Epifanii to prepare an entirely new translation, but his death the following year precluded the completion of this project.[204]

Homiletic

During his sojourn in Moscow, Epifanii was active as a preacher. The restoration of preaching was an important aspect of the program of the zealots of piety. About fifty of his sermons survive in manuscript form. Slavinetskii's homilies, however, "resembled dissertations more than public teachings."[205] He explained the dogmas of the church in academic language, using numerous citations from church writers. In the manuscripts, the citations are written in the original language, though he doubtless translated them when he spoke. He included frequent references to Greek philosophers and poets, and often used highly metaphorical language.[206]

Patristic

Epifanii translated a number of patristic texts, and many of these were published.[207] These include works by John Chrysostom, Basil the Great, Gregory of Nazianzus, Athanasius of Alexandria, John of Damascus, and others. Most of his translations were based on published editions.[208] Scholars take a generally dim view of the style of his translations, as the following citation illustrates:

> In his own compositions, Epifanii's Slavonic is polished, clear, correct, clean—a fine ecclesiastical language. But his translations are totally different, and this is because, in translating, he is too strictly literal, first and above all concerned with reproducing the letter of the original. His translations are literally correct, but unclear and little comprehensible, so that some of them cannot be understood without the original.[209]

Arts and Sciences

A significant body of the Kievan monk's efforts falls within the category of secular knowledge. Epifanii composed a philological lexicon as well as a 7000-word Greek-Slavonic-Latin dictionary, a work which made him famous among his contemporaries.[210] He translated sections from Book I of the *History* of Thucydides,[211] excerpts from Pliny the Younger's panegyric to Trajan,[212] a work on anatomy by the famous Renaissance physician Andreas Vesalius,[213] a cosmology by the Dutch geographer Wilhelm Janszoon Blaeu,[214] and others. According to the Soviet scholar B. Raikov, the latter accomplishment made Epifanii the first Russian to accept the heliocentric view of the world proposed by Copernicus.[215]

Epifanii's interests were certainly broad. This is clearly indicated by the inventory of his books, made after his death by his disciple, the monk Evfimii. This personal library, willed by Epifanii to the Kievan Brotherhood, included works by Plutarch, John Scotus, Aristotle, Hippocrates; several dictionaries and grammars; books on Turkey, Scotland, Hungary, Persia, Belgium; and many others.[216]

iii. Role in the liturgical reforms

Brought to Moscow to translate the Bible, Epifanii proved himself highly useful to the Muscovite government. He was assigned numerous tasks involving the translation of both religious and secular works. Doubtless because of his versatility, Epifanii never became one of the official correctors attached to the Printing Office.[217] Rather, during his entire stay in Moscow, he remained attached to the Foreign Ministry,[218] from which he drew his salary. In Moscow, Epifanii soon established himself as a leader in the grecophile party aligned with the tsar, with Stefan Vonifatiev, and later with Nikon. By far the most educated of this group, he gained their respect and trust. As a result, he was in a position to play a vital role in the program of liturgical reform launched by Nikon.

Epifanii developed a very close friendship with Nikon, a friendship which remained constant even after Nikon's fall from power. The two first met in Moscow, probably during the winter of 1649-1650, when Nikon was in the capital. When Nikon became patriarch in 1652, Epifanii's salary was raised twice, reaching a level of ninety rubles a year— a tremendous sum in those days.[219] Needless to say, Epifanii praised Nikon highly in the introductions he composed for the *Sluzhebnik* and *Skrizhal'*.[220] More significantly, Epifanii was the only important figure to stand up for Nikon, after the patriarch abandoned his throne in 1658. In 1660, Nikon expressed his desire to regain his position, and the tsar convened a council to deal with the problem. The council decided that Nikon had abandoned any claim to the throne and should be defrocked. Epifanii, who had been invited to the council, jumped to Nikon's defense, arguing that while Nikon had indeed left the throne of his own free will, he should not be stripped of his orders. Epifanii carried the day, and the council decided that the see was vacant, but said nothing about defrocking Nikon.[221] Epifanii's brave defense says a great deal about the sincerity of his friendship with Nikon, because his action was highly risky, particularly in those days. It also reveals the high regard in which the tsar held him. Moreover, this public defense of his friend was Slavinetskii's sole foray into political life. He much preferred to sit unnoticed in his cell, toiling away at his translations.

Epifanii played a vital role in the reform of the liturgical books, which he oversaw from his office at the Foreign Ministry. Though not officially a "corrector," he reviewed the liturgical and patristic texts before their publication and wrote many of their introductions. His chief achievements include translating the Acts of the 1593 Council in Constantinople,[222] composing the official Acts of the 1654 Moscow Council,[223] and writing the introductions to the 1655 *Sluzhebnik* [224] and the *Skrizhal'*.[225] As we saw in the first chapter, these documents entrusted to Epifanii were keystones in Nikon's justification of the reform. Such vital tasks could be assigned only to a person in whom the authorities placed great confidence.

Epifanii's effectiveness became evident particularly in the period following Nikon's departure. Even toward the end of his days as patriarch, Nikon had begun to lose interest in the reform. After he left the throne, he paid it no more attention, focusing instead on his ambitious construction program, and later on the defense of his patriarchal prerogatives. Under Epifanii's guidance, however, liturgical and patristic books continued to be printed, and the Kievan monk tirelessly defended the reform, as is clear in the essay against the Old-Believers cited below. Epifanii strongly believed in the rightness of the reform, which he considered necessary because of errors in previous Russian books, caused by the carelessness and ignorance of scribes and correctors. A member of the grecophile party, he naturally considered it best to base the corrections on Greek books. Unlike most of his contemporaries, however, he realized that the changes in the books did not involve any changes in dogma; but his voice was only a cry in the wilderness. To conclude, it might be best to let his words, in an essay against the Old-Believers, speak for themselves:

> The newly-appeared teachers secretly compose false writings, and with them create disputes and confusion among the people. They themselves are ashamed, or afraid to show their faces. But who called them to the task of teaching secretly, or, rather, confusing the people? Not God, not the bishops. With their proud conceit and vain intellects they have come to this. It is not enough that men,

and even women, whom the apostle does not instruct to teach, have started to do this. Blind ignoramuses, hardly able to read one syllable at a time, having no understanding of grammar, not to mention rhetoric, philosophy, or theology, people who have not even tasted of study, dare to interpret divine writings, or, rather, to distort them, and slander and judge men well-versed in Slavonic and Greek languages. The ignoramuses cannot see that we did not correct the dogmas of faith, but only some expressions which had been altered through the careless-ness and errors of uneducated scribes, or through the ignorance of correctors at the Printing Office.

Epifanii continues by comparing the Old-Believers to Korah and Abiram, who rebelled against Moses (Num 16).[226]

NOTES

1. E.g. D. Ia. Sklobovskii, "Patriarkh Nikon po novym istoricheskim ukazaniiam," *PrOb* 1883(2) 690.

2. E.g. L. Lebedev, "Patriarkh Nikon, Ocherk zhizni i deiatel'nosti," *BT* 23(1982) 174.

3. E.g. N.F. Druzhinin, review of KAPTEREV, *NIKON I ALEKSEI, ZhMNP* 1913(Aug.), 297-298.

4. E.g. KLIUCHEVSKII, p. 340. The most complete overview of the historical judgements of Nikon, through the beginning of the 20th century, is to be found in chapter 6 of ZYZYKIN, v. 3, pp. 295-365.

5. *Izvestie o rozhdenii i vospitanii i o zhitii sviateishago Nikona, patriarkha moskovskago i vseia Rossii* (Moscow, 1871). This work was composed in the 1680's by a cleric attached to Nikon and strongly favorable to him.

6. First published in 1938. Strongly favoring Avvakum, Pascal is very negative in his judgement of Nikon.

7. L. Lebedev, "Patriarkh Nikon, Ocherk zhizni i deiatel'nosti," *BT* 23(1982) 154-197; 24(1983) 139-170. This article, published in the official scholarly journal of the Russian Orthodox Church, appears to be the prelude to a possible effort to canonize Nikon. Such a step, in the Soviet Union, would have tremendous significance, particularly because of Nikon's doctrine affirming the total superiority of the church over the state.

8. SHUSHERIN, pp. 3-4, 11, 104-108.

9. *Ibid.*, pp. 118. When Nikon was returning to Moscow in 1666 to face trial, Shusherin, who accompanied him, was arrested, kept in prison in Moscow for three years, then exiled to Novgorod for ten years more.

10. *Ibid.*, pp. 1-3

11. KLIUCHEVSKII, pp. 343-344. See p. 94 below.

12. SHUSHERIN, pp. 2-3.

13. *Ibid.*, pp. 4-5.

14. SHUSHERIN, pp. 5-6. Performing such feats of asceticism was characteristic of the age, so there is little reason to disbelieve Shusherin's account in this matter. Pious lay persons, exemplified by Tsar Alexis himself, would follow the strict fasting rules prescribed by the

Typikon, stand in church five to six hours a day, and make 1000-1500 prostrations a day—cf. KLIUCHEVSKII, p. 345.

15. SHUSHERIN, p. 6. This too, was typical of the times. One has but to look at Avvakum's autobiography to see the similarities.

16. *Ibid.*, p. 7.

17. *Ibid.*, pp. 7-10.

18. Cf. PASCAL, *AVVAKUM*, p. 123.

19. SHUSHERIN, pp. 4-5.

20. MAKARII, *ISTORIIA*, v. 11, p. 163.

21. SOLOV'EV, v. 2, col. 1518.

22. KARTASHEV, p. 134.

23. *Ibid.*, p. 135.

24. SHUSHERIN, pp. 10-11.

25. PASCAL, *AVVAKUM*, pp. 125-126. Cf. also PAUL OF ALEPPO, *ChOIDR* 1898(4) pt. 2, 54, 146-147.

26. *DEIANIE 1649*, p. 49. See p. , note 193.

27. See the discussion about the "provincial" reformers in KAPTEREV, *NIKON I EGO PRO-TOVNIKI*, pp. 152-162.

28. KAPTEREV, *NIKON I ALEKSEI*, v. 1, pp. 62-63.

29. Neronov reminded Patriarch Nikon in 1657: "...formerly, we heard you tell us many times that the Greeks and 'Little Russians' have lost the faith and have no strength or good customs," *MATERIALY* I, p. 150.

30. KAPTEREV, *TSERKOVNO-REFORMATSIONNOE DVIZHENIE*, pp. 331-337. At first, their preaching consisted of nothing more than reading from patristic texts and lives of saints.

31. Paisios' arrival in Moscow is described in KAPTEREV, *SNOSHENIIA*, pp. 126-129. Cf. also NIKOLAEVSKII, *ROSSIIA I VOSTOK*, pp. 253-256. A complete account of Paisios' stay in Moscow appears in KAPTEREV, *PRIEZD PATRIARKHA PAISIIA*.

32. KAPTEREV, *SNOSHENIIA*, pp. 140-141. Pascal considers these meetings with Paisios as the moment of Nikon's conversion to the grecophile side—PASCAL, *AVVAKUM*, p. 203.

33. *Skrizhal'* (Moscow, 1656), "*Slovo otveshchatelnoe*," f. 1v. The "*Slovo*" is Nikon's own introduction to the book.

34. KAPTEREV, *TSERKOVNO-REFORMATSIONNOE DVIZHENIE*, p. 491.

35. NIKOLAEVSKII, *ROSSIIA I VOSTOK*, p. 256.

36. The text of the letter, written on March 14, 1649, is printed in *SOBRANIE GRAMOT*, v. 3, #135, pp. 447-449. A mantia is a monastic mantle.

37. "*Khomovoe*" singing involved the addition of extra vowels or syllables into sung liturgical texts for musical purposes. But this often rendered the text totally incomprehensible. Cf. N.A. Gardner, *Bogosluzhebnoe penie russkoi tserkvi*, 2 vols. (Jordanville, NY: Holy Trinity Monastery, 1978-1982), v. 1, pp. 307-308; v. 2, pp. 41-50. On the musical reform in Novgorod at this time, cf. *ibid.*, v. 2, pp. 35-36, 57-58. On the relation between Nikon's liturgical reform and the musical reform, cf. *ibid.*, v. 2, pp. 35-64.

38. SHUSHERIN, p. 13.

39. Cf. PASCAL, *AVVAKUM*, pp. 163-165. This was a part of the program of the Moscow reformers. The same reform was being pushed throughout Russia.

40. See the description of his accomplishments in Novgorod in KARTASHEV, p. 136. Cf. also SHUSHERIN, pp. 11-21, and PASCAL, *AVVAKUM*, p. 173.

41. SOLOV'EV, v. *2, cols. 1526-1551.*

42. Cf. *MATERIALY* I, pp. 331-332.

43. *MATERIALY* V, pp. 17-19. This passage, from the autobiography of Avvakum, has been cited in chapter one, section 2.

44. Philip was martyred on December 23, 1569, for opposing the cruelty of Ivan the Terrible.

45. "*Theognost*" means "known to God."

46. *AKTY ARKHEOGRAFICHESKOI EKSPEDITSII*, v. 4, #57, pp. 75-76.

47. The events are described by MAKARII, *ISTORIIA*, v. 12, pp. 4-7. A more dramatic description, very unfavorable to Nikon, appears in PASCAL, *AVVAKUM*, pp. 193-195. References to the oath appear also in the introduction to the 1655 *Sluzhebnik*, pp. 3-4, in PAUL OF ALEPPO, *ChOIDR* 1897(4) pt. 3, 47, as well as in the writings of Nikon's opponents, such as Deacon Fedor in his "Letter to his son Maksim," *MATERIALY* VI, p. 197. PASCAL, *AVVAKUM*, p. 194, gives several other references.

48. GIBBENET, v. 1, pp. 9-16.

49. PASCAL, *AVVAKUM*, pp. 123-124.

50. KLIUCHEVSKII, p. 319.

51. PAUL OF ALEPPO, *ChOIDR* 1897(4) pt. 3, 47-48.

52. FLOROVSKII, p. 63.

53. E.g. KAPTEREV, *NIKON I ALEKSEI*, 2 vols., *passim;* KLIUCHEVSKII, pp. 323-326, 335-336, 340; FLOROVSKII, pp. 63-67; KARTASHEV, pp. 137-144, 183-185. Even Pascal, who has little love for Nikon, accepts this view—PASCAL, *AVVAKUM*, pp. 165-167. But there are those who disagree and say that Nikon acted only out of pride and love for power: e.g. N.F. Druzhinin, book review of KAPTEREV, *NIKON I ALEKSEI*, in *ZhMNP* 1913 (Aug.) 297-298. This latter view is based largely on the evaluation of Nikon by his opponents, such as Neronov and Avvakum.

54. On the *Ulozhenie*, see KLIUCHEVSKII, pp. 140-148. On its historical background, cf. M. Gorchakov, *Monastyrskii Prikaz (1649-1725 g.)* (St Petersburg, 1868). On Nikon's opposition to it, see ch. 3 of ZYZYKIN, v. 2, pp. 253-331. The *Ulozhenie* was the first step in the secularization of church lands, which culminated in the reforms of Peter the Great less than a century later.

55. *AKTY ARKHEOGRAFICHESKOI EKSPEDITSII*, v. 4, #5, p. 70. The order is dated February 6, 1651.

56. The text of the letter is published in *SOBRANIE GRAMOT*, v. 3, no. 147.

57. Cf. I. Zuzek, *Kormchaja Kniga* (= *OCA* 168) (Rome: Pont. Institutum Orientalium Studiorum, 1964), pp. 54-55. These interpolations, consisting of sixteen separately-numbered folia, are placed between ff. 641 and 642. An English translation of "The Schism of the Roman Church" appears in PALMER, v. 1, pp. 662-665.

58. Zuzek, *op. cit.*, pp. 100-101.

59. Copious examples of the appropriation of this title by Nikon are cited in MAKARII, *ISTORIIA*, v. 12, pp. 229-231.

60. *Ibid.*, pp. 232-234.

61. Thus, in the introduction to the 1655 *Sluzhebnik*, Nikon and Alexis are presented as the two great gifts which form the diadem of the great Orthodox Church in Great and Little Russia,

pp. 2-3. "Great" Russia was the official designation for Muscovite Russia, while "Little" Russia was what is now known as the Ukraine.

62. KARTASHEV, pp. 140-141. On the issue of patriarchal land holdings, see M. Gorchakov, *O zemel'nykh vladeniiakh vserossiiskikh mitropolitov, patriarkhov i sv. sinoda (988-1738 gg.)* (St Petersburg, 1871).

63. MAKARII, *ISTORIIA*, v. 12, pp. 247-263.

64. This is particularly true of ZYZYKIN, and this notion is accepted by M. Spinka, "Patriarch Nikon and the Subjection of the Russian Church to the State," *Church History* 10(1941) pp. 347-366, and by L. Lebedev, "Patriarkh Nikon, Ocherk zhizni i deiatel'nosti," *BT* 23(1982) 168-170, 198. The most recent study of the issue is by Wolfgang Heller, *Die Moskauer "Eiferer für die Frömmigkeit" zwischen Staat und Kirche (1642-1652)* (Wiesbaden: Otto Harrassowitz, 1988).

65. Cf. W.K. Medlin, *Moscow and East Rome* (=Etudes d'histoire économique, politique et sociale, 1) (Geneva: Librairie E. Droz, 1952), pp. 183-184.

66. I. Zuzek, *op. cit.*, pp. 100-101. On its use by Patriarch Michael Cerularius, see R.J.H. Jenkins, "A Cross of the Patriarch Michael Cerularius," *DOP* 21 (1967) 233-240. The most complete study of the history of this text in the East is that of H. Fuhrmann, "Konstantinische Schenkung und abendlandisches Kaisertum: Ein Beitrag zur Uberlieferungsgeschichte des Constitutio Constantini," *Deutsches Archiv* 22 (1966) 63-178.

67. FLOROVSKII, pp. 66-67.

68. The classic work on this subject is by N. Zernov, *Moscow, the Third Rome* (London: SPCK, 1937) (reprint: New York: AMS Press, 1971). More recent scholarship, however, has tended to minimize the importance of this ideology: e.g. J. Meyendorff, *Byzantium and the Rise of Russia* (London, New York: Cambridge University Press, 1981), esp. pp. 261-278.

69. KAPTEREV, *TSERKOVNO-REFORMATSIONNOE DVIZHENIE*, pp. 484-486, 496.

70. In 1649, Patriarch Paisios of Jerusalem had given a wooden model of this church to Nikon. Arsenii Sukhanov, sent to the Holy Land in the same year, was told to obtain an exact description. This is provided in the *Proskinitarii*, the report of his first journey, published by S. Belokurov in *ChOIDR* 1894(2) pt. 1. The best study on the Monastery of the Resurrection remains that of Archimandrite Leonid (Kavelin), *Istoricheskoe opisanie stavropigial'nogo Voskresenskogo, Novyi Ierusalim imenuemogo, monastyria* (Moscow, 1876).

71. FLOROVSKII, p. 64.

72. KAPTEREV, *NIKON I ALEKSEI*, v. 1, pp. 258-260; KAPTEREV, *ISPRAVLENIE KNIG, BV* 1909(1) 35.

73. KARTASHEV, p. 141.

74. KAPTEREV, *ISPRAVLENIE KNIG, BV* 1909(1) 36.

75. *ZAPISKI*, v. 2, p. 519. See also KAPTEREV, *ISPRAVLENIE KNIG, BV* 1909(1) 24-26. Nikon repeatedly stated this belief, e.g. in *DELO*, pp. 212-213, 223.

76. KARTASHEV, p. 164.

77. As indicated by Deacon Fedor, a leading Old-Believer, in *MATERIALY* VI, p. 150.

78. Various eyewitness accounts appear in *DELO*, pp. 15-16, 20, 52.

79. KAPTEREV, *OSTAVLENIE*, pp. 353-355.

80. *ZAPISKI*, v. 2, p. 515.

81. *Ibid.*, p. 513.

82. KARTASHEV, p. 144.

83. KAPTEREV, *OSTAVLENIE*, pp. 364-367.

84. *AKTY ARKHEOGRAFICHESKOI EKSPEDITSII*, v. 4, #57, p. 86.

85. Cf. *MATERIALY* I, pp. 154-158, 171-178, 184-198.

86. KARTASHEV, p. 144.

87. See chapter one, section 4.

88. See chapter one, section 9.

89. *DELO*, pp. 361-363, 365-368.

90. KARTASHEV, pp. 219-220.

91. There are a number of biographical studies of Alexis. Cf. V. Berkh, *Tsarstvovanie tsaria Alekseia Mikhailovicha* (St Petersburg, 1831); I. Zabelin, *Sochinenie, v. 1: Domashnii byt russkikh tsarei v xvi i xvii st.* (Moscow, 1895); A.I. Zaozerskii, *Tsar' Aleksei Mikhailovich v svoem khoziaistve* (Petrograd, 1917). The most recent work is by J.T. Fuhrmann, *Tsar Alexis, His Reign and His Russia* (Gulf Breeze, FL: Academic International Press, 1981), but though this work contains an adequate bibliography, it is totally devoid of footnotes. Cf. also P. Bartenev, ed., *Sobranie pisem tsaria Alekseia Mikhailovicha* (Moscow, 1856).

92. KLIUCHEVSKII, pp. 343-344.

93. The "*Horologion*," containing the "ordinary" or fixed portions of the office throughout the week.

94. The book which contains the variable portions of the office throughout the week.

95. The book containing the seasonal "proper" for services of the Lenten cycle.

96. On education in Russia during this period, see A.I. Rogov, "Shkola i prosveshchenie," in A.V. Artsikhovskii, ed., *Ocherki russkoi kultury XVII veka*, v. 2 (Moscow: Moscow University, 1979), pp. 142-154.

97. KLIUCHEVSKII, p. 345. Morozov was to be *de facto* head of the government in the first years of Alexis' rule. On Morozov, cf. P. Smirnov, *Pravitel'stvo B.I. Morozova i vosstanie v Moskve 1648g.* (=Trudy Sredne-Aziatskogo gos. Universiteta, series III, Hist. fasc. 2) (Tashkent, 1929).

98. Cf. PASCAL, *AVVAKUM*, pp. 120-122.

99. PAUL OF ALEPPO, *ChOIDR* 1898(3) pt. 3, 94.

100. This refers to the PRES.

101. PAUL OF ALEPPO, *ChOIDR* 1898(3) pt. 3, 131.

102. KLIUCHEVSKII, p. 345.

103. KAPTEREV, *TSERKOVNO-REFORMATSIONNOE DVIZHENIE*, pp. 323-325.

104. *AKTY ARKHEOGRAFICHESKOI EKSPEDITSII*, v. 4, #321, pp. 481-482.

105. *MATERIALY* I, pp. 272-273.

106. KAPTEREV, *TSERKOVNO-REFORMATSIONNOE DVIZHENIE*, pp. 325-328.

107. KARTASHEV, pp. 121-124.

108. As cited by KAPTEREV, *SNOSHENIIA*, p. 137.

109. KAPTEREV, *TSERKOVNO-REFORMATSIONNOE DVIZHENIE*, p. 469.

110. GIBBENET, v. 1, p. 15.

111. PAUL OF ALEPPO, *ChOIDR* 1898(4) pt. 2, 170-171. Cf. also p. 158.

112. GIBBENET, v. 2, pp. 883, 885-887.

113. KAPTEREV, *KHARAKTER OTNOSHENII*, pp. 26-31.

114. *Ibid.*, pp. 38ff; MAKARII, *ISTORIIA*, v. 10, pp. 3-36.

115. MAKARII, *ISTORIIA*, v. 11, pp. 3-7.

116. KAPTEREV, *KHARAKTER OTNOSHENII*, pp. 276-345.

117. KAPTEREV, *TSERKOVNO-REFORMATSIONNOE DVIZHENIE*, pp. 461-466.

118. *Ibid.*, pp. 482-483. The text of Nikon's letter appears in *Pis'ma russkikh gosudarei* (Moscow, 1848), pt. I, #382, p. 302. The "*mnogoletie*" (Gk: *polychronion*) is an *ad multos annos* acclamation, usually done at the end of a liturgical service, asking for "long life" for the tsar and the bishops.

119. PAUL OF ALEPPO, *ChOIDR* 1897(4) pt. 3, 153; *ChOIDR* 1898(4) pt. 2, 111.

120. NIKOLAEVSKII, *ROSSIIA I VOSTOK*, pp. 250-251. Benedict's extreme arrogance alienated the Muscovites, however, and he was soon sent away.

121. KAPTEREV, *TSERKOVNO-REFORMATSIONNOE DVIZHENIE*, pp. 475-476.

122. This is shown, for example, in his 1666 letter to Mt. Athos, referred to above, in which he asks that three learned Athonite monks be sent to Moscow—cf. GIBBENET, v. 2, pp. 883, 885-887. The plans to set up a Greek school in Moscow, however, were not fulfilled until the 1680's—cf. KAPTEREV, *KHARAKTER OTNOSHENII*, p. 493.

123. KAPTEREV, *NIKON I ALEKSEI*, v. 2, pp. 9-10.

124. KAPTEREV, *TSERKOVNO-REFORMATSIONNOE DVIZHENIE*, pp. 467-468.

125. Cf. KAPTEREV, *PRIEZD PATRIARKHA PAISIIA*.

126. Cf. Arsenii Sukhanov, "Preniia s grekami o vere," in BELOKUROV, *ARSENII SUKHANOV*, *ChOIDR* 1894(2) pt. 1, 25-114.

127. *Ibid.*, Appendix, p. xxxvi.

128. The text of the letter is published in *SOBRANIE GRAMOT*, v. 3, #136, pp. 449-450.

129. KAPTEREV, *SNOSHENIIA*, p. 148. The instructions given to Sukhanov are not extant, but the reports he submits, upon his return, include descriptions of Greek liturgical rites (BELOKUROV, *ARSENII SUKHANOV*, *ChOIDR* 1894(2) pt. 1, 105-144). Very few of the books he brought back, however, were liturgical texts. Most were patristic and philosophical works. This already points to the fact that the liturgical reforms were to be based not on ancient texts, but on contemporary Greek books.

130. E.g the *Kormchaia kniga* (Moscow, 1650), based on the Greek book brought by Paisios of Jerusalem; The *Shestodnev* (Moscow, 1650), whose afterword indicates that Slavic sources were used, only because Greek books were not available when the book was printed, and corrections, based on the Greek, are placed in an appendix to the volume; the *Uchitel'noe Evangelie* (Moscow, 1652), based on the Ostrog Bible (1580). Cf. KAPTEREV, *TSERKOVNO-REFORMATSIONNOE DVIZHENIE*, pp. 473-475; KARTASHEV, pp. 148-149.

131. Cf. FLOROVSKII, pp. 62-63; KAPTEREV, *TSERKOVNO-REFORMATSIONNOE DVIZHENIE*, pp. 484-496.

132. Especially over the issue of abolishing *mnogoglasie;* cf. KAPTEREV, *NIKON I EGO PRO-TIVNIKI*, pp. 127ff; *DEIANIE 1649*, pp. 41-46; KAPTEREV, *TSERKOVNO-REFORMATSIONNOE DVIZHENIE*, pp. 482-484.

133. Cf. *DEIANIE 1654*; KAPTEREV, *TSAR I SOBORY*, pp. 649-650.

134. *MATERIALY* V, pp. 17-19.

135. N.F. Kapterev, "Bor'ba protopopa Ioanna Neronova s patriarkhom Nikonom," *BV* 1909(1) 207.

136. Cf. PAUL OF ALEPPO, *ChOIDR* (1898(4) pt. 2, 169. The argument was over Nikon's refusal to bless water twice at Epiphany. The event is described in section 4 of chapter one.

137. Alexis felt quite free to take action on his own in religious matters. On March 10, 1660, for example, he sent a letter to Novgorod, requiring all inhabitants to go to confession and communion at least during the four fasting periods, with the threat that they would otherwise be ineligible for church burial—*AKTY ARKHEOGRAFICHESKOI EKSPEDITSII*, v. 4, #115, pp. 160-162. For the tsar to involve himself in managing the pastoral affairs of the church was, of course, hardly a novelty—e.g. *ibid.*, #321, pp. 481-482; #327, pp. 487-489.

138. Cf. ZERNOVA, pp. 87-96.

139. KAPTEREV, *NIKON I ALEKSEI*, v. 2, p. 11.

140. *MATERIALY* V, pp. 59-60, 119-132.

141. Cf. *DELO*, pp. 250-263; *DEIANIIA 1666-1667*, pt. 1, ff. 7v-9. On the Council of 1666, see chapter one, section 9, part i.

142. *MATERIALY* V, pp. 68-71, 81, 118.

143. On the 1667 Council, see chapter one, section 9, part ii.

144. The acts themselves specify that the tsar requested this: *DEIANIIA 1666-1667*, pt. 2, ff. 11v-12, 13-13v. These practices are enumerated in chapter one, section 9, part ii.

145. *MATERIALY* I, p. 64.

146. As recounted in a biography of Neronov, probably composed by his contemporary, the Abbot Theoktist; *MATERIALY* I, p. 150.

147. *MATERIALY* VI, p. 31. He repeats the charge elsewhere, *ibid.*, pp. 320-321.

148. He was among those tried and convicted at the 1666 Council. The documents relating to his case are published in *MATERIALY* I, pp. 458-464; II, pp. 117-118.

149. *MATERIALY* VII, pp. 31, 61-62. He repeats the accusations in his petition to the tsar, *ibid.*, pp. 266, 314.

150. Cf. "Oproverzhenie raskol'nicheskikh klevet na patriarkha Nikona," *Prib* 19(1860) 302-310. Arsenios is attacked in such major Old-Believer works as the 1723 composition by Andrei and Semen Denisov, *Pomorskie Otvety*, and Semen Denisov's *Vinograd rossiiskii, ili opisanie postradavshykh v Rossii za drevletserkovnoe blagochestie* (Moscow, 1906).

151. The materials regarding his case are kept in the "*Grecheskie dela*" (Greek affairs) section of the foreign affairs archives, the "*Glavnyi Arkhiv Ministerstva Inostrannykh Del*" for the year 7157 (1649), sv. 27, no. 33—presently kept at TsGADA, f. 52, op. 1, 7157g., no. 33 (FONKICH, p. 109). These materials are studied at length in several scholarly articles, and it is on these that we base our account: N.F. Kapterev, "Sledstvennoe delo ob Arsenie greke i ssylka ego v Solovetskii monastyr'," *ChOLDP* 1881(7) 70-96; V. Kolosov, "Starets Arsenii Grek," *ZhMNP* 1881(9) 77-93; MAKARII, *ISTORIIA*, v. 12, pp. 154-164; and KAPTEREV, *KHARAKTER OTNOSHENII*, pp. 208 210.

152. *RBS*, v. 2, p. 304.

153. Each member of a Greek delegation was given a sum of money, whose amount depended on his ecclesiastical rank. The patriarchs and bishops, who led such delegations, thus took on as many persons as they could. Many of these were Greek merchants, who would then give the leader of the delegation a percentage of the funds received. Paisios' delegation in 1649 consisted of over twenty-five people—cf. KAPTEREV, *SNOSHENIIA*, pp. 120-124.

154. *Ibid.*, p. 126.

155. KAPTEREV, *PRIEZD PATRIARKHA PAISIIA*, pp. 207-208; KAPTEREV, *KHARAKTER OTNOSHENII*, p. 209.
156. FONKICH, pp. 119-120. This inventory was taken on July 26, 1649, by order of the tsar.
157. *Ibid.*, pp. 109-116.
158. TsGADA, BMST, no. 3092.
159. BELOKUROV, *ARSENII SUKHANOV, ChOIDR* 1891(1) pt. 3, 185-189.
160. Cited in *ibid.*, p. 189. Nikon subsequently blamed Arsenii Sukhanov for lying about Arsenios out of jealousy—cf. *MATERIALY* I, pp. 150-151. Arsenii Sukhanov's dislike for Greeks is evident in his debates with them, and this may well explain why he was never himself a corrector.
161. Cited in KAPTEREV, *KHARAKTER OTNOSHENII*, pp. 209-210. The complete text is published by BELOKUROV, *ARSENII SUKHANOV, ChOIDR* 1891(2) pt. 4, XLIII-XLV.
162. KAPTEREV, *KHARAKTER OTNOSHENII*, p. 210.
163. *Ibid.*, pp. 211-214.
164. *Ibid.*, pp. 214-215.
165. FONKICH, pp. 110-111. Cf. also "Arsenii grek pri patriarkhe Nikone," *PrSob* 1858(3) 340.
166. V. Kolosov, "Starets Arsenii grek," *ZhMNP* 1881(9) 86-87; MAKARII, *ISTORIIA*, v. 12, pp. 162-163.
167. Cf. "Arsenii grek pri patriarkhe Nikone," *PrSob* 1848(3) 335-337; and "Oproverzhenie raskol'nicheskikh klevet na patriarkha Nikona," *Prib* 19(1860) 302-305.
168. FONKICH, p. 109, note 8; p. 110, note 11—indicates that Nikon intended to make use of Arsenios even while still Metropolitan of Novgorod.
169. On this school, see S. Belokurov, *Adam Olearii o greko-latinskoi shkole Arseniia greka v Moskve v XVII st.* (Moscow, 1888). However, N. Kapterev, in "O greko-latinskikh shkolakh v Moskve V XVII v. do otkrytiia Slaviano-greko-latinskoi Akademii," *Prib* 44(1889) 588-671, argues that, while Arsenios may have given private lessons, no formal school existed at this time. He bases his argument on the lack of any evidence that Arsenios was given any salary as a teacher. S. Brailovskii, *Odin iz "pestrykh" XVIIgo stoletiia* (St Petersburg, 1902), pp. 14-23, rejects Kapterev's arguments. FONKICH, pp. 120-121, guardedly accepts that a school existed and suggests that Arsenii Sukhanov's collection of books and manuscripts from Mt. Athos was intended, at least in part, for Arsenios' school. For our purposes, it is sufficient to know that Arsenios' original occupation in Moscow was that of teacher.
170. NIKOLAEVSKII, *PECHATNYI DVOR, KhCht* 1891(2) 165. On May 6, 1656, Arsenios' salary was raised retroactively to 70 rubles, which made him the highest-paid corrector.
171. *MATERIALY* I, pp. 64, 150.
172. Cf. Filaret [Gumilevskii], *Obzor dukhovnoi literatury.* 862-1863 (St Petersburg, 1884), pp. 239-240; SOBOLEVSKII, pp. 296-297, 311, 326-327, 333-334, 338, 342, 345, 356-359, 364-365; *RBS*, v. 2, pp. 304-307.
173. On this work, see chapter one, section 7.
174. ZERNOVA, p. 89. This is a collection of translations by Arsenios. It includes the lives of Saints Catherine, Theodore Stratilates, and Alexis, the "Man of God," as well as sections from the writings of Maximus the Confessor and Gregory Nazianzen.
175. The first history written in modern Greek, this post-Byzantine work contains the history of the world from creation to the end of the 16th century. Cf. esp. I.N. Lebedeva, "Grecheskaia khronika Psevdo-Dorofeia i ee russkii perevod," *TODRL* 21(1965) 298-308. Begun by Arsenios, who translated the bulk of the work, it was completed by Dionisios the Greek,

who, in 1663, took Arsenios' place as corrector. Dionisios returned to Mt. Athos in 1669. The chronicle was translated from its 1631 Venetian edition (cf. LEGRAND, *XVII ͤ SIÈCLE*, v. 1, no. 211, pp. 290-299). The translation was not published in Russia until 1767. Lebedeva's study of the sources is completed in her later work, *Pozdnie grecheskie khroniki i ikh russkie i vostochnye perevody* (=*Palestinskii Sbornik* 18(81)) (Leningrad: Nauka, 1968). She offers two reasons why the chronicle was not published in Moscow for over a century after its translation: first, after Nikon's fall and Arsenios' second exile to the Solovki, it became difficult to publish anything connected with Arsenios' name; second, Greek influence was sharply curtailed in Russia during the latter half of the 17th century. The significant number of copies made from the original manuscript of the translation, however, indicates that the text was nevertheless rather widely read (cf. pp. 94-100). See also Kh.G. Patrinelis, "Διονύσιος 'Ιβηρίτης μεταφραστὴς τῆς Χρονογραφίας τοῦ Δωροθέου, εἰς τὴν ῥωσσικὴν καὶ μητροπολίτης Οὐγγροβλαχίας," 'Επετηρὶς 'Εταιρείας Βυζαντινῶν Σπουδῶν 32 (1963) 314-318.

176. This is an essay in praise of Tsar Alexis, composed in Greek by Paisios Ligarides, who played a leading role in the 1667 Moscow Council, which condemned Nikon.

177. SOBOLEVSKII, p. 289.

178. V.P. Adrianova-Perets, *Zhitie Alekseia Cheloveka Bozhiia v drevnei russkoi literature i narodnoi slovesnosti* (Petrograd, 1917) (rep: *Slavistic Printings and Reprintings* 165: The Hague, Paris: Mouton, 1969), pp. 107-112.

179. I.N. Lebedeva, "Grecheskaia khronika Psevdo-Dorofeia i ee russkii perevod," *TODRL* 21(1965) 305.

180. N.P. Kiselev, "O moskovskom knigopechatanii XVII veka," *Kniga. Issledovaniia i Materialy,* no. 2 (Moscow, 1960), pp. 145, 153.

181. "Starets Arsenii grek," *ZhMNP* 1881(9) 89. Cf. also I.N. Lebedeva, *Pozdnie grecheskie khroniki i ikh russkie i vostochnye perevody* (=*Palestinskii Sbornik* 18(81)) (Leningrad: Nauka, 1968), p. 79.

182. "Starets Arsenii grek," *ZhMNP* 1881(9) 92-93.

183. *Moskovskaia Sinodal'naia Tipograficheskaia Biblioteka,* FONKICH, pp. 124-125. This collection is now located in Moscow, at the GIM.

184. Cf. *RBS,* v. 2, p. 306; and I.N. Lebedeva, "Grecheskaia khronika Psevdo-Dorofeia i ee russkii perevod," *TODRL* 21(1965) 303; FONKICH, p. 125. Where Arsenios lived after his release is not known.

185. SOBOLEVSKII, pp. 342-343.

186. E. Petukhov, *Russkaia literatura. Istoricheskii obzor glavneishikh literaturnykh iavlenii drevniago i novago perioda,* v. 1, *Drevnii period* (Iuriev, 1911), p. 444. KHARLAMPOVICH, p. 122, categorically states that there is no evidence for affirming White-Russian origin.

187. Exactly when Epifanii studied in Kiev is similarly unknown, KHARLAMPOVICH, p. 122. Cf. also E. Petukhov, *op. cit.,* p. 444.

188. Again, the exact time and place cannot be determined. Cf. Petukhov, *ibid.*; KHARLAMPOVICH, p. 122; N. Kostomarov, *Russkaia istoriia v zhizneopisaniiakh ee glavneishikh deiatelei,* v. 2 (St Petersburg, 1911), p. 299; B. Raikov, *Ocherki istorii geliotsentricheskogo mirovozreniia v Rossii* (Moscow: AN, 1947), p. 118, tentatively suggests that Epifanii may have studied at the Academy in Cracow, but he offers no supporting evidence.

189. B. Raikov, *ibid.,* p. 118. Again, the exact time-frame is uncertain, cf. KHARLAMPOVICH, p. 122.

190. SILVESTER MEDVEDEV, *OGLAVLENIE KNIG,* p. 22. See also SOBOLEVSKII, p. 121.

191. *SOBRANIE GRAMOT,* v. 3, #136, pp. 449-450.

192. No reason is given for the replacement of Damaskin Ptitskii by Epifanii. Damaskin subsequently came to Moscow on December 14, 1650, and became one of his coworkers. Cf. *AKTY IUZHNOI I ZAPADNOI ROSSII,* v. 3, #312, pp. 435-437.

193. *Ibid.,* #263, pp. 328-330.

194. *Ibid.,* #267, pp. 332-336.

195. *Ibid.,* #330, pp. 479-480.

196. NIKOLAEVSKII, *PECHATNYI DVOR, KhCht* 1891(1) 169, note 2. Both subsequently moved to the Chudov Monastery, also inside the Kremlin—Arsenii Satanovskii in 1650, Epifanii only after 1657—cf. KHARLAMPOVICH, p. 123.

197. KHARLAMPOVICH, p. 138; SILVESTER MEDVEDEV, *OGLAVLENIE KNIG,* p. 21.

198. SOBOLEVSKII, p. 199; SILVESTER MEDVEDEV, *OGLAVLENIE KNIG,* p. 22.

199. SILVESTER MEDVEDEV, *OGLAVLENIE KNIG,* p. 21.

200. *Ibid.,* pp. 21-22, lists twenty-five titles. For the list of translations, see SOBOLEVSKII, pp. 64, 98, 121, 164, 183, 199, 213, 231, 268, 284, 286, 288-291, 293, 294, 296-298, 301-303, 306, 308, 324, 334, 338.

201. ZERNOVA, p. 93.

202. KHARLAMPOVICH, p. 138; ROTAR, p. 210. See also GORSKII-NEVOSTRUEV, v. 1, pp. 167-176.

203. The preface is reprinted in its entirety in STROEV, *OPISANIE KNIG TOLSTOVA,* pp. 286-292.

204. ROTAR, pp. 396-398. Before his death, he had succeeded in translating only the New Testament and the Pentateuch; cf. N. Kostomarov, *Russkaia istoriia v zhizneopisaniiakh ee glavneishikh deiatelei,* v. 2 (St Petersburg, 1911), pp. 301-302.

205. N. Kostomarov, *Russkaia istoriia v zhizneopisaniiakh ee glavneishikh deiatelei,* v. 2 (St Petersburg, 1911), p. 302.

206. On Epifanii's preaching, see also Filaret [Gumilevskii], *Obzor dukhovnoi literatury* (St Petersburg, 1884), pp. 236-237; and V. Pevnitskii, "Epifanii Slavinetskii, odin iz glavnykh deiatelei russkoi dukhovnoi literatury v XVII v.," *TDKA* 1861(3) 135-182.

207. The chief editions of his translations are: John Chrysostom, *On the Priesthood* (Moscow, 1664)—cf. ZERNOVA, p. 94; *Sbornik perevodov Epifaniia Slavinetskago* (Moscow, 1665)— cf. ZERNOVA, p. 95. Other translated texts are placed in various editions. Thus the 1650 Moscow Psalter contains his translation of Athanasius' Letter to Marcellinus on the Psalms. The 1656 *Skrizhal'* contains a letter of Athansius to Antiochus, a series of pseudo-Athanasian sermons, as well as other Athanasian texts, all translated from the 1627 Paris edition of Montfaucon. Cf. ROTAR, pp. 200-206, 213-215; Filaret, *op. cit.,* p. 238; Kostomarov, *op. cit.,* p. 301.

208. See the previous footnote, as well as SILVESTER MEDVEDEV, *OGLAVLENIE KNIG,* pp. 21-22; ROTAR, p. 196.

209. Filaret, *op. cit.,* p. 239. Other scholars echo this view, e.g. Kostomarov, *op. cit.,* p. 301.

210. Neither of these was published. Cf. Kostomarov, *op. cit.,* p. 302; B. Raikov, *Ocherki po istorii geliotsentricheskogo mirovozreniia v Rossii* (Moscow: AN, 1947), p. 119.

211. SILVESTER MEDVEDEV, *OGLAVLENIE KNIG,* p. 21.

212. *Ibid.*

213. *Ibid.,* pp. 21-22. His translation was based on a 1641 Brussels edition. The Greek born

scholar was the author of the famous "De corporis humani fabrica" (1543), which revolutionized the science.

214. *Ibid.*, p. 21. The cosmology, a four-volume work comprising an introduction and a geography of the known world, including Muscovy, was published in Amsterdam in 1645.

215. *Ocherki po istorii geliotsentricheskogo mirovozreniia v Rossii* (Moscow: AN, 1947), pp. 117-130.

216. The letter which accompanied the shipment of books from Evfimii to Silvester Golovchich, rector of the Kievan Brotherhood, is printed in V. Undol'skii, "Uchenye trudy Epifaniia Slavinetskago," *ChOIDR* 1846(8) pt. 4, 71-72.

217. NIKOLAEVSKII, *PECHATNYI DVOR, KhCht* 1891(3) 180-181.

218. "Posol'skii Dvor."

219. ROTAR, pp. 347-352.

220. See, for example, the *Sluzhebnik* (Moscow, 1655), pp. 2-3, 4; *Sluzhebnik* (Moscow, 1656), p. 12; *Skrizhal'* (Moscow, 1656), foreword, f. 9.

221. On this matter, cf. esp. ROTAR, pp. 354-371. All the related documents are published in *DELO*.

222. Printed in the *Kormchaia Kniga* (Moscow, 1653), ff. 21-55.

223. Cf. *DEIANIE 1654.*

224. Pp. 1-44. The introduction is reprinted in its entirety in STROEV, *OPISANIE KNIG TOLSTOVA I TSARSKAGO*, pp. 147-169.

225. (Moscow, 1656), ff. 1-18. ROTAR, pp. 199-206, credits Epifanii with composing several significant portions of this work.

226. As cited by N. Kostomarov, *Russkaia istoriia v zhizneopisaniiakh ee glavneishikh deiatelei*, v. 2 (St Petersburg, 1911), p. 306.

Part II

The Contents of the Reform

Introduction

We turn now to take a brief look at the new liturgical books published by Nikon. Our focus will be on the *Sluzhebnik,* not only because this is the most commonly used service book,[1] but because it is to this book that the reformers turned their primary attention. We shall deal primarily with CHR, the most commonly employed liturgy, for the same reason: CHR drew the special attention of the "correctors" and underwent the most significant changes. We begin with a few general remarks about the reform.

A Moscow priest in 1655, picking up a copy of the new *Sluzhebnik,* would be shocked. The book did not look much different on the outside. The contents, however, were a different story! As he prepared to celebrate liturgy, he noted that the pagination was different, that each page was now numbered, rather than each folio. He had not seen this before,[2] and it took him a few extra minutes to find what he was looking for. Only if he had traveled outside the bounds of Muscovy would he know that this was how books were now being printed in Kiev, Lvov, Striatin, and elsewhere. But the real shock would come only later.

As he began to celebrate the liturgy, he would see that nothing was the same as before. Not only were many rubrics changed, particularly for his entrance into church, vesting, and the prothesis, but the text of no single prayer was exactly the same as in the redaction he was accustomed to. The familiar prayers now sounded strange, many word-endings were different, and some words were altogether new. Able to read only with great effort, he found the new book very hard to follow. Accustomed to celebrating almost entirely from memory, he now had to pay very close attention to the text. Even the most familiar texts sounded strange to his ears, as can be seen from the following examples.

Cherubic Hymn	
1655 CHR (Moscow)	**1652 CHR (Moscow)**
Izhe kheruvimy[a] taino obrazuiushche,[a] i zhivotvoriashchei troitse trisviatuiu pesn' pripevaiushche,[b] vsiakoe nyne zhiteiskoe otlozhim popechenie,[c] iako da[c] tsaria vsekh podimem,[d] anggelskimi nevidimo dorinosima[d] chinmi. alliluiia, alliluiia, alliluiia.[e]	*Izhe kheruvimi[a] taino obrazouiushche,[a] i zhivotvoriashchei troitse, trisviatuiu pesn' prinosiashche,[b] vsiaku nyne zhiteiskuiu otverzhem pechal',[c] iako tsaria vsekh pod"emliushche,[d] anggel'skimi nevidimo daronosima[d] chinmi. allilouia.*

Changes in the new text are underlined, and the following is a brief analysis of these changes:

a. Orthographical variations were common in Slavic books and these changes are not significant. In previous Muscovite printed editions, *kheruvimi* consistently ends with an "*i*," the correct grammatical ending for the nominative plural.[3] The "*y*" ending appears in the 1655 and all subsequent Moscow editions.[4] This spelling already existed, however, in the Kievan *Sluzhebniks* published by Peter Moghila in 1629 and 1639, as well as in the 1646 Lvov edition. Since this new translation was the work of Epifanii Slavinetskii,[5] it is hardly surprising to find such South-Russian peculiarities in the new books. With regard to the different spelling of *obrazuiushche,* the explanation is even simpler, for the letter "*u*" can be rendered by either "*u*" or "*ou*," as is clear from any 17th century Slavonic lexicon.[6]

b. The change from *prinosiashche* to *pripevaiushche* corrects an error in the earlier text, probably based on a misreading of the Greek προ-σάδοντες (singing) as προσάγοντες (offering). This, at least, is the explanation given by Cherniavskii[7] and accepted by Taft.[8]

c. These are merely stylistic changes, which do not alter the meaning of the text in any way.

d. This is a mistranslation of the Greek word ὑποδέχεσθαι— a problem that has already been studied.[9]

e. The introduction of the triple alleluia was one of the changes most violently opposed by the Old-Believers. The triple alleluia was used in contemporary Greek practice and indicated in all the printed Venetian euchologies, including the 1602 *Euchologion*, which served as the model for Nikon's edition. All the earlier Muscovite editions prescribed a single alleluia, although they indicated a triple alleluia on Holy Thursday and Holy Saturday, which have special Cherubica. This subject, too, has been amply studied elsewhere.[10]

The following is the text of the gospel prayer, recited by the celebrant prior to the reading of the gospel.[11] Again, changes in the new text are underlined.

THE GOSPEL PRAYER		
1602 BAS (Venice)	**1655 BAS (Moscow)**	**1652 BAS (Moscow)**
Ἔλλαμψον ἐν ταῖς καρδίαις ἡμῶν, φιλάνθρωπε δέσποτα, τὸ τῆς σῆς θεογνωσίας ἀκήρατον φῶς, καὶ τοὺς·τῆς διανοίας ἡμῶν διάνοιξον ὀφθαλμούς εἰς τὴν τῶν εὐαγγελικῶν σου κηρυγμάτων κατανόησιν. Ἔνθες ἡμῖν καὶ τὸν τῶν μακαρίων σου ἐντολῶν φόβον, ἵνα τὰς σαρκικὰς ἐπιθυμίας πάσας καταπατήσαντες, τὴν πνευματικὴν πολιτείαν μετέλθωμεν, πάντα τὰ πρὸς εὐαρέστησιν τὴν σὴν καὶ φρονοῦντες καὶ πράττοντες. Σὺ γὰρ εἶ ὁ ἁγιασμὸς καὶ φωτισμὸς τῶν ψυχῶν καὶ τῶν σωμάτων ἡμῶν, καὶ σοὶ τὴν δόξαν	*Vozsiiai v serdtsakh nashikh <u>chelovekoliubche</u> vladyko, <u>tvoego</u> <u>bogorazumiia</u> <u>netlennyi</u> <u>svet</u>, i mysl<u>ennyia</u> nas<u>ha</u> otverzi ochi, vo evangel'<u>skikh</u> tvoik<u>h</u> propovedanii razumenie. Vlozhi <u>v nas</u> i strakh <u>blazhennykh</u> tvoik<u>h</u> zapovedei, da <u>plotskiia</u> <u>pokhoti</u> <u>vsia</u> popravshe, dukhovnoe zhitelstvo proidem: <u>vsia</u> iazhe ko blagougozhdeniiu tvoemu, i mudrstvuiushche, i <u>deiushche</u>. Tybo esi prosveshchenie <u>dush</u> i teles nashikh khriste bozhe, i tebe slavu vozsylaem, so beznachal'nym ti ottsem, i presviatym i blagim, i zhivotvoriashchim <u>ti</u> dukhom, nyne i prisno i <u>vo</u> <u>veki</u> <u>vekov</u>, amin.*	*Vozsiiai v serdtsakh nashikh vladyko, nepristoupnyi svet bogorazoumiia tvoego, i mysli nasheia ochi otverzi, vo ezhe razumeti evangal'skaia tvoia propovedaniia. Vlozhi zhe nam i strakh bozhestvenykhti zapovedei, iako da telesnaia zhelaniia popravshe, dukhovnoe zhitel'stvo proidem, vsegda iazhe ko blagougozhdeniiu tvoemou, i moudr"stvuem i tvorim. Vozglas. Ty bo esi prosveshchenie doush i teles nashikh khriste bozhe, i tebe slavu vozsylaem, so beznachal'nym ti ottsem, i s presviatym i blagim i zhivotvoriashchim dukhom, nyne i prisno i voveki vekom, amin'.*

THE GOSPEL PRAYER		
1602 BAS (Venice)	1655 BAS (Moscow)	1652 BAS (Moscow)
ἀναπέμπομεν, τῷ Πατρί, καὶ τῷ Ὑίῷ, καὶ τῷ ἁγίῳ Πνεύματι, νῦν καὶ ἀεί, καὶ εἰς τοὺς αἰώνας τῶν αἰώνων, Ἀμήν.		

The Nikonian version is much closer to the 1604 Striatin,[12] and particularly to the 1629 and 1639 Kievan[13] texts, than to the 1652 Moscow version. Most striking, however, is the verbatim correlation between 1655 Moscow and 1602 Venice. The Slavonic text follows the Greek, word for word, with even the Greek word order preserved almost exactly. The differences between the two Moscow versions are more than just stylistic or orthographical, and the 1652 version is clearly based on a variant Greek text.[14]

Of particular interest in the Nikonian version is the change in the closing doxology. All previous Slavonic printed editions, as well as mss., both Muscovite and Ukrainian, ended the doxology with *voveki vekom*, the word *vekom* being in the dative plural. With the new edition, *vekom* was changed to the genitive plural *vekov*. Characteristically, no explanation was provided for this change, which provoked the ire of the Old-Believers who regarded the new form as heretical.[15] Since the doxology occurs countless times in every service, the change was highly noticeable. Yet there is a simple explanation for it. The dative case, in ancient Slavonic, was often used to indicate possession, and so the Greek τῶν αἰώνων was quite naturally translated as *vekom*.[16] The universal use of this form in all Slavic texts is sufficient proof for this assertion. To the 17th century correctors, however, the dative case sounded wrong, and they changed it to the genitive. The fact that the Greek words, τῶν αἰώνων, were in the genitive could only have reinforced their notion that the earlier Slavonic rendering was faulty. The new form, which did not alter the meaning in any way, became standard in Nikonian and post-Nikonian editions, and soon spread to both Orthodox and Catholic Ruthenian books.[17]

These two textual samples indicate well the nature of the reform and its sources. The Nikonian texts are patterned after contemporary Greek and South-Russian editions. The reform, therefore, never intended a return to ancient Slavic or Greek practice, but aimed at bringing Russian practice in line with the Greek. The reformers sought to achieve the greatest possible closeness between the two, to the point that the same word order and grammatical structures were used, even though at times this made the new Slavonic text awkward and hard to understand. The final sentence of the gospel prayer, for example, is much clearer in the 1652 version than in the revised one, which uses multiple participles rather than active verb forms. It is thus not possible to maintain that the reform was a "correction" of the liturgical books.

The rubrical reform was carried out in the same way. Where the existing Russian usage did not agree with the contemporary Greek, it was changed or eliminated. Thus the older, Russian practices, themselves borrowed from the Greeks in earlier centuries, were replaced by later Greek usages. This, in a nutshell, is the substance of the reform. In the rest of this study, we shall examine what changes in Russian practice this entailed, chiefly in CHR.

NOTES

1. The modern *Sluzhebnik*, like the modern Greek *Hieratikon*, or *Leitourgikon*, is an abridged euchology, containing the fixed portions of Vespers and Matins, and the liturgies of CHR, BAS, and PRES. Often variable parts needed by the celebrant, such as weekday and festal dismissals, are also included. Before 1650, however, the *Sluzhebnik* was identical to the *Trebnik* (Ritual) and contained texts for all the sacraments. Cf. DMITRIEVSKII, *OTZYV ORLOVA*, pp. 252-254.

2. No previous edition of any kind in Moscow was paginated. Cf. ZERNOVA, pp. 11-78. After the 1655 *Sluzhebnik*, however, nearly every work published by the Moscow Printing Office was paginated—cf. *ibid.*, pp. 78-136.

3. See, for example, Lavrentii Zizanii, *Grammatika Slovenska* (Vilna, 1596) (rep: *Specimina Philologiae Slavicae*, Bd. 1, Frankfurt, 1972), p. 26; and G. Nandris, *Handbook of Old Church Slavonic*, Part 1: *Old Church Slavonic Grammar* (London: Athlone Press, 1959), pp. 57-58, 73-75.

4. ORLOV, p. 135.

5. See chapter two, section 4, part ii.

6. Cf., for example, Lavrentii Zizanii, *Leksik* (Vilna, 1596) (phototypically reprinted in

Pam'iatki Ukrainskoi Movi XVI-XVII st. (Kiev: AN, 1964) and Pamvo Berinda, *Leksikon slavenorosskii i imen tl"kovanie* (Kiev, 1627) (phototypically reprinted in *Pam'iatki Ukrainskoi Movi XVII st.*, (Kiev: AN, 1961).

7. CHERNIAVSKII, *OB IZMENENIIAKH,* pp. 256-257.

8. TAFT, *GREAT ENTRANCE,* p. 58.

9. *Ibid.,* p. 58, esp. note 24.

10. Cf. CHERNIAVSKII, *OB IZMENENIIAKH,* pp. 273-280, 406-410; I. Nikolaevskii, "K istorii sporov ob alliluia," *KhCht* 1884(1) 690-729; E. E. GOLUBINSKII, *K nashei* polemike s staroobriadtsami (Moscow, 1905), pp. 196-218. ORLOV, p. 135, gives the variants in Slavic practice. The issue is summarized in TAFT, *GREAT ENTRANCE,* pp. 81-83, where he shows that, though the single alleluia is the more ancient practice, the triple alleluia appears in sources as early as the 10th century, probably as a misunderstanding of a rubric instructing that the entire hymn be sung thrice. N.F. Moran, "The Musical 'Gestaltung' of the Great Entrance Ceremony," *Jahrbuch der Osterreichischen Byzantinistik* 28 (1979) pp. 167-193, disagrees with Taft's hypothesis. That debate, however, is outside the scope of the present work.

11. This prayer is a 12th century addition to the liturgical formulary, though it is absent in many later sources, including DOUCAS, *EDITIO PRINCEPS,* cf. TAFT, *PONTIFICAL LITURGY, OCP* 46 (1980) 98. It came originally from JAS, cf. MATEOS, *CÉLÉBRATION,* pp. 139-140. The Greek text has numerous variants, but these are insignificant, cf. TREMPELAS, pp. 53-55. The prayer entered Russian practice in the 15th century and is present in all the Muscovite printed editions, cf. ORLOV, pp. 80-84.

12. 1604 BAS (Striatin): *V"siiai v serdtsakh nashikh chelovekoliubche vladyko, netlennyi svet bogorazoumiia tvoego, i mysl"nyia nasha otvr"zi ochi v ezhe razumeti evangl'skaa tvoa propovedania, v"lozhi zhe v nas, i strakh blazhennykh tvoikh zapovedei, da plot'skyia pokhoti vsia popravshe dukhovnym zhitel'stvom proidem: v'sia iazhe k blago ougozhdeniiu tvoemu, i mudr"stvouiushche i deiushche...*

13. 1629 and 1639 BAS (Kiev): *V"siiai v serdtsakh nashikh chelovekoliubche vladyko, tvoego bogorazoumia netlennyi svet, i myslennyia nasha otverzi ochi v evangel'skikh tvoikh propovedanii razumenie, vlozhi v nas i blazhennykh tvoikh zapovedei strakh, da pl"tskiia pokhoti vsia popravshe, dukhovnoe zhitelstvo proidem, vsia iazhe k blago ugozhdeniiu tvoemu, i mudrstvuiushche, i deiushche...*

14. The variants are given in TREMPELAS, pp. 53-55. Here, we do find readings which agree exactly with the different 1652 text. Undoubtedly, a search of Greek mss. in Russia would reveal the source for the earlier Muscovite version.

15. E.g. *MATERIALY* IV, p. 200.

16. On this use of the dative in ancient Slavonic, see V.F. Krivchik and N.S. Mozheiko, *Staro-slavianskii iazyk* (Minsk: "Vysheishaiia shkola," 1972), p. 174. Many examples of the use of the word *vek* in the dative case are cited in the *Slovnik Jazyka Staroslovenskeho,* I (Prague: Academy of Science, 1966), p. 376. In each case, the Greek equivalent appears in the genitive case.

17. HUCULAK, pp. 248-249.

3

Preparatory Rites, Enarxis,
Liturgy of the Word

1. Preliminary Prayers and Vesting

The new Nikonian *Sluzhebnik* greatly simplified the rites of entrance into church before the liturgy. In previous centuries, these rites had grown increasingly long and complex. The development of these has been studied by Dmitrievskii, who finds at least seven different redactions,[1] and by Petrovskii.[2] This tremendous variety moved the 1551 Stoglav Council to establish one uniform practice,[3] but without much success. Variations continued up to the Nikonian reform.[4] The following are outlines of these rites as they existed just prior to the reform and in the Nikonian version:

1655 (Moscow)	1646 (Moscow[5])
[I. OUTSIDE THE CHURCH]	
1.A. The priest bows to the superior.	1.B. The priest and deacon bow to the superior and receive his blessing. On the way to church, they recite the following: 2.B. *Glas radosti i spaseniia...*[6] 3.B. *Proliiashasia stopy moia...*[7] 4.B. Ps 14(15) 5.B. Ps 22(23)[8]
[II. ENTRANCE]	
1.A. The priest enters the church, joining the deacon.	1.B. They enter the church, and bow 3x saying each to himself: 2.B. *Bozhe milostiv boudi mne greshnomu.* *Bozhe ochisti mia greshnago i pomilui mia.* *Bez chisla sogreshikh gospodi prostimia.*

1655 (Moscow)	1646 (Moscow)
	3.B. Dismissal[9] *Dostoino est'...* *Gospodi pomilui* 2x Daily dismissal, commemorating the Theotokos, the saint of the church, and of the day.
4.A. They bow 3x before the holy doors.	**4.B.** They go before the holy doors.
5. Deacon: *Blagoslovi vladyko.* Priest: Opening blessing. 6. Deacon: *Tsariu nebesnyi...*;[10] Trisagion; Lord's Prayer. Priest: Ecphonesis.	
	7.B. *Gospodi pomilui* 12x *Priidete poklonimsia* 3x And the following troparia:
8.A. *Pomilui nas gospodi...*	**8.B.** *Raduisia dvere bozhiia...*[11]
9.A. Glory: *Gospodi pomilui nas, na tia bo oupovakhom...*	**9.B.** *Pod tvoiu milost'...*[12]
10.A. Now and ever: *Miloserdiia dveri otverzi nam...*[14]	**10.B.** *Gospodi, otimi ot mene...*[13]
	11.B. *Neprokhodimaia dvere...*[15] **12.B.** They bow 3x, once before the holy doors, once to each side, saying; [to the right:] **13.B.** Glory: *Vkhodiai v dom tvoi...* **14.B.** Now and ever: *Boga i k tebe...*[16] [to the left:] **15.B.** *Gospodi oustne moi otverzi na molbou...* **16.B.** *Prechistomu ti obrazu...*[17] **17.B.** *O tebe raduetsia...*[18] and they bow to the ground. **18.B.** Then the following troparia: Resurrection (in tone of week), if it is a Sunday; Annunciation; of day or feast; of patron saint of the church; kontakion of patron saint; troparion of Chrysostom, Basil, or Gregory, according to liturgy being celebrated; of saint of day.

1655 (Moscow)	1646 (Moscow)
19.A. They kiss the icon of Christ, saying: *Prechistomu tvoemu obrazu...*[19]	**19.B.** They kiss the icon of Christ, saying: *Gospodi isuse khriste, izhe sim obrazom.*[20]
20.A. They kiss the icon of Mary, saying: *Miloserdiia sushchi istochnik...*[21]	**20.B.** They kiss the icon of Mary, saying: *Sviataia bogoroditse ne zaboudi...*[22]
	[They kiss the other icons, saying:]
	21.B. Icon of Annunciation: troparion of Annunciation. **22.B.** The cross: *Siloiu i zastupleniem chestnago kresta....* **23.B.** Icon of John the Baptist: *Sviatyi velikii ioanne...* **24.B.** Icon of the archangel: *Sviatyi arkhanggel khristov...* **25.B.** Icon of an apostle: *Sviatyi apostole...* **26.B.** Icon of a prophet: *Sviatyi proroche...* **27.B.** Icon of a saint: *Sviatiteliu khristov...* **28.B.** Icon of a "righteous one:" *Prepodobne i ougodniche bozhii...* **29.B.** Icon of a martyr: *Sviatyi mucheniche...* **30.B.** If there are any other local saints, they kiss their icons and say troparia and kontakia for them.
31.A. Bowing [before the holy doors], they say:	**31.B.** They enter the sanctuary through the small doors, go to the prothesis table, bow 3x, saying:
32. *Gospodi nizposli ruku tvoiu...*[23]	
33.A. They bow toward each side of the church and go to the prothesis table [in the sanctuary] saying: *Vnidu v dom tvoi...* (Ps 5:7-12). **34.A.** They go before the holy table, bow 3x, and kiss the gospel book and holy table.	

1655 (Moscow)	1646 (Moscow)
[III. VESTING][24]	
1. They each get their vestments, and bow 3x towards the East, saying, each to himself:	
2.A. *Bozhe ochisti mia greshnago, i pomilui mia* 3x.	**2.B.** *Bozhe ochisti mia greshnago i pomilui mia.* *Sozdavyi mia gospodi pomilui mia.* *Bezchisla sogreshikh gospodi prostimia.*
3.A. The deacon approaches the priest, with his vestments in his right hand, bows, and says: *Blagoslovi vladyko stikhar' so orarem.*	**3.B.** The deacon approaches the priest, with his vestments on his left shoulder, bows, and says: *Blagoslovi vladyko oblachitisia vo sviatyi stikhar'.*
4.A. The priest says:	**4.B.** Blessing him, the priest says:
Blagoslaven bog nash, vsegda nyne i prisno...	
5.A.i. The deacon puts on his sticharion, saying:	**5.B.** They each put on their sticharion, saying:
Da vozraduetsia dusha moia o gospode...[25]	
6.A. The deacon kisses his stole and puts it on. **7.A.i.** Putting on the epimanikia, he says, for the right hand: *Desnitsa tvoia gospodi proslavisia v kreposti, desnitsa gospodnia voznese mia, desnitsa tvoia gospodi...* **8.A.i.** For the left hand: *Rutse tvoi sotvoriste mia...* **9.A.** Then he goes to the prothesis table and prepares the discos and the chalice. **5.A.ii.** The priest takes his sticharion and puts it on, saying: *Da vozraduetsia...*[=5.A.i.]	
10.A. The priest blesses his stole and puts it on, saying: *Blagosloven bog izlivaiai blagodat' svoiu...*	**10.B.** The priest kisses his stole and puts it on, saying: *Emshe isusa, sviazashe, predasha ego pontiiskomu pilatu igemonu.*

1655 (Moscow)	1646 (Moscow)
	6.B The deacon kisses his stole and puts it on, saying: *Sviat, sviat, sviat, gospod' savaof, ispoln' nebo i zemliu slavy ego.*
11.A. The priest puts on his zone, saying: *Blagosloven bog prepoiasuiai mia siloiu...*	**11.B.** The priest puts on his zone, saying: *Bog prepoiasa mia siloiu...*
7.A.ii. For the epimanikia, as is written above [**7.A.i.**]	**7.B.** For the epimanikia, the priest and deacon say, each to himself, for the right hand: *Desnitsa gospodnia sotvori sila...* [=second half of 1655—**7.A.i.**]
8.A.ii. [=**8.A.i.**]	**8.B.** For the left hand [=**8.A.i.**]
12.A. Then the priest takes the epigonation [if he is permitted to wear it], blesses it, kisses it, and says: *Prepoiashe oruzhie tvoe...*	
13.A. The priest takes the phelonion, blesses it, kisses it, and says: *Sviashchennitsy tvoi gospodi, oblekutsia v pravdu...*	**13.B.** The priest takes the phelonion and says: *Sviashchennitsy tvoi oblekoutsia v pravdu...*
[IV. LAVABO]	
They wash their hands, saying: *Oumyiu v nepovinnykh routse moi...* [Ps 25(26):6-12].	
	III.9.B. The deacon receives a blessing from the priest, then goes to prepare the vessels on the prothesis table.
[V. PENITENTIAL PRAYERS][26]	
	1.B. *Vladyko gospodi vsederzhiteliu, nekhotiai smerti greshnomu...*[27] **2.B.** *Gospodi bozhe nash, edine blagii i chelovekoliubche...*[28] **3.B.** *Gospodi isuse khriste bozhe nash, syne i slove boga zhivago...*[29] **4.B.** *Gospodi isuse khriste syne bozhii, blagii premudryi...*[30] **5.B.** *Gospodi bozhe nash, blagii chelovekoliubche, prizri...*[31]

The differences between the two are striking. The Nikonian edition greatly simplifies the rite, and eliminates altogether the prayers before the entrance into church. Many troparia in the earlier edition are replaced with different texts. Yet the reason behind these changes is simple. The Nikonian edition is a word for word translation of the 1602 Venice *Euchologion,* down to the smallest rubric. This, as will become obvious, is the pattern for the entire reform.

2. Prothesis

The Nikonian edition contains substantial changes in the proskomide, changes which aroused the opposition of the Old-Believers. In particular, the innovations include a reduction in the number of loaves (*prosphora*) from seven to five, and a change in the prosphora seal.[32] The following is an outline of the prothesis rite as it appears in its two versions:

1655 (Moscow)	1646 (Moscow)
[VI. PROTHESIS]	
They go before the prothesis table, bow 3x, saying:	
1.A. *Bozhe ochisti mia…* 3x	1.B. *Bozhe ochisti mia…* *Sozdavyi mia gospodi…* *Bez chisla sogreshikh…*
2. Then they say the troparion: *Iskupil ny esi ot kliatvy…*[33]	
[Opening Blessing]	
3.A. Deacon: *Blagoslovi vladyko.*	3.B. Deacon: *Blagoslovi vladyko zaklati sviatyi agnets.*
Priest: *Blagosloven bog nash….* Deacon: *Amin.*	
[Preparation of the lamb]	
4. The priest takes a prosphora in his left hand, the spear in his right. He makes the sign of the cross 3x over the bread, saying:	
4.A. *V vospominanie gospoda, i boga, i spasa nashego iisusa khrista* 3x.	4.B. *Vospominanie tvorim velikago gospoda boga i spasa nashego isusa khrista* 3x.

1655 (Moscow)	1646 (Moscow)
	4.B. con't. Deacon: *Amin'. Gospodu pomolimsia, gospodi pomilui.*
5. The priest cuts the prosphora on the right side of the seal, saying: *Iako ovcha na zakolenie vedesia.*	
	5.B. At each incision, the deacon says: *Gospodu pomolimsia, gospodi pomilui.*
6. Cutting on the left side, he says:	
6.A. *I iako agnets neporochen priamo strigushchiago ego bezglasen, tako neotverzet oust svoikh.*	**6.B.** *I iako agnets priamo strigoushchemu ego bezglasen, sitse neotverzaet oust svoikh.*
7. On the top side of the seal: *Vo smirenii ego sud ego vziatsia.* **8.** On the bottom side: *Rodzhe ego kto ispovest'.*	
8.A. The deacon looks reverently at this mystery and, for each incision, says: *Gospodu pomolimsia,* holding his orarion in his hand.	
9. Then the deacon says:	
	9.A. *Gospodu pomolimsia*
Vozmi vladyko. The priest cuts the prosphora from the left side and removes the holy lamb, saying: *Iako vzemletsia ot zemli zhivot ego.* Then he puts it on the discos, with the seal facing down.	
10. The deacon says: *Pozhri vladyko.* The priest cuts it cross-wise, saying:	
10.A. *Zhretsia agnets bozhii vzemliai grekh mira...*	**10.B.** *Zhretsia agnets bozhii vzemliai grekhi miru...*
	11.B. The deacon says: *Polozhi vladyko.* The priest puts the lamb down on the discos and says: *Polagaetsia agnets bozhii za zhivot vsego mira.*
12. The deacon says: *Probodi vladyko.* The priest pierces the lamb on the left side with the spear, saying: *Edin ot voin kopiem rebra emu...*	

1655 (Moscow)	1646 (Moscow)
[Preparation of the wine]	
13.A. The deacon pours wine and water into the chalice, first saying to the priest: *Blagoslovi vladyko sviatoe soedinenie.* And the priest blesses them.	**13.B.** The deacon takes the wine in his right hand, the water in his left, and says to the priest: *Blagoslovi vladyko vino i vodu.* Priest: *Blagosloven bog nash...* The deacon pours the two into the chalice and says: *Soedini vladyko.* Blessing, the priest says: *Soedinenie sviatago dukha, iako trie sout' svidetelstvuiushchii dukh, krov' i voda, i trie vo edino sout'.* Deacon: *Amin'.* [Extensive rubrics follow here about what to do if the lamb is still warm from the oven, i.e. recently baked.]
[Commemorations]	
	14.B. In a monastery, the deacon takes the censer, receives a blessing from the priest, and goes out through the holy doors, opening only one side of them. He incenses the icons and all the brothers. While censing, he silently recites all the commemorations which the priest is making at the prothesis table. Then he says the ektene. He reenters the sanctuary through the holy doors, again opening only one side of them, and incenses the altar table and the priest, and together they make the commemorations for the dead. In secular churches, the deacon remains with the priest, doing what is prescribed. [Here follows a warning that the deacon may, under no circumstances, remove any commemorative particles from the prosphora.]

1655 (Moscow)	1646 (Moscow)
[Theotokos]	
15. The priest takes the second prosphora and says:	
15.A. *V chest' i pamiat' preblagoslovennyia vladychetsi nasheia prisnodevy marii. Eiazhe molitvami priimi gospodi zhertvu siiu v prenebesnyi tvoi zhertvenik.*	**15.B.** *Gospodi isuse khriste syne bozhii, priimi prinoshenie sie, v chest' i v pamiat' presviatyia prechistyia, i preblagoslovennyia vladychitse nasheia bogoroditse, i prisno devy marii.* [A special commemoration is also provided if the church is dedicated to Mary, or if it is a Marian feast.] The deacon also repeats this [the commemoration].
Removing a particle, the priest puts it to the right of the holy lamb.	
[the priest] saying: *Predsta tsaritsa odesnuiu tebe, v rizy pozlashchenny odeianna predukrashenna.*	The deacon says: *Amin'.*
[The Saints]	
16. The priest takes the third prosphora and says:	
	16.B. *Gospodi i isuse khriste syne bozhii, priimi prinoshenie sie, v chest' i slavu...*
16.A.i. John the Baptist He takes a particle [from the third prosphora] and puts it to the left of the lamb, beginning the first row.	**16.B.i.** The bodiless powers John the Baptist
16.A.ii. Moses Aaron Elijah Elisha David Isaiah The three youths Daniel and all the prophets. The priest takes out a second particle.	**16.B.ii.** Elijah Moses and all the prophets

1655 (Moscow)	1646 (Moscow)
16.A.iii. Peter Paul the Twelve and all the apostles. The priest takes out a third particle.	**16.B.iii.** Peter Paul Matthew Mark Luke John the Theologian and all the apostles.
16.A.iv. Basil the Great Gregory the Theologian John Chrysostom Athanasius Cyril Nicholas of Myra Peter [of Moscow] Alexis [of Moscow] Jonah [of Moscow] Philip of Moscow Nikita of Novgorod Leontii of Rostov and all the fathers. The priest takes out a fourth particle.	**16.B.iv.** Basil the Great Gregory the Theologian John Chrysostom Athanasius Cyril Nicholas of Myra Peter [Wonderworker of Russia] Alexis [Wonderworker of Russia] Jonah, Wonderworker of Russia John of Novgorod Leontii of Rostov and all the fathers
16.A.v. Stephen Demetrios George Theodore Teron Theodore Stratelates and all the [male] martyrs Thekla Barbara Kyriake Euthymia Paraskeve Catherine and all the [female] martyrs. The priest takes out a fifth particle.	**16.B.v.** Stephen George Demetrios Theodore Teron Theodore Stratelates Nikita Procopius Boris Gleb Prince Michael of Chernigov his wife Theodora and all the holy martyrs
16.A.vi. Anthony Euthymios Sabbas Onuphrios	**16.B.vi.** Anthony Euthymios Sabbas Onuphrios

1655 (Moscow)	1646 (Moscow)

16.A.vi. con't.
Athanasios of Athos
Sergius of Radonezh
Varlaam of Khutyn'
and all the holy fathers.
 	
Pelagia
Theodoule
Euphrosyne
Mary of Egypt
and all the holy mothers.
 	
The Priest takes out a sixth particle.
	16.B.vi. con't.
	Athanasios of Athos
	Theodosius of Palestine
	John Climacus
	John of Damascus
	Anthony of the Caves in Kiev
	Theodosius of the Caves in Kiev
	Sergius of Radonezh
	Varlaam of Khutyn'
	Kirill
	Nikon
	Dimitri of Prilutsk
	Nikita of Pereiaslavl
	Pafnutii of Borov
	Zosima, Wonderworker of
	   the Solovki
	Savatii, Wonderworker of
	   the Solovki
	and all the holy fathers.

16.A.vii. Cosmas Damian Kyr John Panteleimon Hermolaos and all the unmercenary saints. The priest takes out a seventh particle.	**16.B.vii.** Cosmas Damian Kyr John Panteleimon Hermolaos Sampson Diomedes and all the unmercenary saints.
16.A.viii. Joachim Anna	**16.B.viii.** Joachim Anna **16.B.v'.** Thekla Barbara Kyriake Euthymia Paraskeve Catherine **16.B.vi'.** Pelagia Theodosia Anastasia Eupraxia Fevronia

1655 (Moscow)	1646 (Moscow)
	Theodoule Euphrosine Mary of Egypt and all the holy women.
the saint of the day and all the saints. *Ikh zhe molitvami poseti nas bozhe.* The priest takes out an eighth particle.	16.B.viii'. the patron saint of the church, the saint of the day and all the saints.
16.A.ix. John Chrysostom or Basil the Great [according to which liturgy is being celebrated]. The priest takes out a ninth particle.	16.B.ix. The deacon also says this [all the commemorations.] The priest takes out a particle and places it to the left of the lamb.
[The Living]	
17. The priest takes the fourth prosphora and says:	

17.A.i. All the Orthodox episcopate
The ecumenical patriarchs:
  Constantinople
  Alexandria
  Antioch
  Jerusalem
local metropolitan or bishop
the presbyterate
the diaconate
all orders in the clergy
 	
17.A.ii. The hegumen
the concelebrants
all the brethren
 	
The priest takes out a particle and
places it below the lamb.
	17.B.i. Patriarch of Moscow
	All the Orthodox episcopate.
	
	local bishop
	the presbyterate
	the diaconate
	all orders in the clergy
	
	The priest takes out a particle and
	places it under the other particles.

17.A.iii. Then he commemorates the tsar and his family, each by name. The priest takes out one particle for each person he names.	17.B.iii. He takes the fifth prosphora and commemorates: the tsar and his family, each by name, all the princes and boyars and all Orthodox Christians. The priest takes out one particle.

1655 (Moscow)	1646 (Moscow)
	17.B.ii. In a monastery, the priest takes the sixth prosphora and commemorates: the archimandrite or hegumen; the concelebrants; all the brethren.
17.A.iv. Then he commemorates the living by name, as many as he wishes.	**17.B.iv.** The priest and deacon commemorate the living by name, as many as they wish.
The priest removes one particle for each person.	
	17.B.v. The priest commemorates himself and removes a particle for himself.
[The Dead]	
18.A. The priest takes the fifth prosphora and commemorates the dead: Orthodox patriarchs rulers founders bishop who ordained him and any person he wishes to remember by name.	**18.B.** He takes the seventh prosphora and commemorates the dead: rulers founders patriarchs and metropolitans Grand Princes and Princesses archbishops and bishops archimandrites and hegumens all clerical and monastic orders all Orthodox Christians and any person he wishes remember by name.
The priest removes a particle for each.	
19. The priest arranges all the particles on the discos with the sponge.	
[Covering of the Gifts]	
20. The deacon gets the censer, adds incense, and says to the priest:	
20.A. *Blagoslovi vladyko kadilo. Gospodu pomolimsia.* The priest says the prayer of incense. *Kadilo tebe prinosim…*	**20.B.** *Blagoslovi vladyko kadilo i fimiian. Gospodu pomolimsia.* Blessing the censer, the priest says the prayer of incense. [=1655, except for minor stylistic changes]

1655 (Moscow)	1646 (Moscow)
[The Asterisk]	
21.A. Deacon: *Gospodu pomolimsia.* The priest incenses the asterisk and places it over the holy bread, saying: *I prishedshi zvezda, sta verkhu...*	**21.B.** Deacon: *Gospodu pomolimsia. Postavi vladyko sviatouiu zvezdou, na sviatem diskose.* The priest takes the asterisk, incenses it, and places it over the lamb, saying: *Prished zvezda sta verkhu...* Deacon: *Amin'.*
[The First Veil]	
22.A. Deacon: *Gospodu pomolimsia* The priest incenses the first veil and covers the discos, saying: *Gospod' votsarisia...* [Ps 92(93)]	**22.B.** Deacon: *Pokryi vladyko sviatuiu zvezdu siiu.* The priest takes the first veil and covers the discos, saying Ps 92[93]: *Gospod' votsarisia...* The deacon incenses the veils before each covering. Deacon: *Amin'.*
[The Second Veil]	
23.A. Deacon: *Gospodu pomolimsia. Pokryi vladyko.* The priest incenses the second veil and covers the chalice, saying: *Pokryi nebesa...*	**23.B.** Deacon: *Gospodu pomolimsia, pokryi vladyko sviatuiu chashu siiu.* Priest: *Gospodi pomilui.* And he covers the chalice with the second veil, saying: *Pokryi nebesa...* Deacon: *Amin'.*
[The Aer]	
24.A. Deacon: *Gospodu pomolimsia. Pokryi vladyko.* The priest incenses the aer and covers both vessels, saying: *Pokryi nas krovom krylu...*	**24.B.** Deacon: *Gospodu pomolimsia, pokryi vladyko oboia siia sviataia.* Priest: *Gospodi pomilui.* He covers both vessels with the aer, saying: *Pokryi nas krovom krilou...*
25.A. The priest takes the censer and incenses the gifts, saying: *Blagosloven bog nash sitse blagovolivyi slava tebe* 3x. Each time, the deacon replies: *Vsegda nyne i prisno...amin.* And they bow 3x reverently, and the deacon takes the censer.	**25.B.** The priest crosses his arms across his chest, bows, and says: *Blagosloven bog izhe sitse izvolivyi vsegda, i nyne...amin'.*

1655 (Moscow)	1646 (Moscow)
[Prothesis Prayer]	
26. Deacon: *O predlozhennykh chestnykh darekh gospodu pomolimsia.*	
26.A. Priest:	26.B. Priest: *Gospodi pomilui.* Bowing, he prays:
Bozhe bozhe nash...	
[Dismissal and Incensation]	
27.A.i. They do the dismissal there before the prothesis table. 27.A.ii. Priest: *Slava tebe khriste bozhe...* Deacon: *Slava, i nyne. Gospodi pomilui* 3x. *Blagoslovi.* Priest: Dismissal for day.	
27.A.iii. The deacon incenses the gifts, then around the altar table saying:	
	27.B.iv. Together they say the troparion:
Vo grobe plotski...[34]	
	27.B.iii. The priest incenses the gifts 3x. The deacon takes the censer, opens the holy doors, and incenses around the altar table, reciting Ps 50[51]. The priest, standing on the right side of the altar table, also recites Ps 50[51].
27.A.v. Then he [the deacon] incenses the whole sanctuary and the entire church, reciting Ps 50[51]. Returning into the sanctuary, he incenses the altar table and the priest and puts the censer away.	27.B.v. The deacon incenses the gifts and the whole sanctuary. Standing in the holy doors, he incenses the superior, both choirs, and towards the rear of the church. Then he incenses the altar table, the priest, and gives the censer away.
	27.B.ii. The priest, standing in the holy doors, does the dismissal, saying: *Slava tebe bozhe nash...* and the dismissal for the day.

Once again, the prothesis rite, as presented in the Nikonian edition, matches the Venice 1602 *Euchologion* almost exactly, which in turn reflects the final stage of development in Greek practice.[35] Comparing the 1655 text with the earlier Muscovite edition, we see that the role of the deacon is greatly reduced. In the 1646 edition, the deacon repeats all the commemorations together with the priest (13.B.ii; 15.B; 16.B.ix; 17.B.iv). The rubric forbidding him to remove particles from the prosphora (13.B.ii) clearly indicates that this was still being done in some places. All this hearkens to an earlier age, when the deacon alone performed the prothesis except for the offertory prayer.[36] The Nikonian text, however, faithfully reproduces the contemporary Venetian version.

There are only a few, minor differences between 1655 Moscow and 1602 Venice. The first difference is in the commemorations of saints (16.iv-vi), ecumenical patriarchs (17.A.i), and of the tsar and his family (17.A.iii). To the list of saints in the Greek version is added a list of local, Russian saints, though a far shorter one than in the 1646 *Sluzhebnik*.[37] The selection of Russian saints has no parallel in any earlier *Sluzhebnik*. Significantly, the name of Metropolitan Philip of Moscow, whose relics Nikon had brought back to Moscow in 1652, was added to the list of Muscovite metropolitans. This was certainly consistent with Nikon's agenda of increasing the stature of the Muscovite hierarchy vis-à-vis the tsar. The commemoration of the ecumenical patriarchs (17.A.i) also fits in with the program of the tsar and Nikon to make Russia the center of world Orthodoxy, and to reinforce among Russians the notion that the Greeks are fully orthodox. The only rubrical difference within the prothesis, between the 1655 *Sluzhebnik* and the 1602 *Euchologion*, comes in the dismissal (27.A.). The Moscow text specifies that the dismissal is to be done *tamo* ("there"), i.e., in front of the prothesis table rather than at the holy doors, as in the 1646 *Sluzhebnik*. Clearly, the editors want to emphasize the new practice which follows the 1602 Greek *Euchologion*. Hence this minor difference only highlights the strict adherence of Nikon's reformers to the newer, Greek practice.

The Old-Believers complain about four changes in the prothesis rite which they see as significant:

i. The change in the number of prosphora;

ii. The difference in the seal on the prosphora;

iii. The change in the number of particles removed at the commemorations of the saints (16);

iv. The change in the formula "*Zhretsia agnets bozhii*" (10).[38]

In each case, the 1655 *Sluzhebnik* exactly follows Greek practice, as found in the 1602 Venice *Euchologion.* The Old-Believers defend the earlier Muscovite practice.

i. They maintain that seven, not five, prosphora should be used. They appeal to the 1551 Stoglav Council, to scripture (Mt 15—the feeding of the 4,000 with seven loaves), and to pre-Nikonian Moscow *Sluzhebniks.* In fact, however, the Stoglav Council did not specify the exact number of prosphora necessary, and the previous Moscow service books were not consistent.[39] The 1646 *Sluzhebnik*, cited above, requires seven prosphora only in a monastery (17.B.ii), but six at a cathedral or parish church.

ii. The Nikonian edition changes the seal, which is to be placed on the prosphora used for the eucharistic lamb.[40] The new seal is square, with a simple Greek cross in the middle, and with the inscription "IC, XC, NIKA" ("Jesus Christ conquers"). The earlier Muscovite version is quite different. It is round, contains a three-bar cross, an inscription about the edge "This is the lamb of God who takes away the sins of the world"),[41] a depiction of a spear and a lance, and the inscription "IC, XC, *tsar' slavy*" ("Jesus Christ, King of glory") over the cross.[42] The Old-Believers declare that the new seal is heretical, but we need not go into their arguments here.[43] It is evident that the Greek church knew both square and round seals, though seals from the post-Byzantine period all contain a square with a Greek cross, and the inscription "IC, XC, NIKA," from which the lamb is cut out,[44] even if the entire seal may be round.[45] The 1604 Striatin *Sluzhebnik* shows a diagram very similar to what we see in Nikon's edition,[46] as does the 1629 *Sluzhebnik* of Peter Moghila in Kiev.[47] The Greek printed books from this period have no diagrams, so we cannot say with absolute certainty that the new seal comes from the Greeks. The diagram presented by Goar, however, reveals a seal identical to the Nikonian one.[48] This, together with the Moscow reformers' care to follow the Greeks in every detail, does make a convincing argument for a Greek origin.

iii. Regarding the number of commemorative particles, the Nikonian *Sluzhebnik* follows the Venetian edition exactly. The 1646 Moscow

Sluzhebnik indicates that only one particle is removed from the third prosphora at the commemoration of the saints (16.B.i-ix). The Old-Believers reject Nikon's innovation and claim that only one particle may be taken from each prosphora.[49] The practice of removing only one particle for the commemoration of the saints is found in the Diataxis of Philotheos (14th cent.).[50] In the 16th century, however, we see multiple particles being taken from the third prosphora,[51] and eventually we see the nine particles, as in the 1602 *Euchologion*.[52] Among Slavic editions, the 1604 Striatin, and the 1629 and 1639 Kievan *Sluzhebniks*, adopt this practice. Thus, once more, the Nikonian version is simply adopting a more contemporary Greek practice.

iv. Finally, the Old-Believers complain about the formula which accompanies the cutting of the lamb. The pre-Nikonian Moscow edition reads: *Zhretsia agnets bozhii vzemliai grekhi miru* ("Sacrificed is the lamb of God, who takes away the sins of the world"). The Nikonian version reads: *Zhretsia agnets bozhii vzemliai grekh mira*. The only difference, highly significant for the opponents of the reform, is that the word *grekh* (sin) is here in the singular, whereas the former text had it in the plural.[53] The 1604 Striatin and the various Kievan texts (1629, 1639) also have the plural, as do many ancient Slavic mss.[54] The Greek printed books all have the singular. Nikon's correctors, wishing to follow the Greek text as closely as possible, follow suit.

3. The Enarxis

Compared to the entrance and prothesis rites, the rest of eucharistic liturgies was hardly touched. This is to be expected, given the fact that the opening rites continued to evolve significantly, long after the core of the liturgies had been fixed. Our comments about the changes in the liturgies proper will be correspondingly briefer.

i. The Opening Dialogue

The first difference, about which the Old-Believers complain, concerns the opening diaconal invitation in the preliminary dialogue between priest and deacon.[55] The text is as follows:

1655 (Moscow)	1646 (Moscow)
Deacon: *Vremia sotvoriti gospodevi, vladyko blagoslovi.* The priest blesses him and says:	Deacon: *Vremia posluzhiti gospodevi, blagoslovi vladyko.* The priest blesses him by making a sign of the cross over his head and says:
Blagosloven bog nash, vsegda...	

The remainder of the exchange is identical in the two versions. The issue revolves around the proper translation of the Greek text: Καιρὸς τοῦ ποιῆσαι τῷ κυρίῳ, δέσποτα εὐλόγησον. There are no known variants of the word ποιῆσαι. Earlier versions of the Greek text have either a briefer form of the diaconal invitation (Εὐλόγησον δέσποτα), or the present text, though some add the adjective ἅγιε before the word δέσποτα. The controversy, then, is simply over the correct translation of the verb ποιῆσαι. The 1646 edition renders it as *posluzhiti* (to serve or perform): this is a correct translation of the Greek word.[56] The Nikonian text reads *sotvoriti* (to make or create). This is the primary meaning of the Greek,[57] but it does not fit the context anywhere near as well. The 1655 translation first appears in the 1604 Striatin *Sluzhebnik*, then in the Kievan *Sluzhebniks* in 1620, 1629, and 1639. It is hardly surprising that Nikon's correctors, using Greek and Ukrainian books as models, chose this translation.

ii. The Little Entrance

There are a few minor differences in the First Entrance. The rubrics read as follows:

1602 (Venice)	1655 (Moscow)	1646 (Moscow)
[VII. LITTLE ENTRANCE][58]		
1.A. Ὅταν δὲ ἔλθῃ ὁ χορὸς εἰς τὸ Δόξα Πατρί, ὁ ἱερεὺς καὶ ὁ διάκονος στάντες ἔμπροσθεν τῆς ἁγίας τραπέζης, ποιοῦσι προσκυνήματα τρία.	When the singers come to the Glory of the third antiphon, the priest and deacon together, standing before the holy table, bow 3x.	1.B. When the singers begin the Glory of the Beatitudes.

1602 (Venice)	1655 (Moscow)	1646 (Moscow)
2.A. Εἶτα λαβὼν ὁ ἱερεὺς τὸ ἅγιον εὐαγγέλιον, δίδωσι τῷ διακόνῳ καὶ οὕτως ἐξελθόντες διὰ τοῦ βορείου μέρους προπορευομένων αὐτῶν λαμπάδων, ποιοῦσι τὴν μικρὰν εἴσοδον,	The priest then takes the holy gospel, gives it to the deacon, and they go to the right, behind the altar. They go out the north side, preceded by candles, and perform the little entrance.	**2.B.** The priest takes the holy gospel and gives it to the deacon. The deacon takes it and kisses the priest's hand. Turning to the right side, they go out through the small doors. When they pass in front of the prothesis table, the deacon points with his orarion and says to the priest: *Blagoslovi vladyko predlozhenie se.* The priest blesses the holy gifts with his hand, saying: *Blagosloveno predlozhenie sviash-chennykh i bozhestvenyk tvoikh tain, vsegda...* Deacon: *Amin*. And going out through the small doors, they perform the entrance.
3.A. καὶ στάντες ἐν τῷ συνήθη τόπῳ, κλίνουσιν ἀμφότεροι τὰς κεφαλάς, καὶ τοῦ διακόνου εἰπόντος· Τοῦ κυρίου δεηθῶμεν. Λέγει ὁ ἱερεὺς τὴν εὐχὴν τῆς εἰσόδου μυστικῶς· Δέσποτα Κύριε ὁ Θεὸς ἡμῶν . . .	Standing at the usual place, they both bow their heads. The deacon says: *Gospodu pomolimsia.* The priest says the Entrance Prayer silently: *Vladyko gospodi bozhe nash...*	**3.B.** The priest says the entrance prayer silently: *Vladyko gospodi bozhe nash...*
4.A. Τῆς εὐχῆς δὲ τελεσθείσης, λέγει ὁ διάκονος πρὸς τὸν ἱερέα, δεικνύων πρὸς ἀνατολὰς τῇ δεξιᾷ, κρατῶν ἅμα καὶ τὸ ὡράριον τοῖς τρισὶ δακτύλοις· Εὐλόγησον δέσποτα τὴν ἁγίαν εἴσοδον.	When the prayer is finished, the deacon says to the priest, pointing toward the east [the front of the church] with his right hand, holding the orarion with three fingers: *Blagoslovi vladyko sviatyi vkhod.*	**4.B.** The deacon with the gospel book turns to the priest, bows, and says quietly: *Blagoslovi vladyko vkhod sviatyi.* The priest kisses the holy gospel book, makes the sign of the cross over the deacon's head, and says quietly: *Blagosloven vkhod sviatykh tvoikh...*

1602 (Venice)	1655 (Moscow)	1646 (Moscow)
Καὶ ὁ ἱερεὺς εὐλογῶν, λέγει· Εὐλογημένη ἡ εἴσοδος τῶν ἁγίων σου . . .	Blessing, the priest says: *Blagosloven vkhod sviatykh tvoikh...*	
5.A. Εἶτα ὁ διάκονος προσέρχεται πρὸς τὸν ἐπίσκοπον ἢ τὸν ἡγούμενον, εἰ πάρεστιν, εἰ δ᾽ οὔκ, ἀσπάζεται ὁ ἱερεύς.	Then the deacon goes to the bishop or the hegumen, if he is present. If not, then the priest kisses it.	**5.B.** If there is a bishop, the deacon approaches him with the gospel book, and the bishop kisses the gospel book and blesses the deacon. If there is no bishop, the priest kisses it himself. If it is a monastery, the deacon brings the gospel book to the hegumen, and the hegume kisses it and blesses the deacon. The priest kisses the gospel book in the sanctuary.
6.A. Πληρωθέντος δὲ τοῦ τελευταίου τροπαρίου, εἰσέρχεται ὁ διάκονος εἰς τὸ μέσον, καὶ στὰς ἔμπροσθεν τοῦ ἱερέως ἄνυψοι μικρὸν τὰς χείρας, καὶ δεικνύων τοῦ εὐαγγελίου, λέγει μεγαλοφώνως· Σοφία ὀρθοί.	When the last troparion is finished, the deacon goes to the middle, stands in front of the priest, raises his hands slightly to show the holy gospel book and says aloud: *Premudrost' prosti.*	**6.B** The deacons raises the gospel book slightly, does not make a sign of the cross with the book, and says aloud: *Premoudrost' prosti.*
7.A. Εἶτα προσκυνήσας αὐτός τε καὶ ὁ ἱερεύς, κατόπισθεν αὐτοῦ, εἰσέρχονται εἰς τὸ ἅγιον βῆμα, καὶ ὁ μὲν διάκονος ἀποτίθησι τὸ ἅγιον εὐαγγέλιον ἐν τῇ ἁγίᾳ τραπέζῃ.	He bows, as does the priest behind him, and they enter the holy sanctuary. The deacon places the holy gospel book on the holy table.	**7.B.** They enter the holy sanctuary. The deacon places the gospel book on the holy table.

1602 (Venice)	1655 (Moscow)	1646 (Moscow)
8.A. Οἱ δὲ ψάλται ψάλλουσι· Δεῦτε προσκυνήσωμεν . . . καὶ τὰ συνήθη τροπάρια.	And the singers sing: *Priidite poklonimsia...* and the usual troparia.	**8.B.** The singers sing: *Priidite poklonimsia...* and the usual troparia and kontakia.

The 1655 text is obviously much closer to the Greek edition than to the pre-Nikonian Moscow version. The Old-Believers complain that the new recension leaves out the blessing of the prothesis table by the priest as the procession passes by (VII.2.B).[59] This practice is found only in the Muscovite *Sluzhebniks* before Nikon, but not in any other printed service books. It does appear in one 15th century diataxis,[60] so the practice is not a Russian invention. But because this custom is absent in the Venetian edition, it is eliminated from the new service books.

The 1655 text is clearly dependent on the Greek Venetian edition. The content is virtually identical, and even the Greek word-order is preserved almost exactly in the Nikonian rendition. The 1655 *Sluzhebnik* is more precise in describing the route of the procession around the altar table; but beyond that the two texts are identical.

iii. The Trisagion

Here, too, there are some changes:

1655 (Moscow)	1646 (Moscow)
[VIII. TRISAGION]	
	3.B. The priest says the Prayer of the Trisagion: *Bozhe sviatyi, izhe vo sviatykh pochivaiai...*
1.A. When they [the singers] reach the final troparion, the deacon, bowing his head and holding his orarion with three fingers, says:	**1.B.** When they [the singers] start the Gloria Patri and the last kontakion, the deacon says quietly to the priest:
Blagoslovi vladyko vremia trisviatago.	

1655 (Moscow)	1646 (Moscow)
The priest blesses him and says:	The priest turns to the west [facing the people][61] and says:
Iako sviat esi bozhe nash...nyne i prisno.	
2.A. When the troparion is finished, the deacon comes near the holy doors and points with his orarion, first toward the icon of Christ, and says: *Gospodi spasi blagochestivyia, i uslyshi ny.* Then he turns to the people standing outside and says loudly: *I vo veki vekov.*	**2.B.** The deacon points to the outside with his hand and orarion and says loudly: *I voveki vekom.*
Choir: *amin.*	Choir: *amin'.* Trisagion.
3.A. And while they sing the trisagion, the priest says this prayer: Prayer of the Trisagion *Bozhe sviatyi, vo sviatykh pochivaiai...*	
4.A. When this is finished, the priest and the deacon themselves say the trisagion together, bowing before the holy table.	**4.B.** The priest and deacon say the trisagion 3x to themselves and bow 3x before the holy table.

The earlier text prescribes that the Trisagion Prayer be recited before the singing of the Trisagion. This is the more ancient practice.[62] The Nikonian *Sluzhebnik*, following the 1602 Venice *Euchologion*, awkwardly places this prayer during the Trisagion, after the ecphonesis, which is begun by the priest and completed by the deacon. The 1604 Striatin *Sluzhebnik* agrees with Nikon's edition and the Greek version, but the Kievan *Sluzhebniks* retain the earlier practice. The 1655 *Sluzhebnik* also adds the commemoration made by the deacon: *Gospodi, spasi blagochestivyia* ("Lord, save the pious"). This is the remnant of an acclamation to the emperor and the patriarch. The acclamation was commonly found in Pontificals, but rarely in ordinary euchologies, which were destined for priests.[63] In 16th century Russian practice, there was a polychronion at this point, for the tsar and the bishop, but only at hierarchal liturgies.[64] For some reason, the acclamation found its way into the Venetian Greek euchology,[65] including the 1602 edition. From there,

it made its way into the 1604 Striatin, the 1629 and 1639 Kievan, and the
Nikonian Muscovite *Sluzhebniks.*

4. The Liturgy Of The Word

i. The Gospel Reading

The Nikonian editors made a few significant changes in the rites sur-
rounding the reading of the gospel.[66] Once more, the earlier Muscovite
text was replaced by the version presented in the 1602 Venice *Euchologion.* The following is an outline of the two Muscovite versions:

1655 (Moscow)	1646 (Moscow)
IX. GOSPEL READING	
[1. Prayer before the Gospel] *Vozsiiai v serdtsakh nashikh...*	
	2.B. Second gospel prayer: *Gospodi bozhe nash, prikloni serdtsa....*
3.A. The deacon puts away the censer in the usual place.	3.B. Giving away the censer, he [the deacon] takes the holy cross from the altar table, puts it in his right hand over the orarion, and brings it to the priest. The priest takes the holy cross, blesses himself with it, and kisses it saying: *Siloiu i zastupleniem chestnago kresta tvoego, gospodi pomilui mia, i pomozi mi greshnomu.* Then he blesses the deacon. The deacon takes the cross, kisses it, repeats the same [prayer], and places it [the cross] back on the altar table.
4.A. [The deacon] approaches the priest and bows to him, holding his orarion and the holy gospel book with the tips of his fingers, namely, in that place [in front?] of the holy table. *Blagoslovi vladyko blagovestitelia swiatago apostola i evangelista,* name.	4.B. Then the deacon, standing in front of the holy table, bows 3x and says loudly: *Blagoslovi vladyko blagovestiti blagovestie, sviatago slavnago i vsekhvalnago vselenskago blagovestnika, apostola i evangelista,* name. Taking the holy gospel book, he bows to the priest.

1655 (Moscow)	1646 (Moscow)
5.A. The priest blesses him and says: *Bog molitvami sviatago slavnago vsekhvalnago apostola i evangelista,* name, *da dast tebe glagol blagovestvuiushchemu siloiu mnogoiu, vo ispolnenie evangelia vozliublennago syna svoego gospoda nashego iisusa khrista.* The deacon says: *amin'.*	**5.B.** The priest, standing at the high place [behind the altar table] says: *Bog zamolitv sviatago slavnago, i vsekhvalnago vselenskago blagovestnika apostola i evangalista,* name, *dast ti glagol vo ezhe blagovestiti silu mnogu.*
6.A. Bowing to the holy gospel book, the deacon takes it and goes out through the holy doors, preceded by candlebearers, and goes and stands on the ambo, or on the appointed spot. The priest stands in front of the holy table, faces west [toward the people] and exclaims:	**6.B.** The deacon bows and goes out through the holy doors to the usual place. The priest says, aloud:
Premudrost' prosti ouslyshim sviatago evangelia.	
7. Deacon: *Ot* name, *sviatago evangelia chtenie.* Priest: *Vonmem.*	
8.A. When the gospel is finished, the priest says: *Mir ti blagovestvuiushchemu.* Choir: *Slava tebe gospodi.* And the deacon goes up to the holy doors and gives the gospel book to the priest.	**8.B.** When the gospel is finished, the priest comes from the high place, stands in the holy doors, takes the gospel book from the deacon, says to him quietly: *Mir ti,* and kisses the gospel book. If others are [co-]celebrating, they all kiss the gospel book.

The first difference lies in the presence, in 1646, of a second gospel prayer (2.B). Dmitrievskii lists a number of Slavic mss. containing this prayer, but was unable to find a Greek equivalent.[67] A number of 14th and 15th century Greek mss., however, indicate the reading of Ps 85(86) at this point,[68] and the prayer in question is evidently a collect for this psalm. According to Petrovskii, in the 14th century this prayer was recited before the epistle.[69] Though found in the 1583 Vilna *Sluzhebnik* and in all the pre-Nikonian Moscow printed editions,[70] the 1602 Venice *Euchologion* does not have it, nor do any of the Striatin or Kievan books. So Nikon's correctors simply remove it.

Second, Nikon's editors eliminate the veneration of the cross before the gospel reading (3.B). The origin of this practice is unclear, and Dmitrievskii cites only two 16th century sources witnessing to it.[71] Among the printed service books, only the Moscow *Sluzhebniks* contain this rite, and not all of these have the priest say the words *Siloiu i zastupleniem...* ("Through the power and intercession...").[72] No Greek or Ukrainian books mention this usage.

There are also differences in the dialogue between the priest and the deacon (4-5). Once again, the Nikonian version is taken straight from the Venetian euchology. The text of this dialogue has a long and varied history.[73] The Old-Believers complain that Nikon removed the phrase *vselenskago blagovestnika* ("universal evangelist") from both the deacon's (4.B) and the priest's (5.B) exclamations, and that they changed the number of prostrations (4.B).[74] Again, the origin of the phrase *vselenskago blagovestnika* is unclear, and it appears only in 17th century Moscow.[75]

In the 1655 *Sluzhebnik*, it is not clear just when the deacon takes the gospel. When he receives the blessing from the priest (4.A), he is already holding the gospel. Later, after the blessing, the rubrics indicate that he bows, takes the gospel (again?), and goes out (6.A). This is a typical example of several layers of rubrics being superimposed, resulting in conflicting instructions.[76] The 1602 Venice edition has the deacon pick up the gospel before he receives the priest's blessing, as does the Nikonian version cited above (4.A). The 1604 Striatin *Sluzhebnik* instructs the deacon to hold only his orarion for the blessing, and only then to take the gospel from the hands of the priest. Combining these two sets of rubrics, we reach the Nikonian version. The situation is confused even further by the ambiguity about where the priest is to stand during this exchange. The 1646 *Sluzhebnik*, has him stand behind the altar, at the "high place" in the apse, during the gospel reading (5.B). This is clearly the more ancient practice, still seen in the 14th century *Diataxis* of Philotheos.[77] This practice is also kept in the Kievan editions of 1629 and 1639. In the Nikonian version, as in the Venetian text, the priest stands in front of the altar table during the reading of the gospel (6.A). But it is not clear just when he goes there. When the deacon comes to receive the blessing, the priest is standing "in that place of the holy table" (3.A). This is a literal translation of the Greek text in the 1602 *Euchologion*: ἐν ἐκείνῳ τῷ τόπῳ τῆς ἁγίας τραπέζης. So it would appear that the priest is already in front of the altar table at this point. This would agree with the usage in the 1604 Striatin *Sluzhebnik:* the priest gives the gospel book to the deacon after their dialogue, and this obviously requires him to be in front of the altar. As usual, the correctors preferred a literal rendering of the Greek text, hence our ambiguous rubrics.

Following the reading of the gospel, the priest greets the deacon with the peace (8.A). The Nikonian edition follows the Venetian text by giving an expanded version of the greeting (Εἰρήνη σοὶ τῷ εὐαγγελιζομένῳ —"Peace to you who has proclaimed the gospel"). The 1655 *Sluzhebnik,* just as the Venetian *Euchologion,* omits the rubrics that have the priest and all the concelebrants venerate the gospel book (8.B).[78]

i. The Litanies

1602 (Venice)	1655 (Moscow)	1652 (Moscow)
[X. EKTENE]		
1.A. Εἴπωμεν πάντες, ἐξ ὅλης τῆς ψυχῆς . . .	1.A. *Rtsem vsi: otvseia dushi...*	1.B.i. *Rtsem vsi.* 1.B.ii. *Ot vseia dushi...*
2.A. Κύριε παντοκράτωρ . . . ἐπάκουσον καὶ ἐλέησον.	2.A. *Gospodi vsederzhiteliu... uslyshi i pomilui.*	2.B. *Gospode vsederzhiteliu... molimtsia.*
3. Ἐλέησον ἡμᾶς ὁ θεός . . .	3. *Pomilui nas bozhe...*	3. [=1655]
4.A. Ἔτι δεόμεθα ὑπὲρ τῶν εὐσεβεστάτων καὶ θεοφυλάκτων βασιλέων ἡμῶν, κράτους, νίκης . . .	4.A. *Eshche molimsia o blagochestivom i bogokhranimom tsare nashem name, o derzhave, pobede...*	4.B. *Eshche milimsia o blagovernnom i bogom khranimom tsare i velikom kniaze, name, o derzhave i o pobede...*
5. Ἔτι δεόμεθα ὑπὲρ τοῦ ἀρχιεπισκόπου ἡμῶν ...	5. *Eshche molimsia o patriarkhe nashem...*	5. [=1655]
[Here follow petitions for:]		
	6.A. The tsar's wife	6.B. General petition for the the tsar and his wife.
	7. The tsar's son.	7. [=1655]

1602 (Venice)	1655 (Moscow)	1652 (Moscow)
	8. The tsar's daughters	8. [=1655]
	9.A. *Eshche molimsia o vsekh ikh khristoliubivom voinstve...*	9.B. *Eshche molimsia o milosti bozhii.*
10.A. Ἔτι δεόμεθα ὑπὲρ τῶν ἀδελφῶν ἡμῶν . . .	10.A. *Eshche molimsia o bratiiakh nashikh...*	10.B. If in a monastery: *Eshche molimsia o ottse nashem igoumene...*
11.A. Ἔτι δεόμεθα ὑπὲρ τῶν μακαρίων καὶ ἀειδίμων κτητόρων τῆς ἁγίας μονῆς ταύτης· καὶ ὑπὲρ πάντων τῶν προαναπαυσαμένων πατέρων καὶ ἀδελφῶν ἡμῶν, τῶν ἐνθάδε κειμένων καὶ ἀπανταχοῦ ὀρθοδόξων.	11.A. *Eshche molimsia o blazhennykh i prisnopamiatnyk sviateishikh patriarsekh pravoslavnykh, i blagochestivykh tsarekh, i sozdatelei sviatyia obiteli seia: i o vsekh prezhde pochivshikh ottsekh I bratiiakh, zde lezhashchikh, i povsiudu pravoslavnykh.*	
12.A. Ἔτι δεόμεθα ὑπὲρ τῶν καρποφορούντων καὶ καλλιεργούντων ἐν τῷ ἁγίῳ καὶ πανσέπτῳ ναῷ τούτῳ κοπιώντων, ψαλλόντων, καὶ ὑπὲρ τοῦ περιεστῶτος λαοῦ, τοῦ ἀπεκδεχομένου τὸ παρὰ σοῦ μέγα καὶ πλούσιον ἔλεος.	12.A. *Eshche molimsia o plodonosiashchikh i dobrodeiushchikh vo sviatem i vsechestnem khrame sem, truzhdaiushchikhsia, poiushchikh, i predstoiashchikh liudekh, ozhidaiushchikh ot tebe velikiia i bogatyhia milosti.*	12.B.i. *Eshche molimsia o vsekh sluzhashchikh i posluzhjivshikh vo sviatei obiteli sei. If in a secular church: vo sviatim khrame sem, o zhravii i spasenii.* 12.B.ii. *Eshche molimsia o pred'stoiashchikh liudekh, i chaiushchikh iazhe ot tebe veliniia milosti, i o adravii i spasenii.* 12.B.iii. *Eshche nolimsia o tvoriashchikh milostyniu...* 12.B.vi. *Eshche molimsia za vsiu bratiiu, i za vsia khristiany...*
13. Ἐκφώνησις· Ὅτι ἐλεήμων . . .	13. *Iako milostiv...*	13. *Iako milostiv...*

Over the centuries, the ektene has evolved more than any other litany,[79] and there are countless variations in the texts. It is hardly surprising, therefore, that the Nikonian edition contains some significant changes. At the 1654 Council, Nikon had complained that the ektene in the existing service books "contains many petitions, whereas in the Greek and in our old books there are few."[80] The pre-Nikonian, 1652 version represents an earlier redaction of the text of the ektene. The initial petition is divided into two parts, consistent with the earliest sources containing this litany.[81] All the other petitions in this version also have their antecedents in various Greek euchologies.

Once again, the 1655 text is based on the Venetian edition. The chief difference is the addition of extra petitions for the tsar's family (6-8) and for the army (9), which are retained from earlier Moscow books. In the petition for the dead (11), the 1655 text adds commemorations for the Orthodox patriarchs and tsars. These changes are consistent with the official policy of the tsar and Nikon to make Russia the center of the Orthodox world.

The litany for the dead follows in the 1655 text of CHR, but not in BAS. Rubrics before this litany indicate that it is to be said only at memorial liturgies. Once more, there are differences from the earlier Muscovite text:

1655 (Moscow)	1646 (Moscow)
[XI. LITANY FOR THE DEAD]	
1.A. *Pomilui nas bozhe, po velitsei milosti...*	1.B. *Eshche molimsia o ostavlenii sogresheniikh...*
2.A. *Eshche molimsia o upokoenii dush ousopshikh rabov bozhiikh,* names, *i o ezhe prostitisia im...*	2.B. *O prostiti im vsiakoe sogreshenie...*
3. *Iako da gospod' bog...* 4. *Milosti bozhiia, tsarstvo nebesnoe...* 5. The Priest prays: *Bozhe dukhov, i vsiakiia ploti...*[82]	
	6.B. On Meatfare Sunday, the second, third, and fourth Saturdays of Great Lent, and on the seventh Saturday after Easter, the following litany is said instead:

1655 (Moscow)	1646 (Moscow)
	7.B *Eshche nolimsia o ostavlenie sogresheniikh, izhe vo blazhennei pamiati prestavl'shikhsia rab tvoikh, sviateishikh vselenskikh patriarkh...* [there follows a general commemoration of deceased tsars, bishops, clergy, and all Orthodox Christians.]
	8.B. And the rest [of the petitions, as above].

Curiously, no known Greek ms. or printed edition prescribes the memorial litany in the liturgy; only Slavic sources witness to it. All the pre-Nikonian Moscow books include it. The 1604 Striatin Sluzhebnik includes this litany in the rite of blessing the *kolyvo*.[83] The 1629 and 1639 Kievan *Sluzhebniks* do have this litany just as we find it in the 1655 Moscow edition. The text of the Nikonian version of the litany, different from the earlier Moscow text, comes from the funeral service in the Greek *Euchologion*.[84] But a long Slavic mss. tradition witnesses to the earlier Russian recension.[85] Nikon's correctors obviously did not want to remove this litany entirely, though it had no place in contemporary Greek use at the liturgy; but they "updated" it on the basis of the then current Greek funeral rite.

iii. The Unfolding of the Antimension

At the 1654 Council, as reported in the Acts, Nikon addressed the assembly with these words: "In our old Rituals and Euchologies, and in the Greek ones, it is indicated that we are to serve on antimensia. But now this is not done, and we place the antimension under the eiliton."[86] The council directed that this "abuse" be corrected.[87] Following are the rubrics in the 1646, 1652, and 1655 *Sluzhebniks* regarding the unfolding of the eiliton and the antimension at the liturgies of CHR and BAS:

1646 (Moscow)	1652 (Moscow)	1655 (Moscow)
[XII. UNFOLDING OF THE EILITON-ANTIMENSION]		
Gospel reading Gospel book placed on the altar table "behind the *eiliton*" *Eiliton* unfolded	Gospel reading	Gospel reading

1646 (Moscow)	1652 (Moscow)	1655 (Moscow)
Ektene Litany for the dead	Ektene Litany for the dead	Ektene Litany for the dead
Litany for catechumens	Litany for catechumens	Litany for catechumens *Antimension* unfolded during ecphonesis
Dismissal of catechumens	Dismissal of catechumens Unfolding of *eiliton*	Dismissal of catechumens
First prayer of the faithful, "after unfolding the *eiliton*."	First prayer of the faithful "after unfolding the *eiliton*."	First prayer of the faithful, "after unfolding the *antimension*."

The antimension was originally a portable altar, used only when a consecrated altar was unavailable. Eventually, however, it came to be used on all altars, though this was not universally the case even up to Nikon's time.[88] In Muscovite practice before the reform, the antimension was placed on top of the altar table, but under the eiliton, or corporal. Occasionally, the antimensia were sewn onto the altar-cloth, or even nailed directly to the altar table.[89] Thus the pre-Nikonian Moscow books spoke only to the unfolding of the eiliton, as we can see from the two editions cited above. The 1655 *Sluzhebnik*, in accord with the decision of the 1654 Council that the antimension be placed on top of the eiliton, now refers to the unfolding of the antimension. As for the exact time for the unfolding, the 1655 *Sluzhebnik* agrees with both Venice 1602, and Striatin 1604, in placing it at the ecphonesis of the litany for the catechumens.

The issue is clouded, however, by the fact that the terms "eiliton" and "antimension" are used interchangeably in the liturgical sources. Thus the 1604 Striatin *Sluzhebnik* speaks of the eiliton in CHR and BAS, but of the antimension in PRES. The 1629 Kiev *Sluzhebnik* follows 1604 Striatin exactly, but the 1639 Kievan version speaks of unfolding the "eiliton and the antimension inside it" at the ecphonesis of the litany for the catechumens, in both CHR and BAS.[90] All the printed Greek euchologies in this period refer only to the unfolding of the eiliton at the liturgies and make no mention of the antimension. Patriarch Paisios of Constantinople, writing in reply to Nikon's questions after the 1654 Council, however, clearly refers to the unfolding of the antimension at the ecphonesis of the litany of the catechumens.[91]

In addition to changing the position of the antimension on the altar and the time for its unfolding, Nikon also introduced new, Greek-style antimensia. During the 16th and 17th centuries, the Greeks had begun to use antimensia with depictions of the entire threnos, or burial scene of Christ.[92] The Russians, meanwhile, still used plain white cloths, decorated only with a three-bar cross and the inscription "IC XC, NIKA" ("Jesus Christ conquers").[93] At the 1655 Moscow Council, Nikon mandated the acceptance of the new format, and then had a large number of these Greek-style *antimensia* printed and distributed.[94]

NOTES

1. DMITRIEVSKII, *BOGOSLUZHENIE V XVI VEKE*, pp. 57-81.

2. PETROVSKII, *RÉDACTION SLAVE*, pp. 862-926.

3. *STOGLAV*, ch. 9, pp. 88-90. This council simply took one ms. *Sluzhebnik* and declared it to be the norm. DMITRIEVSKII, *BOGOSLUZHENIE V XVI VEKE*, pp. 67-69, identifies this ms. as *Moscow Synod 612*, described in GORSKII-NEVOSTRUEV III, pt. 1, pp. 59-65.

4. DMITRIEVSKII, *BOGOSLUZHENIE V XVI VEKE*, pp. 67-69.

5. We cite from this edition because this section is missing in the copy of the 1652 *Sluzhebnik* at the library of the Pontifical Oriental Institute in Rome.

6. This prayer first appears in the Russian books in the 15th century, PETROVSKII, *RÉDACTION SLAVE*, pp. 892-893. I was unable to locate its Greek equivalent, but it appears to be a collect for Ps 46(47).

7. *Ibid.* This is a collection of psalm verses: Pss 72(73):2; 121(122):1; 65(66):13.

8. The recitation of Pss 14(15) and 22(23) enters Slavic practice in the 14th century. They were read as the priest entered the sanctuary, *ibid.*, p. 879. In the 15th century, some documents instruct the priest to recite these psalms as he kisses the icons in church, *ibid.*, p. 892. The earliest printed Moscow *Sluzhebniks* place the psalms before the priest's entrance into church, as they appear here, *ibid.*, p. 925.

9. DMITRIEVSKII, *BOGOSLUZHENIE V XVI VEKE*, pp. 64-65. This corresponds to one of the 16th century redactions of the entrance rite, which divides it into two distinct parts, with a dismissal separating them. This is found, for example, in *Moscow Synod 617*, except that in the printed *Sluzhebnik* the dismissal is done inside the church rather than at the outside door.

10. A troparion for Pentecost.

11. Theotokion for the apostikha at Vespers of December 13. It appears among the entrance prayers in Russian practice in the 14th century, PETROVSKII, *RÉDACTION SLAVE*, p. 879.

12. A dismissal troparion for Vespers during Great Lent. It first appears as an entrance prayer in the 15th century, *ibid.*, p. 891.

13. This troparion appears among the entrance prayers in the 15th century, *ibid.*, p. 891. I was unable to locate its Greek equivalent.

14. These troparia (8.A, 9.A, 10.A) are taken from the second stasis of Great Compline.

15. Theotokion for the aposticha of Monday evening Vespers in tone 2. It also appears in the 15th century, PETROVSKII, *RÉDACTION SLAVE*, p. 891.

16. These two prayers appear in Slavic mss. in the 15th century, *ibid.*, p. 892.

17. This troparion, originally from the 6th Hour, enters Slavic practice in the 14th century, *ibid.*, p. 879.

18. This theotokion, for the second kathisma of Matins in tone 8, appears among the entrance prayers in the 15th century, *ibid.*, p. 892. Later it was also used as the Hymn to the Theotokos in BAS, cf. G. Winkler, "Die Interzessionen der Chrysostomusanaphora," *OCP* 36 (1970) 323.

19. See note 17 above.

20. A 15th century addition, this prayer is a reworking of *Prechistomu ti obrazu,* cf. PETROVSKII, *RÉDACTION SLAVE,* p. 893.

21. Theotokion of the 6th Hour.

22. I was unable to identify the Greek equivalent of this troparion, used here from the 15th century, *ibid.*, p. 893.

23. This prayer enters Russian (and Greek) practice in the 14th century via Philotheos, who has it in his diataxis as the only preparatory prayer. Cf. TREMPELAS, p. 1; and PETROVSKII, *RÉDACTION SLAVE,* p. 886. The prayer first appears in some early Palestinian sources. Cf. *Sinai gr. 959* (11th cent.) (DMITRIEVSKII, *OPISANIE* II, p. 53) and the contemporary Georgian version of CHR (A. Jacob, "Une version géorgienne inédite de la liturgie de saint Jean Chrysostome," *Le Muséon* 77 (1964) 79, 85-86). From these, it apparently entered the monastic diataxes, including Philotheos' version.

24. There is tremendous variety in the formulae which accompany the vesting of the clergy. As with the entrance prayers, no comprehensive study has yet been done. Some indications are given in PETROVSKII, *RÉDACTION SLAVE*; in S. Muretov, *Istoricheskii obzor chinoposledovaniia proskomidii do "Ustava liturgii" konstantinopol'skago patriarkha Filofeiia* (Moscow, 1895); and in DMITRIEVSKII, *BOGOSLUZHENIE V XVI VEKE.*

25. This troparion comes from the office to the Angelic Powers, GOAR, p. 11.

26. These are the "episcopal" prayers about which Nikon complains at the 1654 Council, cf. chapter one, section 3.

27. This formula of absolution from the rite of confession appears as a preparatory prayer already in the 12th century, PETROVSKII, *RÉDACTION SLAVE,* p. 862. On its origin, cf. AL-MAZOV, v. 2, pp. 229-230.

28. This prayer appears here only in the 15th century, PETROVSKII, *RÉDACTION SLAVE,* p. 895. It is originally a prayer of "cleansing from any iniquity." On its origin, cf. ALMAZOV, v. 2, pp. 237-238; appendix, p. 63; v. 3, pp. 219ff.

29. This prayer, found here only in the 15th century, PETROVSKII, *RÉDACTION SLAVE,* p. 895, appears in some early mss. of JAS, cf. B. Ch. Mercier, *La Liturgie de saint Jacques* (=PO 26, Fasc. 2) (Paris, 1946), pp. 248-249. Originally, however, it comes from the rite of confession, as a prayer over the penitent, cf. ALMAZOV, v. 2, pp. 177-179, 198-199. It was used mostly as a prayer of absolution by the bishop over the priest, *ibid.*, pp. 219-227.

30. Neither PETROVSKII, *RÉDACTION SLAVE,* nor DMITRIEVSKII, *BOGOSLUZHENIE V XVI VEKE,* mention this prayer. Judging by its content, it is a prayer of preparation for receiving communion.

31. This is a prayer of blessing over the wine. It appears here in the 15th century, PETROVSKII, *RÉDACTION SLAVE,* p. 895. A Greek text is found in GOAR, p. 553.

32. These changes are discussed by CHERNIAVSKII, *OB IZMENENIIAKH,* pp. 5-192.

33. This troparion is from Matins of Holy (Good) Friday, where it serves as the kathisma of the 15th antiphon, and as the apolytikion (dismissal troparion). It is also found in the Oc-

toechos, as the first kathisma of Wednesday and Friday Matins in tone 4.

34. A troparion from the Hours of Easter Sunday.

35. The development of the prothesis rite has been amply studied. Cf. S. Muretov, *Istoricheskii obzor chinoposledovaniia proskomidii do "Ustava liturgii" konstantinopol'skago patriarkha Filofeia* (Moscow, 1895); and particularly the more recent studies of MANDALÀ and LAURENT.

36. Cf. MANDALÀ, pp. 74-96.

37. On the history of this dismissal, cf. DMITRIEVSKII, *BOGOSLUZHENIE V XVI VEKE*, pp. 99-100. In the 16th century, this practice existed only in the city of Novgorod. At the Stoglav Council, however, it was decided to institute this practice throughout Muscovite Russia—*STOGLAV*, ch. 41, question 12, p. 175.

38. These are enumerated in CHERNIAVSKII, *OB IZMENENIIAKH*, pp. 5-186.

39. The arguments of the Old-Believers and rebuttals to them are to be found in *ibid.*, pp. 6-77. On the many variations in Russian practice, cf. DMITRIEVSKII, *BOGOSLUZHENIE V XVI VEKE*, pp. 84-88.

40. A picture of the new seal is printed in the 1655 Moscow *Sluzhebnik*, p. 188.

41. This, of course, is based on one of the formulae from the prothesis (VII.10).

42. CHERNIAVSKII, *OB IZMENENIIAKH*, p. 80, has a diagram.

43. The arguments of the Old-Believers are spelled out in *ibid.*, pp. 79-116.

44. On the development of bread seals in the Byzantine tradition, cf. G. Galavaris, *Bread and the Liturgy, the Symbolism of Early Christian and Byzantine Bread Stamps* (Madison, Milwaukee, and London: Univ. of Wisconsin Press, 1970). This work is highly unreliable with regard to the history of the liturgy however; cf. the review by R. Taft, *OCP* 40 (1974) 209-210. For illustrations of post-Byzantine Greek seals, see Galavaris, pp. 99-107.

45. *Ibid.*, ρ. 67. The two figures represent contemporary Greek and Russian seals. The Russian seal depicted is identical to the one depicted in Nikon's *Sluzhebnik*. For a comparison of modern Greek and Russian usages, see E.S. Drower, *Water into Wine, a Study of Ritual Idiom in the Middle East* (London: John Murray, 1956), pp. 123-139.

46. Pp. 24, 26.

47. P. 121.

48. GOAR, p. 99.

49. CHERNIAVSKII, *OB IZMENENIIAKH*, p. 147.

50. TREMPELAS, p. 3.

51. MANDALÀ, pp. 138-139.

52. Cf. also GOAR, pp. 71-72; SWAINSON, pp. 105-107.

53. CHERNIAVSKII, *OB IZMENENIIAKH*, pp. 177-186.

54. DMITRIEVSKII, *BOGOSLUZHENIE V XVI VEKE*, pp. 88-90; PETROVSKII, *RÉDACTION SLAVE*, p. 873. All the Greek texts they cite, however, have the word in the singular.

55. Cf. CHERNIAVSKII, *OB IZMENENIIAKH*, pp. 187-191.

56. C.W.H. Lampe, *A Patristic Greek Lexicon* (Oxford: Clarendon Press, 1961), pp. 1107-1108, gives this as the secondary meaning.

57. *Ibid.*, pp. 1107.

58. On the history and development of the Little Entrance, cf. MATEOS, *CÉLÉBRATION*, pp. 71-90.

59. CHERNIAVSKII, *OB IZMENENIIAKH*, pp. 210-216.

60. *Vatic. gr.* 573, cf. KRASNOSEL'TSEV, *MATERIALY*, p. 103.

61. In the 1651 and 1652 Moscow editions, however, the priest faces the altar table, FILARET, *OPYT SLICHENIIA*, p. 88.

62. MATEOS, *CÉLÉBRATION*, pp. 115-118.

63. On the history of this acclamation, cf. *ibid.*, pp. 122-123.

64. DMITRIEVSKII, *BOGOSLUZHENIE V XVI VEKE*, p. 105.

65. SWAINSON, p. 115, note 6.

66. Cf. CHERNIAVSKII, *OB IZMENENIIAKH*, pp. 217-233.

67. DMITRIEVSKII, *BOGOSLUZHENIE V XVI VEKE*, p. 110.

68. Cf. MATEOS, *CÉLÉBRATION*, p. 140; TREMPELAS, pp. 54-55.

69. PETROVSKII, *RÉDACTION SLAVE*, p. 902. Petrovskii does not cite his sources, but I was able to find this in a 14th century *Sluzhebnik, Moscow Synod 346 (950)* (GORSKII-NEVOSTRUEV III, 1, p. 29).

70. ORLOV, p. 85.

71. DMITRIEVSKII, *BOGOSLUZHENIE V XVI VEKE*, p. 110.

72. FILARET, *OPYT SLICHENIIA*, p. 89.

73. Cf. MATEOS, *CÉLÉBRATION*, pp. 141-143.

74. CHERNIAVSKII, *OB IZMENENIIAKH*, pp. 217-218.

75. *Moscow Synod 899*, ORLOV, pp. 85-87, and all the printed Moscow *Sluzhebniks* up to 1652. TREMPELAS, pp. 53-54, does not mention this variant.

76. See for example the rubrics about waiving the aer over the gifts during the recitation of the Creed, TAFT, *GREAT ENTRANCE*, pp. 421-422.

77. TREMPELAS, p. 8. Here, the priest is told to stand behind the altar, in the apse, unless there is insufficient room, in which case he is to stand in front of the altar.

78. On this practice, cf. MATEOS, *CÉLÉBRATION*, pp. 145-146; DMITRIEVSKII, *BOGOSLUZHENIE V XVI VEKE*, pp. 109-110; ORLOV, p. 88.

79. On the origin and development of the ektene, see MATEOS, *CÉLÉBRATION*, pp. 148-156. On its Greek variants, cf. TREMPELAS, pp. 57-61. On its Slavonic redaction, see ORLOV, pp. 88-103. On the variants in the Kievan and Ruthenian books, cf. HUCULAK, pp. 293-302. Only this litany is properly called the *ektene*. Among the Slavs, the word *ekteniia* has come to mean any litany. We use the term *ektene* in its original sense.

80. Cf. *DEIANIE 1654*, ff. 16-16v, and chapter one, section 3, above.

81. MATEOS, *CÉLÉBRATION*, pp. 150-152. Mateos cites *Grott. Gb. VII (324)* (10th cent.), *Paris Coislin 214* (12th cent.), *Sinai 1040* (12th cent.), *et. al.*

82. This ancient prayer, used today in funeral and memorial services, is found already in the 4th century, where it appears as an inscription on an Egyptian tomb dating to 344—cf. H. Leclerq, "Âme," DACL I, l, 1531-1534. Cf also *Apostolic Constitutions* VII, 41 (F.X.,Funk, ed., *Didascalia et Constitutiones Apostolorum*, vol. 1 [Padeborn, 1905], pp. 550-552). The prayer also appears in the 8th century codex *Barberini 336*—cf. the description of A. Strittmatter, "The 'Barberinum S. Marci' of Jacques Goar," EL 47 (1933) 364, No. 295. On the use of this prayer in the funeral service, cf. V. Bruni, *I funerali di un sacerdote nel rito bizantino secondo gli eucologi manoscritti di lingua greca* (Jerusalem: Franciscan Printing Press, 1972), pp. 146-158.

83. A sweet dish, traditionally used in both Greek and Slavic lands to commemorate the dead, reminiscent of the ancient *refrigerium*, or meal honoring the departed. For the Greek text of the prayer of blessing the *kolyva*, cf. GOAR, p. 524.

84. GOAR, p. 424.

85. Cf. DMITRIEVSKII, *BOGOSLUZHENIE V XVI VEKE*, pp. 111-112. On this litany in Ukrainian usage, cf. HUCULAK, pp. 298-302.

86. *Deianie 1654*, f. 19v.

87. See the discussion on this council in chapter one, section 3.

88. There are a number of detailed studies on the antimension. The most recent and complete is that of IZZO. Cf. also K. Nikol'skii, *Ob antiminsakh pravoslavnoi russkoi tserkvi* (St Petersburg, 1872); A. Petrovskii, "Antimins," *Pravoslavnaia Bogoslovskaia Entsiklopediia* I (Petrograd, 1900) 797-809; and A. Raes, "Antimension, Tablit, Tabot," *POC* 1 (1951) 59-65.

89. IZZO, pp. 103-104, 114.

90. See the discussion on this in K. Nikol'skii, *Ob antiminsakh pravoslavnoi russkoi tserkvi* (St Petersburg, 1872), pp. 121-125.

91. PAISIOS OF CONSTANTINOPLE, p. 563.

92. This development was connected to the interpretation of the Great Entrance and deposition of gifts as the funeral cortege and burial of Christ. See TAFT, *GREAT ENTRANCE*, pp. 216-219.

93. IZZO, pp. 37-38; and cf. PAUL OF ALEPPO, *ChOIDR* 1898(3) pt. 3, 170.

94. Cf. chapter one, section 5. above; PAUL OF ALEPPO, *ibid.*

4

The Liturgy Of The Eucharist

1. The Great Entrance

The following is the outline of the Great Entrance in the Nikonian and
pre-Nikonian editions:

1655 (Moscow)	1646 (Moscow)
[XIII. THE GREAT ENTRANCE][1]	
	1.B. The deacon enters the sanctuary, bows 3x before the altar table, and asks forgiveness of the priest. He then takes the censer and incense. The priest blesses it, saying the prayer of incense.
	The deacon incenses the altar table, and the holy things [on the prothesis table], and the entire sanctuary, silently reciting Ps 50(51).
2. While the Cherubic Hymn is being sung, the priest says the Prayer of the Cherubic Hymn: *Niktozhe dostoin…*[2]	
3.A.	3.B. After the incensation, the deacon reverently stands to the left of the altar table and waits for the prayer to end.
When the prayer is finished they say the Cherubic Hymn 3x, bowing once after each conclusion:	When it is finished, they each say the Cherubic Hymn to themselves, as is the custom in the universal church:
Izhe kheruvimy…[3]	

1655 (Moscow)	1646 (Moscow)
1.A. The deacon then takes the censer, adds incense, and approaches the priest. Receiving the blessing from him, he incenses around the altar table, the entire sanctuary, and the priest. He recites Ps 50(51) and, if he wishes, the penitential troparia,[4] together with the priest.	
	4.B. They bow 3x before the altar table, saying to themselves: *Bozhe ochisti mia greshnago i pomilui mia. Sozdavyi mia gospodi pomilui mia. Bezchisla sogreshikh gospodi prostimia.* [=II.2.B; VI.1.B] And they do the rite of forgiveness before the altar table. They kiss the altar table
5.A. They go to the prothesis table, the deacon going first, incense the gifts, praying to themselves: *Bozhe ochisti mia greshnago* 3x.	5.B and go to the prothesis table. The priest takes the censer and incenses the gifts and the deacon. He [the priest] gives the censer to the deacon, who incenses the priest.
6.A. [The deacon] says to the priest: *Vozmi vladyko.*	6.B. and [the deacon] says: *Gospodu pomolimsia. Vozmi vladyko sviataia.*
7.A. The priest takes the aer and places it on his [the deacon's] left shoulder saying:	7.B. The priest takes the aer and places it on the deacon's right shoulder, saying:
Vozmite ruki vasha vo sviataia... (Ps 133(134):2)	
8.A. Taking the holy discos, [the priest] places it on the head of the deacon, who also holds the censer with one of his fingers. He himself [the priest] takes the chalice,	8.B. Taking the holy discos, [the priest] places it on the head of the deacon, who takes it with great care. The priest takes the holy chalice,
9.A. and they go out through the north side, preceded by candlebearers; and they go around the church, praying and saying:	9.B. and they perform the Great Entrance. The deacon goes first, holding the censer in one finger of his right hand, and the discos. He walks erect, without bowing, preceded by a candlebearer. Entering the church, they say to themselves, first the deacon, then the priest:

1655 (Moscow)	1646 (Moscow)
[10. Commemorations][5]	
10.A.i. *Blagochestiveishago gosudaria nashego, tsaria...* [Commemoration of the tsar and his family] **10.A.ii.** *Sviateishago* name, *arkhiepiskopa moskovskago...*	
10.A.iii. *Vsekh vas pravoslavnykh khristian...*	**10.B.iii.** *Vsekh vas da pomianet gospod' bog...* And standing opposite the west doors [i.e. facing the people], they say: *Da pomianet gospod' bog vsekh vas...* And turning to the south [left] side *Vsekh vas da pomianet gospod' bog...* **10.B.i.** If the tsar is present, they say: *Da pomianet gospod' bog blagorodie tvoe...* **10.B.ii.** If a bishop is present, they also say: *Da pomianet gospod' bog sviatitel'stvo tvoe...* **10.B.iv.** In a monastery, if the hegumen is present: *Da pomianet gospod' bog sviashchenstvo tvoe...*
10.A.v. This is said if only one priest is celebrating without a deacon, and whether the tsar is there or not. If there are many concelebrating priests, they say the following: First priest: for the tsar. Second priest: for the tsarina. Third priest: for the tsar's son. Fourth priest: for the tsar's daughter. Fifth priest: for the Patriarch of Moscow. Sixth priest: *Vsekh vas...*	
11.A. Entering through the holy doors, the deacon stands to the right. When the priest wants to enter, the deacon says to him: *Da pomianet gospod' bog sviashchenstvo tvoe...* And the priest says to him: *Da pomianet gospod' bog sviashchenno diakonstvo tvoe...*	**11.B.** Entering through the holy doors, the priest says to himself quietly: *Blagosloven griadyi vo imia gospodne, bog gospod' i iavisia* name (Ps 117(118):26a, 27a)[6]

1655 (Moscow)	1646 (Moscow)
[Deposition of the Gifts]	
12.A. And the priest places the holy chalice on the holy table. Taking the discos from the head of the deacon, he places it on the holy table saying: 　i. *Blagoobraznyi iosif...* 　ii. *V grobe plotski...* 　iii. *Iako zhivonosets...*[9]	12.B. And the priest places the holy chalice on the holy table. Then he takes the holy discos from the head of the deacon and places it on the holy table, close to and to the left of the holy chalice.
13.A. Then taking the veils off the discos and chalice, he puts them to one side of the altar table. Removing the aer from the deacon's shoulder, he incenses it and covers the the gifts with it, saying: *Blagoobraznyi iosif...*[10] [=12.A.i]	13.B. The priest removes the veils and puts them on the holy altar, and taking the aer, he covers the gifts, saying: *Blagoobraznyi iosif...*
14. The priest takes the censer from the deacon and incenses the gifts 3x, saying: *Oublazhi gospodi...* (Ps 50(51):20–21).	
	15.B. Then they bow 3x to the floor, saying to themselves: *Bozhe ochisti mia greshnago...* [=II.2.B and XIII.4.B] Then, crossing their hands across their chests, they do the forgiveness,[11] as written above [XIII.4.B].

Not surprisingly, the Old-Believers have numerous complaints regarding the many changes in the Great Entrance rites.[12] And, once more, the Nikonian version is based almost exclusively on the 1602 Venetian *Euchologion*. The pre-Nikonian version, of course, also has antecedents in Greek practice.[13] The main difference between the two is that the 1655 edition has added commemorations during the entrance and troparia at the deposition of the gifts on the altar. We have already discussed the changes in the text of the Cherubic Hymn.

i. The Commemorations

The 1646 version has only one commemoration "for all," which is repeated silently three times (10.B.iii). Only if the tsar, bishop, or monastic superior is present are there any additional commemorations. The Nikonian text, however, contains commemorations for the tsar and his family

(10.A.i), the patriarch (10.A.ii), as well as "for all" (10.A.iii), which are done whether the notables are present or not. These commemorations, which interrupt the flow of the Cherubic Hymn, are a very late addition to the liturgy. They first appear in the 12-13th centuries, originally just one commemoration for all the people.[14] At first, the commemoration was done silently and did not interrupt the Cherubic Hymn.[15] Later, the emperor and the patriarch were also commemorated, but only if they were present, as in the 14th century *De officiis*.[16] In the 15-16th centuries, some of the commemorations came to be chanted aloud.[17] This is what we find in the pre-Nikonian Moscow *Sluzhebnik*: a general commemoration is said silently, but if the tsar or patriarch is present, each is commemorated aloud, individually. The final stage of this evolution has multiple commemorations for the rulers, bishops, and other classes, all said out loud.[18] This is what we find in the Nikonian edition. Following the Venetian edition, the 1655 Moscow *Sluzhebnik* also adds commemorations by the deacon and the priest, for each other, as they reenter the sanctuary. These are already found in the 12-13th century Diataxis *Ethnike bibl. 662*, as well as in Philotheos' Diataxis in the 14th century.[19] The 1604 Striatin *Sluzhebnik*, as well as the Kievan editions of 1629 and 1639, also contain this exchange.

Among early Slavic printed editions, the 1604 Striatin *Sluzhebnik* has only the general commemoration "for all." The rubrics do not specify whether this is said aloud, but the printed text of the Cherubic Hymn has a new *incipit* at *Iako da tsaria*, which strongly suggests that the hymn was interrupted for the intercession at the entrance. The 1629 and 1639 Kievan editions contain intercessions for the rulers, the bishop, and the monastic superior, and the rubrics specify that they are said aloud.[20] Thus the South-Slavic editions, also patterned after contemporary Greek euchologies, show the same evolution as the Muscovite books.

ii. The Deposition Troparia

In the 1646 *Sluzhebnik*, the priest says nothing as he takes the discos from the deacon and puts it on the altar (12.B). Only when he covers the gifts with the aer does he recite the Holy Friday troparion (13.B). This pre-Nikonian edition gives the longer recension of this troparion, found only in the *Octoechos* and the *Pentecostarion*. Among Slavic sources, only the 1583 Vilna and all the pre-Nikonian Moscow *Sluzhebniks* contain this longer recension.[21] Among Greek sources, the Philothean Diataxis and all the Greek printed editions give the Triodion version of this troparion, though some later Greek texts indicate that the longer recension, with its resurrectional conclusion, is to be said on Sundays.[22]

In the Nikonian edition, the priest recites three different troparia at the deposition of the discos (12.A). All these troparia speak of Christ in the tomb, and hence are related to the traditional Byzantine mystagogical interpretation of the Great Entrance as the funeral cortege of Christ. The first of these troparia, "The Noble Joseph," appears already in the 14th century. The latter two are among a group of troparia, which makes its appearance at the deposition only in the 16th century. The number, order, and exact placement of these troparia vary widely in the sources.[23] Among printed editions, the 1604 Striatin *Sluzhebnik* has only "The Noble Joseph," which is said at the covering of the gifts with the aer (13.A). The Kievan editions in 1629 and 1639 have only the second two (12.A.ii–iii), but *V grobe plotski* (12.A.ii) is said at the deposition of the chalice, and *Iako zhivonosets* (12.A.iii) at the deposition of the discos. Only in the Venetian *Euchologion*, including the 1602 edition, do we find exactly the same arrangement as in Nikon's *Sluzhebnik*.[24]

2. The Dialogue after the Entrance

One of the most curious changes brought about by Nikon's reform is in the dialogue between the priest and deacon, immediately following the deposition of the gifts. The texts read as follows:

1655 (Moscow)	1646 (Moscow)
[XIV. THE "ORATE FRATRES" DIALOGUE][25]	
1.A. [The priest] lowers his phelonion, bows his head, and says to the deacon: *Pomiani mia brate i sosluzhiteliu.* The deacon [says] to him: *Du pomianet gospod' bog sviashchenstvo tvoe vo tsarstvii svoem.*	

1655 (Moscow)	1646 (Moscow)
2.A. Then the deacon himself bows his head, holding his orarion with three fingers of his right hand, and says to the priest: *Pomolisia o mne vladyko sviatyi* And the priest: *Dukh sviatyi naidet na tia i sila vyshniago osenit tia* (Lk 1:35). And the deacon: *Toizhde dukh sodeistvuet nam, vsia dni zhivota nashego.*	2.B. The deacon incenses the priest, saying: *Dukh sviatyi naidet na tia, i sila vyshniago osenit tia.*
3.A. Then again [the deacon]: *Pomiani mia vladyko sviatyi.* And the priest: *Da pomianet tia gospod' bog vo tsarstvii svoem, vsegda nyne i prisno i vo veki vekov.* Deacon: *Amin.*	3.B. Again, the deacon says: *Pomiani mia vladyko sviatyi.* Priest: *Pomianet tia gospod' bog vo tsarstvii svoem, vsegda i nyne i prisno i voveki vekom.* Deacon: *Amin.*

This dialogue is one of the preparatory rites for the anaphora which is to follow, and has nothing to do with the Great Entrance which has just been completed. This preparation was, at one time, more important than the transfer of gifts (later called the "Great Entrance") which preceded it and, finally, overshadowed it.[26] We need not repeat here the exhaustive studies on this dialogue by Raes[27] and, more recently, by Taft;[28] but we shall base our remarks on their conclusions.

The 1646 edition reflects a more primitive, simple, and *correct* version of the "orate fratres" dialogue, as it is found in the Constantinopolitan recension of the liturgy in the 12th century, and later in the Diataxis of Philotheos. Part 1 (1.A) is absent, and it is the deacon who addresses the chief celebrant with the angelic words from Lk 1:35 ("The Holy Spirit will descend upon you, and the power of the Most High will overshadow you").[29] This is the form in which the dialogue appears in the 1583 Vilna and in all the pre-Nikonian Moscow *Sluzhebniks.*[30]

The 1655 Nikonian text is quite different. A preliminary exchange (1.A.) is added, part 2 (2.A) is turned around, so that the words of Lk 1:35 are now addressed by the priest to the deacon(!), and the deacon is given a new response. This version of the dialogue appears in the 1602 Venice

Euchologion, in the 1604 Striatin and in the Moghilan *Sluzhebniks* of 1629 and 1639 in Kiev. The first part (1.A) is to be found in no Greek or Slavic mss., and first appears in the 1571 Venice *Euchologion.* Taft and Raes see it merely as an extension of the commemorations exchanged between the priest and deacon, as they enter the sanctuary at the Great Entrance (XIII.11.A).[31] From the Venetian editions, it enters first South-Slavic practice and then, through Nikon's reform, Muscovite practice as well.

The change in part 2 (2.A), however, is more peculiar. In the vast majority of mss., it is the deacon who prays for the descent of the Spirit upon the priest. In only a few sources, all of them from the 15th century and later, are the priest's and deacon's parts reversed.[32] How did this confusion occur? Originally, the dialogue took place between the bishop and his concelebrants. The chief celebrant would bow to the presbyters on either side and then ask for their prayers. They, in turn, would respond with the traditional verse from Lk 1:35. A difficulty arose, however, at a presbyteral liturgy, where the priest celebrated either alone, or with a deacon. Either the dialogue had to be omitted, or the priest had to pray for the descent of the Spirit upon himself, or the deacon had to take the role of the concelebrants. If the third option was taken, however, then the priest would address the deacon as "master" (δέσποτα)—an incongruity. Yet this is exactly what we find in some sources, including Philotheos' Diataxis.[33] This awkward situation led to several further solutions. The first was simply to drop the celebrant's request altogether; this is exactly what we find in the 1646 Moscow edition, where part 2.B contains only the gospel verse, addressed by the deacon to the priest. Another solution was to reverse the roles. The deacon, addressing the priest as "Master," asked for his prayers, and the priest prayed for the descent of the Spirit upon the deacon![34] Thus one incongruity led to an even greater one. This is the redaction which entered first the Venetian *Euchologia,* then Ukrainian editions, and finally, in 1655, the Moscow service books. Only in the *Chinovnik (Archieratikon)* did the Muscovites keep the proper form of the dialogue, where the bishop asks all his concelebrants to pray for him, and they all reply with the text from Lk 1:35.[35] These two practices coexist in the Russian books to this day.

3. The Kiss of Peace and the Creed

There are several differences between the Nikonian *Sluzhebnik* and the earlier Muscovite books at the Kiss of Peace and the Creed. First, the earlier editions all contain a "Prayer before the Kiss of Peace" (*Gospodi isuse khriste bozhe nash, liubvi tvorche...*), which is absent both in the Venetian editions and in Nikon's *Sluzhebnik*. Taft indicates that the use of this prayer here is a Slavic peculiarity, which entered Slavic tradition under the influence of JAS, which had such a prayer.[36] The text of the Slavic prayer seems to be a reworking of a Greek prayer for the reconciliation of enemies.[37] Because this prayer is absent in the Venetian edition, Nikon's correctors remove it.

At the Kiss of Peace, the rubrics in the pre-Nikonian *Sluzhebniks* indicate that the clergy kiss each other "on the mouth." The Nikonian version, however, instructs the clergy to kiss one another on the shoulder. The Greek books are silent on this matter. The pre-Nikonian Moscow books preserve a practice which had gradually disappeared among the Greeks, as sources witness from the 11th century on.[38] The Venetian editions say nothing about how the kiss is exchanged, but Nikon's correctors specify that the kiss is to be made on the shoulders of the concelebrant, in order to bring Russian practice in line with the then-current Greek usage.

The wrath of the Old-Believers is focused particularly on the changes in the text of the Creed of Nicea-Constantinople.[39] The following is the text of the Creed in its pre- and post-Nikonian recensions. Changes made by Nikon's correctors are underlined.

1655 (Moscow)	1640 (Moscow)[40]
[XV. THE CREED]	
1.A. *Veruiu vo edinago boga, ottsa vsederzhitelia, tvortsa nebu i zemli, vidimym zhe vsem i nevidimym.*	1.B. *Veruiu vo edinago boga ottsa vsederzhitelia, tvortsa nebu i zemli, vidimym zhe vsem i nevidimym.*
2.A. *I vo edinago gospoda <u>iisusa</u> khrista syna <u>bozhia</u> edinorodnago, izhe ot ottsa rozhdennago <u>prezhde</u> vsekh vek. Sveta ot sveta, boga istinna ot boga istinna. Rozhdenna, ne <u>sotvorenna,</u> edinosushchna ottsu, imzhe vsia bysha.*	2.B. *I vo edinago gospoda <u>isusa</u> khrista syna <u>bozhiia,</u> edinorodnago, izhe ot ottsa rozhdennago <u>prezhe</u> vsekh vek. Sveta ot sveta, bogo istinna, otboga istinna. Rozhdenna <u>a nesotvorena,</u> edinosushchna ottsu, imzhe vsia bysha.*

1655 (Moscow)	1640 (Moscow)[40]
3.A. *Nas radi chelovek, i nashego radi spaseniia, s"shedshago s nebes, i voplotivshagosia ot dukha sviata, i marii devy, i vochelovech'shasia.*	3.B. *Nas radi chelovek, i nashego radi spaseniia soshedshago s nebes, i voplotivshagosia ot dukha sviata, i marii devy vochelovech'shasia.*
4.A. *Raspiatago zhe za ny, pri pontiistem pilate.I stradavsha i pogrebena,*	4.B. *Raspiatago zany pri pontiistem pilate. Stradavsha i pogrebena,*
5.A. *i voskresshago v tretii den' po pisaniem.*	5.B. *i voskresshago v tretii den' po pisaniikh.*
6.A. *I vozshedshago na nebesa, i sediashcha odesnuiu ottsa,*	6.B. *I vozshedshago na nebesa, i sediashcha odesnuiu ottsa,*
7.A. *i paki griadushchago so slavoiu, suditi zhivym, i mertvym, egozhe tsarstviiu ne budet kontsa.*	7.B. *i paki griadushchago so slavoiu, suditi zhivym i mertvym, egozhe tsarstviiu nest' kontsa.*
8.A. *I v dukha sviatago, gospoda, zhivotvoriashchago, izhe ot ottsa iskhodiashchago, izhe so ottsem, i synom s"pokloniaema, i s"slavima, glagolavshago proroki.*	8.B. *I v dukha sviatago gospoda istinnago i zhivotvoriashchago, izhe ot ottsa iskhodiashchago, izhe so ottsem i s synom s pokloniaema i s slavima, glagolavshago proroki,*
9.A. *Vo edinu sviatuiu sobornuiu i apostol'skuiu tserkov'.*	9.B. *I vo edinu sviatuiu sobornuiu i apostol'skuiu tserkov'.*
10.A. *Ispoveduiu edino kreshchenie vo ostavlenie grekhov.*	10.B. *Ispoveduiu edino kreshchenie, vo ostavlenie grekhov.*
11.A. *Chaiu voskreseniia mertvykh,*	11.A. *Chaiu voskreseniia mertvym,*
12.A. *i zhizni budushchago veka, amin'.*	12.B. *i zhizni budushchago veka, amin'.*

The 1655 text is taken from the Acts of the 1654 Council. The new translation is the work of Epifanii Slavinetskii.[41] All but one of the changes are merely stylistic, and they need not concern us here. The one significant change is in the eighth article, which refers to the Holy Spirit. The pre-Nikonian text adds the word *istinnago* ("true"): *I v dukha sviatago gospoda istinnago i zhivotvoriashchago* ("And in the Holy Spirit, the Lord, *true* and the giver of life"). The Old-Believers complain about the removal of this adjective from the text of the Creed. In fact, however, the word is an interpolation, and this is one of the few cases where the

Nikonian reformers actually corrected the old books in any real sense.

The word *istinnago* first appears in the eighth article of the Creed in the 14th century. At first, it replaced the word *gospoda* ("Lord"), so it was a mistranslation of the Greek κύριον.[43] Gezen suggests that this curious translation may have been influenced by the gospel text in Jn 15:26 ("The Spirit of truth, who proceeds from the Father...").[44] Though the adjective *istinnago* at first replaced the word *gospoda,* by the 15th century some sources combine the two, and the phrase *gospoda istinnago* ("true Lord") appears.[45] In the late 16th century, the majority of Russian mss. contained this variant in the Creed, so it is hardly surprising that this was the reading chosen by the pre-Nikonian Muscovite editors. A number of 16th and 17th century service books outside Moscow, however, retained either the original reading, or have the word *istinnago* replacing *gospoda.*[46] The other changes, which do not alter the meaning of the text in any way, are listed by Gezen.[47]

In addition to the changes in the Kiss of Peace and the Creed, the Nikonian reformers also introduced some changes in the removal of the veil from the gifts, before the anaphora.

1655 (Moscow)	1646 (Moscow)
[XVI. REMOVAL OF THE AER]	
1.A. [As the Creed begins,] the priest raises the aer and holds it over the holy gifts. If other priests are concelebrating, they also raise the holy aer and hold it over the gifts, wave it, and say the Creed to themselves, just as the people.	1.B. [As the Creed begins,] the priest raises the aer above his head and holds it over the holy gifts, saying the Creed silently. If there are concelebrating priests and deacons, they too raise the aer over the holy gifts and also recite the Creed with the people.
2.A. [After the Creed,] the priest removes the aer from the gifts, kisses it, and places it to one side.	2.B. [After the Creed,] all kiss the aer, each saying to himself *Sviatyi bozhe, sviatyi krepkii...* And they place the aer on the holy altar table.

There are two changes: first, the new edition introduces the practice of waving the aer over the gifts; second, the recitation of the Trisagion disappears in the Nikonian text. The practice of holding the aer over the gifts during the recitation of the Creed appears by the 15th century, as witnessed by Symeon of Thessalonika.[48] The Trisagion appears at the removal of the veil, in the Byzantine tradition, in the 12th century.[49] The practice of waving the aer over the gifts while removing it, probably originated in Syria, a custom witnessed to there as early as the sixth century.[50] When, in the 15th century, the Byzantines began to lift up the aer *before* the Creed, some Greeks probably began to wave it at the same time, during the recitation of the Creed. The first evidence for this is in the 15th century codex *Sinai Gr. 986.*[51] This is still the practice we find in Nikon's edition. The rubrics in the 1655 *Sluzhebnik* still betray the earlier practice: the directions after the Creed (2.A.) instruct the priest to remove the aer from the gifts, even though the aer has already been removed at the beginning of the Creed. As for the Trisagion, Nikon's correctors suppress it because it is absent in the 1602 Venice *Euchologion.* It was kept, however, in the *Chinovnik* (Pontifical) approved by the 1667 Moscow Council, where the bishop recites it silently as he kisses the gifts before the Creed.[52]

4. The Anaphora

Not even the anaphora escapes the "correctors'" attention. Once again, most of the changes are stylistic, and these need not detain us. Significant changes, however, are made in the opening dialogue, in the rubrics at the words of institution and the epiclesis, as well as in the intercessions.

i. The Opening Dialogue

There are two interesting changes in the dialogue with which the anaphora begins. The texts read as follows:

1655 (Moscow)	1652 (Moscow)
[XVII. OPENING DIALOGUE]	
1.A. Deacon: *Stanem dobre, stanem so strakhom, vonmem sviatoe voznoshenie v mire prinositi.*	1.B. Deacon: *Stanem dobre, stanem sostrakhom, vonmem sviatoe voznoshenie, vo smirenii prinositi.*
2.A. Choir: *Milost' mira, zhertvu khvalenia.*	2.B. People: *Milost' mir zhertvu i penie.*

1655 (Moscow)	1652 (Moscow)
3. Priest: *Blagodat' gospoda nashego…*	
4.A. Choir: *I so dukhom tvoim.*	4.B. People: *I sodukhom tvoim.*
5.A. Priest: *Gore imeim serdtsa.*	5.B. Priest: *Gore imeem serdtsa.*
6. Priest: *Blagodarim gospoda.*	
7.A. Choir: *Dostoino i pravedno est', poklaniatisia ottsu, i synu, i sviatomu dukhu, troitse edinosushnei i nerazdelnei.*	7.B. *Dostoino i pravedno.*

The change in the diaconal admonition, from *vo smirenii* (1.B) to *v mire* (1.A), is of no significance; it is merely a stylistic change. The change in the response is more interesting. The 1652 text reads: "Mercy, peace, sacrifice and singing" (2.B), with each word in the accusative case. In the 1655 rendition, the first and third words are in the accusative, the other two in the genitive. The 1646 text has yet a third rendition, this time all in the nominative case: *Milost' mir zhertva i penie*. Thus we find three variant recensions in the Muscovite service books in less than a decade! Yet these variations in Russian sources reflect similar variations in the Greek sources.[53] The primitive Greek rendition of this text, Taft has demonstrated, is Ἔλεον, εἰρήνην, θυσίαν αἰνέσεως ("mercy, peace, sacrifice of praise"). Eventually, however, a variant reading, Ἔλεον εἰρήνης, θυσίαν αἰνέσεως ("mercy of peace, sacrifice of praise") came to predominate. This text was used in all the printed Greek euchologies and is the *textus receptus* today, even though "mercy of peace" makes no sense.[54] Among Slavic editions, the variations continued up to the Nikonian reform, when the current Greek text served as a model for the new edition. The two versions in the 1646 and 1652 *Sluzhebniks* offer peculiar variants of the text (1646: *zhertva i penie;* 1652: *zhertvu i penie*). The translation of the Greek word αἰνέσεως as *penie* ("singing") is technically correct, but is arguably not the best choice. But the use of the conjunction *i* ("and"), as well as of the nominative, or accusative case for the word *penie,* is extremely odd and has no known Greek antecedent.[55] This variant first appears in 15th century Slavic sources,[56] and is used in all the printed Moscow *Sluzhebniks,* from the *editio princeps* in 1602 until 1652. These editions, however, retain the more ancient and correct recension of the first half of the phrase Milost' mir ("Mercy, peace"), later changed in the Nikonian edition.

The second major change made in the pre-anaphoral dialogue by the reformers is the use of the expanded version of *Dostoino i pravedno* ("Αξιον καὶ δίκαιον). The Old-Believers complain about the addition,[57] showing that the longer form was not used in Russian practice before the reform. All the pre-Nikonian service books in Moscow contain the short recension. The 1604 Striatin edition is the first Slavic edition to have the longer version in both CHR and BAS. The 1629 and 1639 Kiev *Sluzhebniks* have the short recension for CHR, the long one for BAS. This poses something of a problem, for it could well be that the so-called "short recension" is, in fact, simply the incipit of the people's response. This is common in both Greek and Slavic euchologies, which are intended for use by clergy, not by lay people. In Moscow, however, it would appear that the short recension was indeed the rule prior to the Nikonian reform. Two pieces of evidence strongly favor this conclusion: first, the Old-Believers complain about this change, as we mentioned above; second, the longer text appears in only one 17th century Slavic ms., *Sofia 903*, before the Nikonian reform.[58] Among the Greeks, the expanded version appears earlier, and the longer redaction is found already in Doucas' *editio princeps* (Rome, 1526). Following the 1602 *Euchologion* and the 1604 Striatin Sluzhebnik, the Moscow correctors used the expanded version for both CHR and BAS.

ii. The Institution Narrative

Up to this point in the Nikonian edition, all the rubrics for CHR and BAS have been identical. At the words of institution, however, we find a curious divergence. The pre- and post-Nikonian texts of CHR read as follows:

1602 (Venice)	1655 (Moscow)	1646 (Moscow)
[XVIII.A. INSTITUTION NARRATIVE (CHR)]		
1. [No rubrics for CHR]		
2. Λάβετε, φάγετε . . . Ὁ χορός· ᾽Αμήν.	2. *Priimite, iadite...* The choir: *Amin.*	2. *Priimite, iadite...* The people: *Amin.*

1602 (Venice)	1655 (Moscow)	1646 (Moscow)
3.A. Τούτου δὲ λεγομένου, δεικνύει τῷ ἱερεῖ ὁ διάκονος τὸν ἅγιον δίσκον, κρατῶν καὶ τὸ ὡράριον τοῖς τρισὶ δακτύλοις τῆς δεξιᾶς· ὁμοίως καὶ ὅταν λέγει ὁ ἱερεὺς τό· Πίετε ἐξ αὐτοῦ πάντες, συνδεικνύει καὶ αὐτὸς τὸ ἅγιον ποτήριον.	**3.A.** As this is said, the deacon shows the holy discos to the priest, holding his orarion with three fingers of his right hand. Similarly, when the priest says "Drink of this, all of you," he also points with him to the holy cup.	**3.B.** Saying this, the priest points to the holy discos with his right hand. The deacon points with his orarion and says *amin*.⁵⁹
4. Ὁ ἱερεὺς μυστικῶς· Ὁμοίως καὶ ποτήριον μετὰ τὸ δειπνῆσαι λέγων·	**4.** The priest says silently: *Podobne i chashu povecheri glagolia*	**4.** The priest says silently: *Podobne i chashu povecheri glagolia*
5. Ἐκφώνως·	**5.** Exclamation:	**5.** Exclamation:
6. Πίετε ἐξ αὐτοῦ πάντες . . . . Ὁ χορός· Ἀμήν.	**6.** *Piite ot neia vsi...* Choir: *Amin.*	**6.** *Pite ot neia vsi...* People: *Amin.*
		7.B. Saying this, the priest points to the holy cup with his hand. And the deacon also points to the cup with his orarion.

Except for the wording of the rubrics, there is no substantial difference between the two Moscow versions. The rubric (3.A) in the 1655 text is an exact translation of the Venetian text. Even the ambiguity, as to whether the priest also points to the paten, remains in the Nikonian text. This demonstrates the close dependence of Nikon's *Sluzhebnik* on the 1602 Venetian edition, because the 1604 Striatin and the Kievan *Sluzhebniks* have totally different rubrics here, rubrics which have aroused considerable controversy.

The same moment in BAS is quite different:

1602 (Venice)	1655 (Moscow)	1646 (Moscow)
[XVIII.B. INSTITUTION NARRATIVE (BAS)]		
1.A. Ὁ ἱερεὺς κλίνει τὴν κεφαλήν, αἴρων τὴν δεξιὰν αὐτοῦ μετὰ εὐλαβείας, εὐλογεῖ τὸν ἅγιον ἄρτον, ἐκφώνως λέγων·	**1.A.** The priest bows his head, raises his right hand with reverence, blesses the holy bread, [and] exclaims, saying:	
2. Ἔδωκε τοῖς ἁγίοις . . . Ὁ χορὸς ψάλλει· Ἀμήν.	**2.** *Dast sviatym svoim...* Choir: *Amin.*	**2.** *Dast sviatym svoim...* People: *Amin.*
3.A. Τότε ὁ ἱερεὺς καὶ ὁ διάκονος τὰ αὐτὰ κἀνταῦθα, ὡς ἐν τῷ Χρυσοστόμῳ.	**3.A.** The priest and deacon do the same here as in the Liturgy of Chrysostom.	**3.B.** The priest points to the holy discos with his right hand. The deacon similarly points [to the discos] with his orarion.
4. Ὁ ἱερεὺς μυστικῶς· Ὁμοίως καὶ τὸ ποτήριον...	**4.** The priest silently: *Podobne i chashu...*	**4.** The priest silently: *Podobne i chashu...*
5.A. Ἐκφώνως ὁ ἱερεύς, τὴν χεῖρα ἔχων ἄνωθεν μετὰ εὐλαβείας καὶ εὐλογῶν, λέγει·	**5.A.** The priest exclaims, holding his hand above [the gifts] with reverence, and blessing says:	**5.B.** Exclamation:
6. Ἔδωκε τοῖς ἁγίοις αὐτοῦ μαθηταῖς . . . Ὁ χορὸς ψάλλει· Ἀμήν.	**6.** *Dast sviatym svoim ouchenikom...* Choir: *Amin.*	**6.** *Dast sviatym svoim ouchenikom...* People: *Amin.*
		7.B. The priest points to the holy cup. And the deacon similarly points [to the cup] with his orarion.

Here again, the Nikonian text is an exact translation of the Greek text. Even the inconsistent rubric, instructing the priest and deacon to do the same as in CHR (XVIII.B.3.A), is kept exactly as it appears in the Venetian text. This is another evident case of conflicting rubrics being superimposed. The 1604 Striatin *Sluzhebnik,* unlike the Nikonian and Venetian text, has virtually identical rubrics in both CHR and BAS:

[XVIII.C. INSTITUTION NARRATIVE (1604 Striatin *Sluzhebnik*)]	
CHR	**BAS**
1.A. And [the priest] bows his head with humility, raises his right hand, points over the holy bread, and blesses it, saying:	1.B. The priest bows his head, raises his right hand with fear, blesses the holy bread, [and] exclaims, saying:
2.A. *Priimite i iadite...* Choir: *Amin'.*	2.B. *Dast sviatym svoim ouchenikom...* Choir: *Amin'.*
3.A. And the deacon points to the holy discos with his orarion, [holding it][60] with three fingers of his right hand.	3.B. The priest and the deacon do the same here, as in the Liturgy of John Chrysostom.
5.A. Then he again raises his right hand over the holy cup and blesses it, saying aloud:	5.B. The priest exclaims, raising his hand with fear, and as he blesses says:
6.A. *Piite ot neia vsi...* Choir: *Amin'.*	6.B. *Dast sviatym svoim ouchenikom...* Choir: *Amin'.*
7.A. The deacon also points to the holy cup.	

It is clear that, except for a few stylistic differences,[61] BAS of the 1655 Moscow agrees completely with BAS in the 1604 Striatin *Sluzhebnik*. But for CHR, as we saw, the Nikonian editors chose to follow the Greek text from the 1602 Venice *Euchologion.* The Kievan editions in 1620, 1629, and 1639 follow the 1604 redaction, though in the books published by Peter Moghila (1629, 1639), the rubrics become much more specific and latinized.[62] These rubrical developments have sparked intense controversy. The issue, of course, is the moment of consecration. In a recent article, N. Uspenskii, the Russian liturgical scholar, sharply criticizes the introduction of these new rubrics into the Muscovite books.[63] In doing this, he is but repeating statements made by Dmitrievskii half a century earlier.[64]

Dmitrievskii has traced the source of these rubrics, and we present his conclusions here. The instructions for the priest to bless the gifts at the words of institution first appear in the *editio princeps* of the Greek liturgies, published in Rome in 1526 by Demetrius Doucas. Doucas was a professor of Greek, in Rome, and without any doubt a Catholic.[65] The corrections of the text in this edition were done by Livio Podocrator, as is stated in the introduction to the text. Livio, too, was a Catholic Greek. His uncle was a cardinal, and he himself became the Latin archbishop of Nicosia, in Cyprus (1524–1553); though he never actually took up residence in his see, preferring to remain in Venice.[66] No known Greek mss. before the 17th century contain these rubrics, so it can safely be assumed that they are latinizations.

Subsequently, the Doucas edition was reprinted verbatim by Iakovos Leonginos in Venice in 1578.[67] This text, which included the "latinized" rubrics, now entered Greek-Orthodox usage and became the model for later Venetian editions from 1589 on. These Venetian editions, including our 1602 *Euchologion*, were used in turn by editors in Striatin, Kiev, and later Moscow, as the basis for their Slavonic editions.[68] Metropolitan Peter Moghila, who accepted the scholastic, Latin teaching that the moment of consecration came at the Words of Institution, made the rubrics even more specific by adding a reference to the proper intention of the priest.[69]

In Moscow, the issue sparked a debate which lasted until the end of the 17th century. Epifanii Slavinetskii, one of the chief figures in Nikon's reform, was himself drawn into this discussion.[70] In Muscovite Russia, however, the issue was not simply theological. Rather, it was caught up in a broader national debate over whether Moscow would lean toward the Greeks, or the Latins. The grecophile side was represented by Epifanii, and later by his student and disciple, the monk Evfimii. The pro-Latin faction was led by Simeon of Polotsk, and then by his disciple Silvester Medvedev. In the end, the controversial rubrics in BAS were removed in the 1699 *Sluzhebnik* published under Patriarch Adrian, but they remain in the Russian *Chinovnik* (Pontifical) to the present day.[71]

This theological dispute, however, had no direct connection with the Nikonian book reform, whose sole purpose was to align Greek and Russian practices. This is demonstrated by the fact that in the 1655 *Sluzhebnik*, while the latinized rubrics were added in BAS, a different set of latinized rubrics, the bows at the Words of Institution,[72] were removed from CHR. The reasons for these changes were not at all theological: the correctors simply followed the contemporary Greek books exactly—in this case the 1602 Venice *Euchologion*. In Moscow, the strongly Latin theological influence was in fact felt much later, with the publication of the 1671 *Trebnik* (Ritual),[73] the 1676 *Sluzhebnik*,[74] and the 1677 *Chinovnik* (Pontifical).[75] In fact, the "latinized" rubrics in BAS could very well be understood in a sense which is totally different from that expressed in the scholastic theology of Peter Moghila. The instruction to bless the gifts at the words of institution could simply be the ritualizing of the words of the anaphora: "The Lord...took the bread into his holy and pure hands, showed it to you, the God and Father, gave thanks, *blessed* it and hallowed it..." *(*BAS). The editors of liturgical books were not, after all, scriptural or Hebrew scholars who could understand the original sense of these words. It is quite likely, therefore, that the Greek Orthodox publishers in Venice, as well as the grecophile correctors working for Nikon, understood the text precisely in this "literal" sense when they allowed these rubrics into the text. As we have already seen, Epifanii Slavinetskii later strongly maintained that the moment of consecration came at the epiclesis, and he would never have accepted the Latin teaching on this matter (though of course the very acceptance of the existence of a moment of consecration implies a scholastic frame of reference). But the fact that these rubrics were added to the *Sluzhebnik* had nothing whatever to do with accepting Latin theology. Rather, it was but one more instance of the strict, uncritical imitation of current Greek practice.

iii. The Elevation of the Gifts

The Nikonian edition introduces the new practice of raising the gifts at the exclamation *Tvoia ot tvoikh* ("Your own of your own..."). The rubrics read as follows:

1655 (Moscow)	1646 (Moscow)
[XIX. ELEVATION OF GIFTS]	
1. Exclamation: *Tvoia ot tvoikh...*	
2.A. As this is said, the deacon puts aside the ripidion, crosses his hands, lifts the holy discos and the holy cup, and bows humbly.	
3.A. Choir: *Tebe poem...*	3.B. People: *Poem tia...*

1655 (Moscow)	1646 (Moscow)
	2.B. The priest points to both [the discos and the chalice] with his hand. The deacon also points to the holy things with his orarion.

No previous Muscovite book indicated the elevation, nor did any printed Venetian text. Before the 17th century, only one 15th century Greek ms. had such a rubric.[76] But the practice is undoubtedly of Greek origin. It is mentioned in the description of the hierarchal liturgy, made by Patriarch Athanasios Patellarios during his visit to Moscow in 1653, which was then included in the Acts of the 1667 Moscow Council.[77] The same practice is mentioned in the conciliar answer sent by Patriarch Paisios of Constantinople to Nikon in 1655.[78] Goar, in his notes on CHR, similarly describes the elevation.[79] The authors of the *Lithos* (Kiev, 1644), a treatise defending the Orthodox from accusations made by Cassian Sakowicz, indicate that, in both Greek and Russian (Kievan) practice, either the priest, or the deacon could elevate the gifts at the exclamation *Tvoia ot tvoikh*.[80] Cassian had criticized the Orthodox custom, saying that only the priest or bishop could to this, as in Latin practice.[81] In Kievan Russia, the elevation was introduced at the beginning of the century, first in the 1604 Striatin *Sluzhebnik*, then in the Kievan editions. There is a peculiarity in the 1604 Striatin text, in that if two deacons are present, each takes one vessel, and they do the elevation together, their arms crossed over each other. The rubric for the elevation appears in CHR only. The 1629 Kiev edition has the elevation rubric in both CHR and BAS, but lacks the instruction for the elevation by two deacons. In the 1639 Kiev *Sluzhebnik*, however, both CHR and BAS have the elevation rubric and the instruction for the two deacons to do it. The 1655 Moscow *Sluzhebnik*, following the 1604 Striatin edition, has the elevation only in CHR, with nothing about the two deacons. However, the instruction at the words of institution in BAS, to do everything "as in the liturgy of Chrysostom," (XVII.B.3.A) could apply here as well.

iv. The Epiclesis

There are several significant changes in the epiclesis in both CHR and BAS, none of them very fortunate. The following are the respective texts:

1655 (Moscow)	1646 (Moscow)
[XX.A. EPICLESIS (CHR)]	
1. The priest prays: *Eshche prinosim ti slovesnuiu siiu...*	
2.A. The deacon puts aside the ripidion and approaches the priest. They both bow 3x before the holy table, praying to themselves and saying:	2.B. If the priest wishes, he invokes the Holy Spirit. The deacon puts aside the ripidion or veil[82] and approaches the priest. They both bow 3x before the holy table, praying to themselves and saying:
3.A. *Gospodi izhe presviatago tvoego dukha...*[83]	3.B. *Gospodi izhe presviatyi svoi dukh...*
4.A. [Deacon,] verse:	4.B. The deacon says the verse:
Serdtse chisto sozizhdi vo mne... (Ps 50(51):10)	
verse:	deacon:
Ne otverzhi mene ot litsa tvoego... (Ps 50(51):11) [The priest repeats the troparion after each verse.]	
5.A. The deacon bows, points to the holy bread with his orarion, and says quietly: *Blagoslovi vladyko sviatyi khleb.* The priest raises his hand, blesses the holy gifts 3x, saying: *I sotvori oubo khleb sei...* Deacon: *Amin.*	5.B. The deacon points to the discos with his orarion and says: *Blagoslovi vladyko sviatyi khleb sei.* The priest blesses the holy bread and says quietly: *Sotvori oubo khleb sei...* Deacon: *Amin'.*
6.A. And the deacon again [says]: *Blagoslovi vladyko sviatuiu chashu.* And the priest, blessing [the cup], says: *A ezhe v chashi sei...* Deacon: *Amin.*	6.B. And the deacon again, pointing to the holy cup [says]: *Blagoslovi vladyko sviatuiu chashu siiu.* The priest, blessing the holy cup, says: *I ezhe v chashi sei...* Deacon: *Amin'.*
7.A. Again the deacon, pointing to both, says: *Blagoslovi vladyko oboia.* The priest blesses both and says: *Prelozhiv dukhom tvoim* sviatym. Deacon: *Amin, amin, amin.*	7.B. And the deacon points to the gifts with his orarion and says: *Blagoslovi vladyko oboia siia sviataia.* The priest blesses both the holy discos and the holy cup and says: *Prelozhi ia dukhom tvoim sviatym.* Deacon: *Amin'.*

The chief difference between the two versions is that the troparion of the Third Hour, optional in the 1646 edition, is made a regular part of the text in the Nikonian edition. The 1655 text agrees with both the 1602 Venice *Euchologion* and the 1604 Striatin edition. The troparion first appears in Greek sources from the 14th century. In the Diataxis of Philotheos, the priest and deacon bow three times as they "pray to themselves," but no indication is given as to what they say.[84] The slightly later 14-15th century diataxis of *Vaticanus gr. 573*, however, has the troparion recited at the option of the priest.[85] By the 16th century, the troparion has entered the Greek ms. euchologies, but, here again, it is recited at the option of the celebrant.[86] We find the same development in Slavic practice. The troparion appears in a few 15th century sources.[87] As with the Greek euchologies before the 17th century, the Moscow *Sluzhebniks* leave the recitation of the troparion to the discretion of the priest (2.B). The Nikonian text "updates" the rubrics by eliminating this option. Thus the troparion, which interrupts the text of the anaphora in mid-sentence, becomes a fixed element in the formulary. The same addition is made in BAS.

In BAS, there is another significant addition at the conclusion of the epiclesis. The following are the formulae pronounced by the celebrants over the gifts:

1655 (Moscow)	1652 (Moscow)
[XX.B. EPICLESIS (BAS)]	
[after the troparion of the Third Hour and the verses:]	
5.A. Bowing his head, the deacon points to the holy bread with his orarion and says quietly: *Blagoslovi vladyko sviatyi khleb.* Rising, the priest blesses the holy gifts 3x and says: *Khleb oubo sei, samoe chestnoe telo, gospoda i boga i spasa nashego iisusa khrista.* Deacon: *Amin.*	5.B. Then the deacon, pointing to the holy discos with his orarion, says: *Blagoslovi vladyko sviatyi khleb sei.* The priest blesses over the holy bread and says quietly: *Khleb oubo sei samoe chestnoe telo, gospoda boga i spasa nashego isusa khrista.* Deacon: *Amin'.*
6.A. And again the deacon [says]: *Blagoslovi vladyko sviatuiu chashiu.* Blessing [the cup] the priest says: *Chashiu zhe siiu, samuiu chestnuiu krov' gospoda i boga i spasa nashego iisusa khrista.* Deacon: *Amin.*	6.B. And again the deacon says: *Blagoslovi vladyko sviatouiu chashiu siiu.* And the priest blesses over the holy cup and says: *Chasha zhe siia samaia chestnaia krov' gospoda boga i spasa nashego isusa khrista.* Deacon: *Amin'.*

1655 (Moscow)	1652 (Moscow)
7.A. Priest: *Izliiannuiu za mirskii zhivot.* Deacon: *Amin.* And again the deacon, pointing to both holy gifts with his orarion, says: *Blagoslovi vladyko oboia.* And the priest, blessing both holy gifts with his hand, says: *Prelozhiv dukhom tvoim sviatym.* Deacon: *Amin, amin, amin.*	7.B. And the deacon again points to the holy gifts with his orarion and says: *Blagoslovi vladyko oboia siia sviataia.* The priest, blessing both the holy discos and the holy cup, says: *Izliiannaia za mirskii zhivot.* Deacon: *Amin'.*

The Nikonian edition adds to BAS the CHR formula *Prelozhiv dukhom tvoim sviatym* ("changing [them] by your Holy Spirit"), which appeared in no previous Muscovite books. Nikon's correctors took this interpolation from the 1602 Venice *Euchologion*. Though absent from the 1604 Striatin *Sluzhebnik*, the Moghilan editions in Kiev (1629, 1639) already contain this addition. The interpolated text first appears in the 11th century Greek euchology *Grottaferrata Codex Arsenii* (AD 1101),[88] and subsequently in numerous Greek mss.[89] The *editio princeps* of Doucas (1526), and nearly all the printed Venetian euchologies, contain the addition.[90] In Slavic practice, this text appears in no known ms.[91] It enters Muscovite practice only through Nikon's reform. The accretion of this text, which completely breaks both the flow and the sense of the anaphora of BAS, is a typical example of the transfer of elements from CHR into BAS. Perhaps it was added by the Greeks because they failed to understand the epiclesis of BAS in a consecratory sense. In the context of the centuries-long debate with the Latins over the "moment of consecration," this is certainly plausible.

The only other change, in both CHR and BAS, is the introduction of the triple amen at the end of the epiclesis (XX.A.7.A and XX.B.7.A). This insignificant change is also an adaptation to contemporary Greek practice.

v. Intercessions

There are several differences in the final section of the anaphora, which contains the diptychs for the living and the dead. The following are the texts from CHR:

1655 (Moscow)	1646 (Moscow)
[XXI. INTERCESSIONS]	
1. *Eshche prinosim ti slovesnuiu sluzhbu...*	
2.A. The deacon incenses around the holy table and commemorates whom he wishes among the living and the dead.	2.B. The deacon puts aside the ripidion, and takes the censor and incenses. Receiving a blessing from the priest, he incenses the holy table.
3. Priest: *Izriadno o presviatei, prechistei...*	
Choir: *Dostoino est'.*	The people: *Dostoino est'...*
4.A. The deacon commemorates from the diptychs, i.e., the list of the dead.	4.B. Then the deacon incenses around the holy table, the whole sanctuary, and the priest. While he does this, he commemorates to himself the founders of the church, or of the monastery, by name, whomever he wants. If the priest is celebrating alone, he incenses the altar table 3x from in front.
5.A. The priest prays: *Sviatago ioanna proroka...*	5.B. Bowing, the priest prays: *Sviatago ioanna proroka...*
6.A. The deacon turns to the doors of the holy sanctuary, holding his orarion with the tips of his fingers, and says: *I o vsekh i za vsia.* And the choir sings: *I o vsekh i za vsia.*	
7.A. [The priest:] *V pervykh pomiani gospodina nashego sviateishago arkhiepiskopa moskovskago*, name, *vseia velikiia i malyia rossii patriarkha, egozhe darui sviatym tvoim tserkvam...*	7.B. Ecphonesis: *V pervykh pomiani gospodi, gospodina nashego sviateishago patriarkha*, name, *egozhe dazhd' sviatym tvoim tserkvam...*

1602 (Venice)	1655 (Moscow)	1646 (Moscow)
8.A. Καὶ ὁ διάκονος λέγει, πρὸς τῇ θύρα στάς· Τοῦ δεινὸς πανιερωτάτου μητροπολίτου, ἢ ἐπισκόπου, ὅστις ἂν ᾖ, καὶ ὑπὲρ τοῦ	8.A. Standing by the doors, the deacon says: *Sviateishago* name, *arkhiepiskopa moskovskago, vseia velikiia i malyia rossii patriarkha. I mitropolita*	8.B.

1602 (Venice)	1655 (Moscow)	1646 (Moscow)
προσκομίζοντος τὰ ἄγια δῶρα ταῦτα εὐλαβεστάτου ἱερέως τοῦδε καὶ ὑπὲρ σωτηρίας τῶν εὐσεβεστάτων καὶ θεοφυλάκτων βασιλέων ἡμῶν, καὶ πάντων καὶ πασῶν.	**8.A con't.** *nashego, egozhe est' oblast'. I o prinosiashchem sviatyia dary siia blagoveineìshem sviashchennìtse, name. I o spasenii blagochestivago gosudaria nashego tsaria, i velikago kniazia,* name: *i ego blagochestivyia tsaritsy i velikiia kniagini,* name: *i blagovernago tsarevicha i velikago kniazia,* name: *i blagovernykh tsareven, names. I o vsei polate, i o voinstve ikh.* The choir sings: *I o vsekh i za vsia.*	

1655 (Moscow)	1646 (Moscow)
9.A The deacons commemorates the list of the living.	**9.B** Then the deacon commemorates the founders of the church, or the monastery, who are alive. In a monastery [he commemorates] also the hegumen and the brethren. [And he commemorates] also any other living persons, whomever he wishes.
10.A. And the priest prays: *Pomiani gospodi grad sei, vnem zhe zhivem, i vsiakii grad i stranu... Pomiani gospodi plavaiushchikh, puteshestvuiushchikh... Pomiani gospodi plodonosiashchikh i dobrotvoriashchikh...*	**10.B.** Bowing, the priest says: *Pomiani gospodi obitel' siiu, vneizhe zhitel'stvuem, i vsiak grad i stranou... Pomiani gospodi plavaiushchikh pout' shestvuiushchikh... Pomiani gospodi plodonosiashchikh i dobrotvoriashchikh...* And the priest commemorates the living by names, whomever he wishes.
	11.B. Then for himself: *Pomiani gospodi po mnozhestvu milosti tvoeia, i moe nedostoin'stvo...*
12. Ecphonesis: *I dazhd' nam edinemi ousty...*	

The changes in the Nikonian edition are as follows:

i) the addition of the diaconal exclamation, *I o vsekh i za vsia*, with its repetition by the choir (6.A);

ii) the addition of the diaconal intercession, aloud, for the bishops, the celebrant, and the civil authorities (8.A);

iii) the elimination of the celebrant's intercession for himself (11.B).

In each case, the 1655 *Sluzhebnik* follows the 1602 Venice *Euchologion*, except that the diaconal intercession (8.A) is expanded to include the patriarch and the tsar's family. The history of the intercessions has been studied in depth by G. Winkler, and there is little point in repeating that complex development here.[92] The diaconal exclamations (6.A and 8.A) are the conclusion of the diptychs, which were originally recited aloud by the deacon. By the 14th century, as for example in Philotheos' Diataxis, these were already recited silently by the deacon,[93] with no diaconal exclamations. This is what we find in the pre-Nikonian Moscow books. The *editio princeps* (Rome, 1526), however, contains the diaconal conclusions to the diptychs of the dead (6.A) and the living (8.A). The Venetian editions follow suit, and then the South-Russian *Sluzhebniks* in Striatin (1604) and Kiev (1620, 1629, 1639). Finally, the Nikonian correctors also adopt this usage from the Venetian text. The prayer of the priest for himself, an interpolation borrowed from BAS, is absent from the Venetian editions and is consequently removed by the correctors.[94]

5. Communion Rites

The Old-Believers complain about a number of rubrical and textual changes in the communion rites in CHR.[95] For BAS, the rubrics follow CHR in each instance:

1655 (Moscow)	1646 (Moscow)
[XXII. PRE-COMMUNION RITES]	
[Elevation]	
1. The priest prays: Prayer of Elevation: *Vonmi gospodi…*	

1655 (Moscow)	1646 (Moscow)
2.A. And he bows. Then the priest and the deacon, who is standing at his place [on the solea], together say quietly, 3x: *Bozhe ochisti mia greshnago i pomilui mia.* When the deacon sees the priest stretching out his hands and nearing the holy bread for the elevation, he exclaims: *Vonmem.*	2.B. When the time comes to elevate the holy lamb, the deacon, [standing] before the holy doors, bows and says aloud: *Vonmem.*
3.A. The priest raises the holy bread and exclaims: *Sviataia sviatym.*	3.B The priest takes the holy bread, with three fingers of both hands, and exclaims: *Sviataia sviatym.* And he makes a sign of the cross over the holy discos with the lamb.
4.A. The choir: *Edin sviat...* Then the koinonikon for the day, or for the saint.	4.B The people say: *Edin sviat...* Then the communion hymn [*prichasten*] for the day.
[Fraction]	
5.A. Then the deacon wraps his orarion around himself cross-wise, enters the holy sanctuary, stands to the right of the priest, who is holding the holy bread, and says: *Razdrobi vladyko sviatyi khleb.*	5.B. The deacon enters the holy sanctuary and stands to the left of the holy altar table.
6.A. The priest, dividing it into four parts with care and reverence, says: *Razdrobliaetsia i razdeliaetsia agnets bozhii, razdrobliaemyi i nerazdeliaemyi, vsegda iadomyi i nikogda zhe izhdevaemyi, no prichashchaiushchyiasia emu osviashchaiai.*	6.B. The priest divides the holy bread into four pieces and places them cross-wise on the holy discos, as indicated below. As he divides it, he says this: *Razdrobliaetsia i razdeliaetsia agnets bozhii, nerazdeliaiasia, izhe vsegda iadomyi, i nikolizhe skonchavaemyi.*
7.A. About the fraction of the holy lamb. [This excursus contains the following instructions: a) how the four parts of the lamb are placed on the discos, with a diagram; b) which parts are used for the communion of the clergy and of the lay people; c) directions to cut sufficient particles for communion;	7.B. [A more expanded excursus with the same instructions, appears in this edition after the communion of the people, ff. 161–162v.]

1655 (Moscow)	1646 (Moscow)
7.A. con't. d) forbidding communion from the commemorative particles; e) to pour enough zeon so that there is sufficient communion for the people.]	
[Commixture]	
8.A. The deacon points to the holy cup with his orarion and says: *Ispolni vladyko sviatyi potir'.* The priest, taking the part on top [the back side of the discos], i.e. IC, makes a sign of the cross with it over the holy cup, saying: *Ispolnenie dukha sviatago.* And he puts it into the holy cup. Deacon: *Amin.*	8.B. The deacon points to the holy cup with his orarion and says: *Ispolni vladyko sviatuiu chashiu.* The priest, taking the top portion with three fingers of both hands, makes a sign of the cross [with it] over the holy cup, saying: *Ispolnenie sviatago dukha.* And he puts it into the holy cup.
[Zeon]	
9.A. And [taking] the zeon, [the deacon] says to the priest: *Blagoslovi vladyko teplotu.* The priest blesses [it] saying: *Blagoslovena teplota sviatykh tvoikh, vsegda nyne i prisno… Amin.* The deacon pours it, cross-wise, into the holy cup, so that there is enough, saying: *Teplota very, ispoln' dukha sviatago, amin.* And putting aside the zeon, [the deacon] stands a bit further off [from the altar table].	9.B. And the deacon takes the vessel containing the zeon and says to the priest: *Blagoslovi vladyko teplotu.* The priest blesses it and says: *Teplota sviatago dukha.* Deacon: *Amin'.* And he [the deacon] pours it into the holy cup.

With the exception of the excursus on the fraction of the lamb, the 1655 *Sluzhebnik* is, once again, an exact translation of the 1602 Venice *Euchologion*. The chief differences from the earlier Moscow editions are as follows:

i) the addition of the penitential verses before the elevation (2.A);

ii) the addition of the diaconal instruction to the priest, just before the fraction (5.A);[96]

iii) the expansion of the fraction formula (6.A);

iv) a change in the time when the deacon wraps his orarion around himself in preparation for communion (5.A);

v) the excursus about the fraction of the lamb (7.A), in a different redaction and location within the text;

vi) the expansion of the zeon formulae (9.A).

i) The 1646 redaction is close to Philotheos' Diataxis.[97] The deacon, standing at his place before the holy doors, simply bows once before making his exclamation. The penitential verses, to my knowledge, appear in no mss. We find them first in the *editio princeps* of Doucas (Rome, 1526), and from there they get into the Venetian euchologies. The verses appear in the 1604 Striatin, and in the 1620, 1629, and 1639 Kiev *Sluzhebniks*. The Nikonian editors, working from the 1602 Venice euchology, added them too.

ii) The diaconal instruction, *Razdrobi vladyko sviatyi khleb* ("Divide, master, the holy bread") (5.A.), first appears in the 14-15 century *Vat. gr. 573*.[98] It is not found in the Diataxis of Philotheos, or in any of the pre-Nikonian Moscow books. The Greek *editio princeps*, the Greek Venetian editions, and the South-Russian books of Striatin and Kiev, all have it, however, and from these it makes its way into the Nikonian text as well.

iii) A slightly variant redaction of the current (Nikonian) fraction formula first appears as an addition in the margin of an 11th century ms., *Paris gr. 391*.[99] The Diataxis of Philotheos contains the shorter redaction, exactly as it is found in the pre-Nikonian Moscow texts (6.B).[100] The expanded version appears in a number of 16th century mss. cited by Trempelas,[101] as well as in Doucas' *editio princeps* and the 1602 Venice *Euchologion*. This longer version also enters the 1604 Striatin *Sluzhebnik*, though not the Kievan editions. Nikon's correctors, working on the basis of the 1602 Venice and 1604 Striatin editions, adopt the longer redaction.

iv) In the Nikonian edition cited above, the deacon wraps his orarion around himself just prior to the fraction (5.A). In the earlier Moscow texts, he does this after all the preparatory rites, just before receiving communion (XXIII.1.B). The reason for doing this is simply to get the orarion out of the way during communion. The pre-Nikonian rubric agrees exactly with Philotheos' Diataxis.[102] In 16th century mss.,[103] as well as in the *editio princeps*, this rubric is moved up from just before communion to before the fraction. The Venetian editions adopt this change, and the new rubric appears in the Striatin and Kievan editions, as well as in Nikon's *Sluzhebnik*.

v) The Nikonian edition contains a long excursus instructing the priest about the fraction of the lamb, about the placement of the four parts of the lamb on the discos, and about the communion of both clergy and people (7.A). This text appears in no Greek editions. The Nikonian correctors follow the redaction of the instruction printed in the 1604 Striatin *Sluzhebnik*, but place it at the fraction, just as in the Striatin edition, rather than after communion (XIII.8.B), as in the pre-Nikonian *Sluzhebniks*. This digression is of particular interest, because it specifies that the faithful are to be communed only from the two remaining pieces of the lamb, "NI" and "KA," and not from any of the particles commemorating the saints, the living, or the dead. The origin of these instructions is not clear. They first appear in the 1604 Striatin *Sluzhebnik*, and then in the Kievan editions of Elisei Pletenetskii (1620) and Peter Moghila (1629, 1639). Most likely, the excursus is in response to polemics with the Latins, concerning whether or not the commemorative particles are consecrated together with the lamb.[104] A version of the instruction first appeared in Muscovite service books published under Nikon's two predecessors, Joasaph and Joseph. This indicates that the debate had reached Muscovite Russia as well.[105]

vi) The Nikonian correctors changed the formulae accompanying the zeon (9.A). In the 1646 Moscow edition, the deacon asks for the priest's blessing, and then only says "Amen" as he pours the hot water into the chalice (9.B). This agrees exactly with the Diataxis of Philotheos,[106] and thus represents an earlier practice. The 1655 text expands the formulary (9.A). The new version is an exact translation of the rite from the 1602 Venice *Euchologion*. This version appears in 16th century Greek mss.,[107] as well as in the *editio princeps* (Rome, 1526) and the Venetian Greek editions. It enters Slavic practice in the 1604 Striatin *Sluzhebnik* and in subsequent Kievan editions. The Moscow correctors, under Nikon, follow suit.

1655 (Moscow)	1646 (Moscow)
[XXIII. COMMUNION]	
[Communion of the Clergy]	
	1.B. The priest and deacon together bow 3x before the holy altar, each saying to himself: *Bozhe ochisti mia greshnago i pomilui mia. Sozdavyi mia gospodi pomilui mia. Bezchisla sogreshikh gospodi prostimia.* [=III.2.B; VI.1.B; XIII.4.B] Then they bow down to the floor, with all reverence, and do the forgiveness rite, each saying to himself: *Prosti mia otche sviatyi,* to the end. Then the deacon wraps his orarion around himself cross-wise [see XXII.5.A] and stands a bit further away [from the altar table] [see XXII.9.A]
2.A. The priest says: *Diakone pristupi.* The deacon approaches, bows reverently, and asks for forgiveness. The priest, holding [a piece of] the holy bread, gives it to the deacon. The deacon kisses the [priest's] hand and takes the holy bread, saying: *Prepodazhd' mne vladyko chestnoe, i sviatoe telo gospoda i boga i spasa nashego iisusa khrista.* The priest says: Name, *sviashchennodiakonu, prepodaetsia chestnoe, i sviatoe, i prechistoe telo, gospoda i boga i spasa nashego iisusa khrista, vo ostavlenie grekhov ego, i v zhizn' vechnuiu.* And he [the deacon] goes behind the holy table, bows his head, and prays just as the priest.	**2.B.** [See below]
3.A. The priest also, having taken one piece of the holy bread, says: *Chestnoe i presviatoe telo gospoda i boga i spasa nashego iisusa khrista, prepodaetsia mne,* name, *sviashchenniku, vo ostavlenie grekhov moikh i v zhizn' vechnuiu.*	**3.B.** The priest takes the bottom portion of the holy lamb with three fingers of his right hand, puts it in the palm of his hand, and holding it in his palm says to himself: *Chestnoe i prechestnoe telo gospoda boga i spasa nashego isusa khrista, podaetsia rabou bozhiiu iereiu,* name, *ot prestola gospoda boga i spasa nashego isusa khrista, v khrame,* name [of church], *na pamiat' sviatago,* name [of saint], *egozhe est' den', vo ostavlenie grekhov i v zhizn' vechnuiu.*[108]

1655 (Moscow)	1646 (Moscow)
	2.B. The priest takes another portion [of the lamb], with three fingers of the same right hand, and says quietly to the deacon: *Pristupi.* The deacon approaches, bows down to the floor with all reverence, and kisses the holy table. And the priest gives him the particles which he is holding with three fingers and says: *Chestnoe i prechestnoe telo gospoda boga.* The deacon kisses the hand which gives him the portion of the holy bread. And he kisses the priest on the mouth. The priest says to the deacon: *Khristos posrede nas.* The deacon says: *Est' i boudet.* If it is Bright Week [Easter Week], then the priest says instead: *Khristos voskrese.* And the deacon answers: *Voistinu voskrese.* This is also said until the Apodosis of Easter. And the deacon goes to the side of the holy table.
4.A. And bowing his head he [the priest] prays, saying:	**4.B.** They say the prayer, each to himself:
Veruiu gospodi i ispoveduiu... *Vecheri tvoeia tainyia...*[109]	
Da ne v sud ili vo osuzhdenie budet mne prichashchenie...	Then they say this prayer: *Vladyko gospodi chelovekoliubche, da ne vo osuzhdenie mi boudet prichastie...*
5.A. And they commune from that which they hold in their hands, with fear and all care.	**5.B.** And they commune of the most pure body of Christ with fear and great reverence. Then they wipe the palms of their hands over the eiliton, so that no small crumb remains in the palms of their hands, which would be a great sin.
6.A. Rising, [the priest] takes the holy cup with both hands and with a cloth, and communes from it 3x, saying: *Chestnyia i sviatyia krove gospoda boga i spasa nashego iisusa khrista, prichashchaiusia az rab bozhii sviashchennik name, vo ostavlenie grekhov moikh, i v zhizn' vechnuiu, amin.*	**6.B.** Then the priest, taking the cup in both hands with the holy cloth, says: *Bogotvoriashchuiu krov', ouzhasnisia cheloveche zria...* The deacon says the same thing. Then the priest says: *Chestnaia i bogotochnaia krov' gospoda boga i spasa...* [ending as in 3.B]

1655 (Moscow)	1646 (Moscow)
6.A. con't. Then, having wiped his mouth and the holy cup with the cloth, which he holds in his hands, he says: *Se prikosnusia oustnam moim i ot imet bezzakoniia moia, i grekhi moia ochistit.*	**6.B con't.** And he communes 3x of the holy, most pure, and life-giving blood of the Lord. Then he wipes his mouth and the edge of the holy cup with the cloth with which he holds the holy cup.
7.A. [The priest] calls the deacon saying: *Pristupi.* The deacon approaches and bows once, saying: *Se prikhozhdu k bezsmertnomu tsariu:* and *Veruiu gospodi i ispoveduiu:* all [to the end]. And the priest says: *Prichashchaetsia rab bozhii diakon,* name, *chestnyia i sviatyia krove gospoda i boga...*[ending as in 11.A] As the deacon communes, the priest says: *Se prikosnusia oustnam tvoim, i ot imet bezzakonia tvoia, i grekhi tvoia ochistit.*	**7.B.** Then he [the priest] again calls the deacon, saying: *Pristupi.* The deacon approaches, bows to the priest, and asks his forgiveness. The priest says: *Chestnaia i bogotochnaia krov',* as written above [6.B]. And the deacon communes of the blood from the cup 3x. The priest holds the cup with the holy cloth. After communing, he [the deacon] wipes his mouth with the holy cloth and kisses the holy cup.
**[Communion of the People]**	
8.A. [Instructions about cutting the "NI" and "KA" portions of the lamb for the communion of the people] Deacon: *So strakhom bozhiim i veroiu pristupite.* Then those who wish to commune approach. They come one by one, bow with all humility and fear, their arms folded across their chests, and receive the divine mysteries. As he gives each person communion, the priest says: *Prichashchaetsia rab bozhii,* name *chestnago i sviatago tela i krove gospoda i boga...* And he wipes the person's mouth with the holy cloth, and the person kisses the holy cup and, bowing, leaves.	**8.B.** [see below]
9.A. Then the deacon takes the holy discos, [holds it] over the holy cup, wipes	**9.B.** Then the deacon takes the holy discos, and the sponge which is placed

1655 (Moscow)	1646 (Moscow)
9.A. con't. [all the particles] off it thoroughly with the holy sponge, with care and reverence, and covers the holy cup with a veil. Then he puts the asterisk and [the other] veils on the discos Meanwhile, the priest says the prayer of thanksgiving:	**9.B. con't.** for this purpose on the eiliton, and puts all the particles and crumbs, which are on the discos, into the holy cup with great care, so that not a single small crumb falls, or remains and perishes through carelessness. As this is done, the priest says the prayer of thanksgiving:
Blagodarim tia vladyko chelovekoliubche...	
10.A. Then they open the doors of the holy sanctuary, and the deacon bows once, takes the chalice with reverence, comes to the doors, raises the holy cup and shows it to the people saying:	**10.B.** The priest takes the censer. The deacon opens the holy doors and takes the chalice. Turning to the west, he shows it to those outside and says:
So strakhom bozhiim i veroiu pristupite.	
	The people: *Blagosloven griadyi vo imia gospodne, bog gospod i iavisia nam* (Ps 117(118):26a, 27a). Turning around, the deacon places the chalice on the holy table.
[Instructions in both editions indicate that the communion of the people takes place here.]	
11.A. The priest blesses the people, saying aloud: *Spasi bozhe liudi tvoia i blagoslovi dostoianie tvoe.* Then the deacon and the priest turn back to the holy table, and the deacon incenses 3x, saying to himself: *Voznesisia na nebesa bozhiia, i po vsei zemli slava tvoia* (Ps 56(57):5).[110] Outside, they sing: *Videkhom svet istinnyi...*[111]	**11.B.** The priest says: *Spasi bozhe liudi svoia, i blagoslovi dostoianie svoe.* And he [the priest] incenses the gifts 3x, saying quietly: *Voznesisia na nebesa bozhe, i po vsei zemli slava tvoia.*
	8.B. If there are some who wish to commune of the most pure mysteries, the priest takes the holy cup and the spoon from the deacon, goes out of the sanctuary, and communes them, saying: *Chestnoe i prechistoe telo i krov'*

1655 (Moscow)	1646 (Moscow)
	8.B con't. *gospoda boga*...And the singers sing: *Telo khristovo priimite...*, until all have communed. The last time, they sing it with alleluia. After communion, the priest enters the sanctuary and places the gifts on the holy table. [Here follows the excursus on the fraction of the lamb and about the communion of the people. See XXII.7 and XXIII.8.A]
[Removal of the Gifts]	
12.A. Then the priest takes the holy discos and places it on the head of the deacon. The deacon takes it with reverence, facing out toward the doors and, saying nothing, goes to the prothesis table and puts it down. The priest bows, takes the holy cup, turns to the doors and faces the people, and says quietly: *Blagosloven bog nash* and aloud: *Vsegda nyne i prisno...* Choir: *Amin. Da ispolniatsia ousta nasha...alliluia* 3x.	**12.B.** [The priest] gives the censer to the deacon and places the holy discos on the head of the deacon, with the asterisk on the top of the veils. The priest himself takes the holy cup. The deacon says quietly: *Blagoslovi vladyko.* The priest: *Blagosloven bog nash*, and turning to the west [toward the people], standing in the holy doors, he says aloud: *Vsegda nyne i prisno...* People: *Amin'. Da ispolniatsia ousta nasha...alliluia* [once]. Then they take the gifts to the prothesis table. The deacon goes first, and there they put down the gifts. The deacon incenses the holy gifts.

The differences between the two are, in fact, minor:

i) in the pre-Nikonian text, the priest takes his portion of the bread before giving one to the deacon: the Nikonian book reverses this order;

ii) the Nikonian *Sluzhebnik* eliminates the Kiss of Peace between the priest and deacon at communion, but expands the formulary;

iii) there are minor textual variations in the pre-communion prayers;

iv) at the communion of the clergy, from the cup, the Nikonian correctors remove the prayer *Bogotvoriashchuiu krov'* (6.B), but again expand the formulary;

v) after communion, the Nikonian text adds the troparion from Pentecost (10.A).

In each of these cases, the 1655 *Sluzhebnik* follows the 1602 Venice *Euchologion* exactly.

i) In the Diataxis of Philotheos, as in the 1646 Moscow *Sluzhebnik*, the priest and deacon bow three times as they pray; then they ask each other's forgiveness (1.B). After this, the priest first takes his own portion of the communion bread, then gives the deacon his.[112] I was unable to find any evidence before the 16th century indicating the order followed by Nikon's *Sluzhebnik*. The *editio princeps* (1529), however, has it precisely this way, and this order is then adopted by the Venetian texts, then the Striatin (1604) and Kievan (1620, 1629, 1639) editions, and finally by Nikon's correctors.

ii) The Nikonian text, following the Venetian 1602 edition, eliminates the Kiss of Peace, exchanged by the priest and deacon, as the priest hands the deacon his portion of the eucharistic bread (2.B). The Kiss of Peace existed in Slavic practice at this point, from at least the 12th century.[113] A number of Greek mss. indicate the same practice.[114] Even when, in the 15th century, the Russians adopted the Philothean rubrics, which lacked the Kiss of Peace at communion, they kept the practice. The Kiss of Peace at communion, however, does not exist in any printed Greek euchologies; these indicate only that the deacon is to kiss the hand of the priest as he receives the bread. This is what we find also in the Striatin and Kievan editions. Following the Venetian and Striatin texts, the 1655 *Sluzhebnik* also adds the deacon's request, addressed to the priest ("Give me, master, the righteous and holy body..."). These same editions also indicate that the deacon is to stand behind (2.A), rather than to the side (2.B) of the altar table, and the Nikonian edition follows suit.

iii) The pre-communion prayers recited by the clergy are virtually identical in the two editions cited above (4.A. and B). The Nikonian edition has a slightly abbreviated version of the third prayer, which agrees exactly with the text found in the 1602 Venetian edition.

iv) The Nikonian correctors suppress the prayer recited by the clergy before they commune from the cup (6.B). This prayer, found in the pre-Nikonian *Sluzhebniks*, is one of many different formulae found at this point in the Slavic sources.[115] This prayer, of course, is of Greek origin,[116] but because the correctors cannot find it in the Venetian euchology, they omit it from the new edition. Following the Venetian text, the editors also expand both the priest's (6.A) and deacon's (7.A) formulary at the communion from the cup.

v) Finally, after the exclamation "O Lord save your people" (11), the Nikonian *Sluzhebnik* adds a polychronion (εἰς πολλὰ ἔτι δέσποτα) and the Pentecost troparion ("We have seen the true light") (11.A). The polychronion first appears in Greek sources of the 15-16th century.[117] The 1602 Venice *Euchologion*, as well as the Striatin (1604) and Kiev (1620, 1629, 1639) *Sluzhebniks*, all contain this addition. As usual, Nikon's editors follow suit, even though the polychronion was usually reserved for hierarchal services. It is removed from the priest's service book in Russia only in the 18th century.[118] The introduction of the Pentecost troparion is more problematic. It appears neither in the 1602 Venice *Euchologion*, nor in any of the Ukrainian books in the first half of the 17th century. According to Dmitrievskii the use of this troparion comes from Greek practice, though he gives no evidence to support his view.[119] At any rate, the 1667 Moscow Council orders it included in the hierarchal liturgy as well.[120] The content of the troparion, as well as of the verse from Ps 56(57) with which it appears, fits in with the life-of-Christ symbolism of the liturgy, prevalent in Greek Orthodox mystagogy at the time, which interprets this part of the liturgy as the Ascension of Christ and the Descent of the Holy Spirit.[121] Undoubtedly, the troparion was introduced as the result of verbal suggestions by one of the Oriental patriarchs who visited Moscow at this time and encouraged Nikon in his reform.

6. Dismissal

The Nikonian edition shows no changes in the final litany, in the Prayer behind the Ambo, in the singing of Ps 33(34), in the distribution of the antidoron, and in the consummation of the gifts. The dismissal, however, is changed significantly, which the Old-Believers do not fail to notice.[122]

1655 (Moscow)	1646 (Moscow)
[XXIV. DISMISSAL]	
1.A. The priest comes out [of the sanctuary] after the end of the psalm [33(34)] and the distribution of the antidoron and says: *Blagoslovenie gospodne na vas, togo blagodatiiu i chelovekoliubiem, vsegda nyne i prisno...* Choir: *Amin.*	1.B. [After distributing the antidoron, the priest] enters the sanctuary, turns to the west [facing the people] and exclaims: *Blagoslovenie gospodne na vsekh vas, vsegda nyne i prisno...* As he says this, he blesses the people with the cross in his hand.
	2.B. Then he says: *Molitvami prechistyia ti materi, i vsekh sviatykh tvoikh, gospodi isuse khriste bozhe nash pomilui nas.* People: *Amin'. Dostoino est'.* Deacon: *Premudrost'.* Priest: *Presviataia bogoroditse spasi nas.* People: *Chestneishuiu kheruvim.*
3.A. Priest: *Slava tebe khriste bozhe upovanie nashe slava tebe.* Choir: *Slava, i nyne, gospodi pomilui 3x, blagoslovi.*	3.B. Priest: *Slava tebe bozhe nash, oupovanie nashe slava tebe.* People: *Slava, i nyne, gospodi pomilui 2x, gospodi blagoslovi.*
4.A. Priest: *Khristos istinnyi bog nash...*	4.B. The priest does the dismissal: *Khristos istinnyi bog nash...* People: *Amin'.*

Originally, the liturgy ended with the Prayer behind the Ambo, which the celebrant read on his way out of the church. The above dismissal rite, which comes from the monastic office, entered the liturgy only in the 12th century, when, at the Constantinopolitan Monastery of the Evergetis, elements of the office of the Typika were merged with the liturgy.[123] This brief office was originally a Palestinian monastic presanctified communion service, as is evident in the 9th century *Horologion, Codex Sin. gr. 863.*[124] When it was combined with the Divine Liturgy, the "typical psalms" (Pss 102, 145, and the Beatitudes) replaced the old Constantinopolitan antiphons (Pss 91, 92, and 94) at the beginning of the Liturgy, and the conclusion of the Typika, consisting of Ps 33(34), the distribution of the antidoron, and the apolysis, or dismissal from the Palestinian office, was added to the end.[125]

The Nikonian editors change the dismissal, so that it agrees exactly with the 1602 Venetian text, which has it according to the Philothean redaction. The 1646 *Sluzhebnik* gives a considerably longer version of the dismissal, which we find also in one 14-15th century Greek diataxis, *Vat. gr. 573*,[126] and in numerous Slavic mss. from the 15th century.[127] The pre-Nikonian version of the dismissal is identical to that in the major hours of the daily office, and it is undoubtedly from the daily office that this dismissal was borrowed for the liturgy.

NOTES

1. On the history and development of the Great Entrance, see the definitive study of TAFT, *GREAT ENTRANCE*.

2. On this prayer, see *ibid.*, pp. 119–148.

3. On changes in the text of the Cherubic Hymn, see the introduction to Part II. For BAS, both editions give the alternate texts for Holy Thursday (*Vecheri tvoeia tainyia...*) and Holy Saturday (*Da molchit vsiakaia plot*).

4. I.e. the *troparia katanyktika*, which are also recited by the clergy when they enter the church (II.8.A, 9.A, 10.A).

5. On the history and development of the commemorations, cf. TAFT, *GREAT ENTRANCE*, pp. 227–234.

6. On the early use of this verse, cf *ibid.*, pp. 234–235. On its use in other Slavic published books, cf. HUCULAK, pp. 329–332. These verses appear today only in the hierarchal liturgy.

7. Troparion of Holy Friday Vespers and Holy Saturday Matins. The text in the Nikonian *Sluzhebnik* has the Triodion recension of the troparion, which refers to the sealing of Christ's tomb, but makes no mention of the resurrection.

8. =VI.27.A.iv. A troparion from the Hours of Easter Sunday.

9. This troparion is also from the Paschal Hours.

10. *Pentecostarion* recension of the same troparion, i.e. with the final phrase referring to the resurrection. This version is used on the Sunday of the Myrrhbearing Women, as well as in the *Octoechos*, at tone 2 Matins.

11. On the various texts of this rite of forgiveness, cf. DMITRIEVSKII, *BOGOSLUZHENIE V XVI VEKE*, pp. 141–142.

12. These complaints are enumerated by CHERNIAVSKII, *OB IZMENENIIAKH*, pp. 234–295.

13. Cf. TREMPELAS, pp. 70–83.

14. *Moscow Synod 381* (KRASNOSEL'TSEV, *MATERIALY*, p. 25); *Ethnike bibl. 662* (TREMPELAS, p. 9); cf. TAFT, *GREAT ENTRANCE*, p. 228.

15. TAFT, *GREAT ENTRANCE*, p. 231.

16. J. Verpeaux, ed., *Pseudo-Kodinos, Traité des offices* (Paris: Centre National de la Recherche Scientifique, 1966), p. 266. The text is also cited by TAFT, *GREAT ENTRANCE*, pp. 201–202.

17. As in the Diataxes of *Sabas 305* and *Leningrad 423* (15th century) (KRASNOSEL'TSEV, *MATERIALY*, p. 89); *Sofia bibl. 875* (16th century) (ORLOV, p. 139). All these references are found in TAFT, *GREAT ENTRANCE*, pp. 231–232.

18. *Ibid.*, pp. 233–234.

19. TREMPELAS, pp. 9–10. On these commemorations, cf. TAFT, *GREAT ENTRANCE*, pp. 241–242.

20. A more complete account concerning these intercessions is given in HUCULAK, pp. 323–328.

21. Cf. *ibid.*, pp. 329–331; and CHERNIAVSKII, *OB IZMENENIIAKH*, pp. 265–272.

22. Cf. TAFT, *GREAT ENTRANCE*, pp. 248–249. The Greek sources for this are cited on p. 249, note 146.

23. *Ibid.*, pp. 244–249.

24. Cf. also GOAR, p. 75.

25. For the division of this dialogue into three parts, we follow the schema presented by RAES, *DIALOGUE*, pp. 40–41, and followed by TAFT, *GREAT ENTRANCE*, p. 285.

26. TAFT, *GREAT ENTRANCE*, pp. 279–283.

27. RAES, *DIALOGUE*.

28. TAFT, *GREAT ENTRANCE*, pp. 285–310.

29. *Ibid.*, pp. 294–295.

30. Cf. HUCULAK, pp. 337–338.

31. TAFT, *GREAT ENTRANCE*, p. 290; RAES, *DIALOGUE*, p. 41.

32. TAFT, *GREAT ENTRANCE*, p. 301.

33. TREMPELAS, p. 10.

34. This entire reconstruction is based upon TAFT, *GREAT ENTRANCE*, pp. 301–304.

35. Cf. *DEIANIIA 1666–1667*, II, f. 53v; and TAFT, *GREAT ENTRANCE*, p. 304.

36. TAFT, *GREAT ENTRANCE*, pp. 392–394. The prayer appears in many Slavic mss., beginning in the 14th century. These are listed on pp. 393–394. Cf. also ORLOV, p. 159; DMITRIEVSKII, *BOGOSLUZHENIE V XVI VEKE*, pp. 118–119; PETROVSKII, *RÉDACTION SLAVE*, pp. 884, 908.

37. TAFT, *GREAT ENTRANCE*, p. 394; PETROVSKII, *RÉDACTION SLAVE*, pp. 884, note 2; GOAR, p. 706.

38. TAFT, *GREAT ENTRANCE*, pp. 390–392.

39. CHERNIAVSKII, *OB IZMENENIIAKH*, pp. 296–338.

40. The text of the Creed is taken from the *Horologion* (Moscow, 1640), ff. 37–37v, because the Moscow *Sluzhebniks* give only the incipit.

41. Cf. chapter one, section 3. *DEIANIE 1654*, ff. 6v–7. A photo–reproduction of the Greek text of the Creed, sent from Constantinople in 1593, from which the text is translated, is attached in *ibid.*, between ff. 6 and 7.

42. CHERNIAVSKII, *OB IZMENENIIAKH*, pp. 300–317.

43. We present here the summary of the study by A. Gezen, *Istoriia slavianskago perevoda simvolov very* (St Petersburg: AN, 1884). The mss. containing this variant reading are listed on p. 57, note 2.

44. *Ibid.*, pp. 57–59.

45. *Ibid.*, pp. 59–60.

46. *Ibid.*, pp. 62–65. The Stoglav Council, ch 9, ruled that either *gospoda* (Lord) or *istinnago* (true) may be used, but not both together.

47. *Ibid*, pp. 66–67. Gezen also includes, in Appendix 3, pp. 126–128, a draft by Epifanii Slavinetskii of a translated Creed, and a brief article by him, explaining the proposed changes. In this translation, Epifanii strives to be even closer to the Greek: the Greek word σταυροθέντα is rendered as *oukrestvovan*, rather than *raspiatago*. Cf. also CHERNIAVSKII, *O izmeneniiakh*, pp. 318–338.

48. *Expositio de divino templo, PG* 155:732. Cf. TAFT, *GREAT ENTRANCE*, p. 421.

49. TAFT, *GREAT ENTRANCE*, p. 424. Taft cites the 12th century Latin translation of CHR by Leo Tuscan, cf. A. Jacob, "La traduction de la Liturgie de saint Jean Chrysostome par Leon Toscan. Edition critique," *OCP* 32 (1966) 152–153.

50. TAFT, *GREAT ENTRANCE*, pp. 418–420.

51. DMITRIEVSKII, *OPISANIE* II, p. 611. Cf. TAFT, *GREAT ENTRANCE*, pp. 421–422; PETROVSKII, *RÉDACTION SLAVE*, p. 868.

52. *DEIANIIA 1666–1667*, II, f. 55.

53. See the study on these by R. Taft, "Textual Problems in the Diaconal Admonition before the Anaphora in the Byzantine Tradition," *OCP* 49 (1983) 340–365. On p. 352, there is a list of Greek mss. with all the variant readings of this text.

54. *Ibid.*, pp. 353–354.

55. *Ibid*, pp. 352–354.

56. ORLOV, p. 163.

57. CHERNIAVSKII, *OB IZMENENIIAKH*, pp. 339–348. Cherniavskii errs, however, when he states that "Greek books always had the addition" (p. 343).

58. ORLOV, p. 167. The date of the ms. is indicated on p. xxxviii.

59. In CHR, in the 1651 and 1652 Moscow *Sluzhebniks*, the priest is instructed to bow here, and at the words over the cup (7.B); cf. USPENSKII, p. 155.

60. The word is missing in the Slavonic text—an obvious lacuna.

61. The Greek word εὐλαβείας (XVIII.B.1.A and B.5.A) is translated as *blagogoveniem* (reverence) in the 1655 *Sluzhebnik*, and as *strakhom* (fear) (XVIII.C.1.B and C.5.B) in the 1604 edition.

62. For example, the rubric before the words over the bread in the 1639 Kievan *Sluzhebnik* (CHR) reads as follows: "Then the priest bows his head with humility, and thinking with great attention that the holy bread will change into the body of our crucified Christ God, adds to this his own will [i.e. intention]; and he raises his right hand, holding his fingers as for a blessing, looks at the holy bread, points over it, blesses it, and exclaims, saying: *Priimete, iadite...*"

63. Cf. USPENSKII, pp. 152–154, and *passim*.

64. DMITRIEVSKII, *OTZYV ORLOVA*, pp. 235–242.

65. This is evident from the Bull by Pope Clement VII, in which Doucas is called "*dilectus filius*." The text of this bull is reprinted by LEGRAND, *XVe et XVIe SIÈCLES*, I, pp. 194–195.

66. His biography appears in *Archives de l'orient latin*, v. 2 (Paris, 1884), pp. 320–324.

67. DMITRIEVSKII, *OTZYV ORLOVA*, pp. 235–236. Cf. LEGRAND, *XVe ET XVIe SIÈCLES*, II, p. 26. Like Doucas' edition, Leonginos' is entitled: Αἱ θεῖαι Λειτουργείαι τοῦ ἁγίου Ἰωάννου τοῦ Χρυσοστόμου, Βασιλείου τοῦ Μεγάλου, καὶ ἡ τῶν Προηγιασμένων (Venice, 1578).

68. DMITRIEVSKII, *OTZYV ORLOVA*, pp. 236–239.

69. On the Latin influence on Moghila's sacramental theology, see my article, "The Liturgical

Reforms of Peter Moghila: A New Look," *SVTQ* 29(1985) 101–114; see also the following basic studies: E.M. Kryzhanovskii, "O Trebnike kievskago mitropolita Petra Mogily," *Sobranie sochinenii*, v. 1 (Kiev, 1890), pp. 87–165; M. Jugie, "Moghila, Pierre," *Dictionnaire de Théologie Catholique*, v. 10 (Paris, 1929), cols. 2063–2081; and especially A. Wenger, "Les influences du Rituel de Paul V sur le Trebnik de Pierre Moghila," *Mélanges en l'honneur de Monseigneur Michel Andrieu* (=*Revue de Sciences Réligieuses*, vol. hors série) (Strasbourg, 1956), pp. 477–499.

70. On the eucharistic debate in Russia, see FLOROVSKII, pp. 73–80; and esp. G. Mirkovich, *O vremeni presushchestvlenie sv. darov* (Vilna, 1886).

71. DMITRIEVSKII, *OTZYV ORLOVA*, pp. 187–188.

72. See the 1651 and 1652 *Sluzhebniks*.

73. This *Trebnik* is the first Russian edition to include in the rite of confession the Latin formula of absolution, taken over from Peter Moghila's *Trebnik* (Kiev, 1646). Nikon's 1658 *Trebnik*, based chiefly on the Greek *Euchologion*, does not contain this prayer. Cf. USPENSKII, pp. 166–168.

74. In this book, at PRES, the priest is instructed not to commune from the chalice, since "it is not the blood of the Lord," because it has not been consecrated as at CHR or BAS. Cf. USPENSKII, pp. 161–162. On this issue see I.A. Karabinov, "Sviataia chasha na Liturgii prezhdeosviashchennykh darov," *KhCht* 1915(1) 737–753; 1915(2) 953–964; and A. Raes, "La Communion au Calice dans l'Office des Présanctifiés," *OCP* 20(1954) 166–174.

75. This book was influenced by the *Trebnik* of Peter Moghila (Kiev, 1646). Cf. USPENSKII, pp. 162–164. In CHR, for example, the concelebrating priests are instructed to recite the words of institution together with the bishop, but under no circumstances to pronounce the words before him. There is, however, an ongoing debate as to whether this is, strictly speaking, a latinization — cf. R. Taft, *Beyond East and West* (Washington, D.C.: Pastoral Press, 1984), pp. 83–84, and p. 96, note 13.

76. (A.D. 1475) *Ist. Patr. 87* (90), CHR, f. 17v. In the 17th century, *Sinai gr. 1047* (A.D. 1685), f. 197, has an illustration in the margin indicating this practice. I am grateful to R. Taft for these references.

77. *DEIANIIA 1666–1667*, pt. 2, f. 56.

78. PAISIOS OF CONSTANTINOPLE, p. 544.

79. GOAR, p. 120.

80. *Lithos*, p. 142 (p. 154 in the edition of the *Lithos* published in *Arkhiv Iugo–zapadnoi Rossii*, pt. 1, v. 9 (Kiev, 1893)).

81. *Perspectiwa* (Cracow, 1642), pp. 49–50.

82. The deacon used one of the veils to fan the gifts, if no ripidion was available.

83. The Troparion of the Third Hour. The differences between the 1655 and 1646 editions are only stylistic.

84. TREMPELAS, p. 11.

85. KRASNOSEL'TSEV, *MATERIALY*, p. 110.

86. TREMPELAS, pp. 112–113; ORLOV, p. 204; KRASNOSEL'TSEV, *MATERIALY*, p. 64, note 2.

87. ORLOV, pp. 203–205; PETROVSKII, *RÉDACTION SLAVE*, p. 908.

88. This ms., now lost, is erroneously dated A.D. 1041 by Goar, p. 151, and this dating is followed also by SWAINSON, p. xxiii; ORLOV, p. xviii; and H. Engberding, *Das eucharistische Hochgebet des Basileiusliturgie* (=*Theologie des christlichen Ostens*, 1) (Munster:

Verlag Aschendorff, 1931), p. xxviii. On this ms. cf. A. Strittmatter, "The *Barberinum s. Marci* of Jacques Goar," *EL* 47 (1933) 331; and particularly TAFT, *GREAT ENTRANCE*, p. 343, note 116.

89. Cf. TREMPELAS, p. 115; ORLOV, p. 208; and DMITRIEVSKII, *OPISANIE* II, p. 249.

90. Only the 1564 Venice *Euchologion,* published by Hyppolitus Valerides, lacks the text. Cf. DMITRIEVSKII, *OTZYV ORLOVA,* pp. 236–237.

91. Cf. ORLOV, p. 209.

92. Cf. G. Winkler, "Die Interzessionen der Chrysostomusanaphora in ihrer geschichtlichen Entwicklung," *OCP* 36 (1970) 301–336; 37 (1971) 333–383.

93. *Ibid.,* *OCP* 37 (1971) 377.

94. On this intercession from BAS (BRIGHTMAN, p. 333:14ff), see *ibid., OCP* 37 (1971) 357–359. On its development in Slavic practice, cf. ORLOV, pp. 246–253.

95. CHERNIAVSKII, *OB IZMENENIIAKH,* pp. 373–385.

96. The 1652 *Sluzhebnik,* however, does have this in BAS.

97. TREMPELAS, p. 12.

98. KRASNOSEL'TSEV, *MATERIALY,* pp. 112. For later mss., cf. TREMPELAS, pp. 132–133.

99. This reference will appear in the chapter on the fraction, in the forthcoming study of the liturgy by R. Taft. I am grateful to him for allowing me access to his notes.

100. TREMPELAS, p. 12.

101. *Ibid.,* p. 133.

102. *Ibid.,* p. 13. Cf. also DMITRIEVSKII, *BOGOSLUZHENIE V XVI VEKE,* pp. 127–128.

103. TREMPELAS, p. 132.

104. On the debate about whether the commemorative particles are consecrated, see the following: I.M. Hanssens, *Institutiones liturgicae de ritibus orientalibus,* v. 2 (Rome, 1930), pp. 200–206; MANDALÀ, pp. 170–179; A. Pavlov, *Nomokanon pri Bol'shem Trebnike,* 2nd ed. (Moscow, 1897), pp. 406–413; M. Andrieu, *Immixtio et consecratio. La consécration par contact dans les documents liturgiques du moyen âge* (=*Bibliothèque de l'Institut de Droit Canonique,* II) (Paris, 1924), pp. 208–212.

105. A similar instruction was printed in Nomocanon #213, published at the conclusion of the Muscovite *Trebniks* (Rituals) published under these two patriarchs in 1639 and 1651. This is cited in A. Pavlov, *Nomokanon pri Bol'shem Trebnike,* 2nd edition (Moscow, 1897), p. 407.

106. TREMPELAS, p. 13; ORLOV, p. 283.

107. TREMPELAS, pp. 136–137.

108. The 1652 Moscow edition, however, already has the same reading as Nikon's edition here, and at 6.B.

109. The Cherubic Hymn for Holy Thursday.

110. This psalm verse is used as the prokeimenon (responsorial psalm) for Ascension.

111. A troparion from Vespers on the eve of Pentecost.

112. TREMPELAS, p. 13.

113. Cf. PETROVSKII, *RÉDACTION SLAVE,* pp. 870, 876, 910. On the history of the Kiss of Peace at communion, cf. Van de Paverd, *Zur Geschichte der Messliturgie in Antiocheia und Konstantinopel gegen Ende des vierten Jahrhunderts* (=OCA 187) (Rome: Pont. Inst. Orientalium, 1970), pp. 224–235.

114. Cf. for example the 13–14th century *Moscow Synod 381* (KRASNOSEL'TSEV, *MATERIALY,* p. 28), and the 14-15th century *Vat. gr. 573* (*ibid.,* p. 113). PETROVSKII, *RÉDACTION SLAVE,* p. 910, note 3, cites other sources as well, as does TREMPELAS, pp. 138–139.

115. Cf. DMITRIEVSKII, *BOGOSLUZHENIE V XVI VEKE,* p. 126; PETROVSKII, *RÉDACTION SLAVE,* pp. 910–911.

116. See for example *Vat. gr. 573* (15th century) (KRASNOSEL'TSEV, *MATERIALY,* p. 113).

117. Cf. A. Dmitrievskii, "O stikhire 'Videkhom svet istinnyi' v chinakh liturgii sv. Ioanna Zlatousta i sv. Vasiliia Velikago," *Rukovodstvo dlia sel'skikh pastyrei* 27 (1886) 266–271; and CHERNIAVSKII, *OB IZMENENIIAKH,* p. 381.

118. A. Dmitrievskii, "O stikhire...," p. 271.

119. *Ibid.,* p. 272.

120. *DEIANIIA 1666–1667,* pt. 2, f. 61. This text, we have seen, is based on the description of the hierarchal liturgy by Patriarch Athanasios Patellarios, who came to Moscow in 1653. Cf. chapter one, section 4.

121. Cf. PAISIOS OF CONSTANTINOPLE, pp. 334–346, and A. Dmitrievskii, "O stikhire...," pp. 269–270. On the development of this symbolical understanding of the liturgy see the studies of R. Bornert, *Les commentaires byzantins de la Divine Liturgie* (=*Archives de l'Orient chrétien* 9) (Paris: Institut Français d'Etudes Byzantines, 1966); and H. J. Schulz, *Die byzantinische Liturgie* (=Sophia, Bd 5) (Freiburg im Breisgau: Lambertus-Verlag, 1964). For the influence of this tradition in Russia, see FELMY, particularly chapter 3, pp. 80–111.

122. CHERNIAVSKII, *OB IZMENENIIAKH,* pp. 386–389.

123. MATEOS, *CÉLÉBRATION,* pp. 69–71. For the text of the Typicon of Evergetis, showing this development, cf. DMITRIEVSKII, *OPISANIE* I, p. 603.

124. Cf. J. Mateos, "Un Horologion inédit de Saint-Sabas," (*Mélanges Eugène Tisserant,* vol. 3, pt. 2 (=Studi e testi 233) (Vatican, 1964), pp. 47–76.

125. The antidoron ("instead of gifts") was introduced in the Studite Monastery in Constantinople, where communion was not received daily. Cf. the *Hypotyposis* of St Theodore the Studite (DMITRIEVSKII, *OPISANIE* I, p. 233, and *PG* 99:1713). Originally, communion was distributed at this point, accompanied by the singing of Ps 33(34), the ancient communion psalm in Jerusalem practice. Cf. MATEOS, *CÉLÉBRATION,* pp. 69–70. See also A. Raes, "L'antidoron," *POC* 3(1953) 6–13.

126. KRASNOSEL'TSEV, *MATERIALY,* p. 114. For later examples, cf. also TREMPELAS, p. 159.

127. ORLOV, p. 315; PETROVSKII, *RÉDACTION SLAVE,* p. 913.

Excursus:

The Later Nikonian Editions

One of the frequent criticisms leveled at the Nikonian books was that they do not agree even among themselves.[1] Of course, the earlier Muscovite editions also contained numerous variations, but this hardly prevented the Old-Believers from using any excuse to attack the new books. It is true, however, that the subsequent Nikonian editions all contain further changes, though these are generally insignificant. In this section, we shall take a brief look at the variations in the text of CHR, in the five *Sluzhebniks* published under Nikon from 1656 to 1658, and finally at the 1667 edition issued after the 1667 Moscow Council.

1. The 1656 Edition

This *Sluzhebnik*, Nikon's second edition released on July 31, 1656, contains quite a few changes from the first edition. According to Dmitrievskii,[2] these are based on the following sources:

i) the conciliar letter sent to Nikon by Patriarch Paisios of Constantinople in 1655;[3]

ii) the 1620 Kiev *Sluzhebnik* published by Elisei Pletenetskii;

iii) and the 1629 Kiev *Sluzhebnik* of Peter Moghila.

Most of the changes are merely stylistic. The text of the Prayer of the Third Antiphon is a typical example. Differences between the two versions are underlined:

1656 (Moscow)	1655 (Moscow)
[Prayer of the Third Antiphon]	
Izhe obshchyia siia, i soglasnyia darovavyi nam molitvy, izhe i dvema ili trem soglasuiushchimsia o imeni tvoem, prosheniia podati obeshchavyi: sam i nyne rab tvoikh prosheniia k poleznomu	*Izhe obshchiia siia, i soglasnyia darovavyi name molitvy, dvema ili trem soglasuiushchim o imeni tvoem, prosheniia podati obeshchavyi: sam i nyne rab tvoikh prosheniia k poleznomu*

213

1656 (Moscow)	1655 (Moscow)
ispolni, podaia nam v nastoiashchem vetse poznanie tvoeia <u>istiny</u>, i v budushchem zhivot vechnyi daruia.	*ispolni, podaia nam v nastoiashchem vetse poznanie tvoeia <u>istinny</u> i v budushchem zhivot vechnyi daruia.*

These variants, merely orthographical and stylistic, do not change the meaning in any way. Many texts are similarly altered, however, and all these further innovations could easily frustrate a priest who, only a year earlier, had had to adapt to completely new service books.

Other changes in this new edition were more significant. First, in the prothesis, the 1656 text restores the commemoration by the celebrating priest, for himself, though it places it after the final commemoration for the dead. In the pre-Nikonian Moscow editions, this commemoration was placed at the conclusion of the commemorations for the living (VI.17.B.v). The Striatin and Kievan texts, however, had this commemoration at the conclusion of all the commemorations, and this is where the Nikonian editors placed it.

The second significant change involved the expansion of the excursus on the fraction of the lamb. The revised instruction, placed immediately after the fraction, is a composite text. Dmitrievskii has studied this text and discovered its sources:[4]

i) the first part of the excursus is taken from the 1620 Kiev *Sluzhebnik*, where it appears after CHR;

ii) the second and longest section (5pp. in the 1656 *Sluzhebnik*) is taken from the conciliar letter sent by Paisios of Constantinople to Nikon.[5] The text is repeated almost verbatim; the only change is that the verbs are all shifted from third to second person;

iii) the third section is taken from the twenty-fourth commentary of John Chrysostom on Corinthians,[6] as is indicated in the text itself;

iv) and the final section is, again, taken from the 1620 Kiev *Sluzhebnik*.

The main point of the instruction is to ensure that communion is distributed only from the consecrated lamb, and not from the commemorative particles, which were not consecrated.

Third, the new edition adds a number of troparia to be recited by the deacon, before he wipes all the commemorative particles into the chalice after communion. First, the three paschal troparia:

   i) *Voskresenie khristovo videvshe...*[7]

   ii) *Svetisia, svetisia novyi ierusalime...*[8]

   iii) *O paskha velikaia...*[9]

These refrains do not appear at this point in any previous Greek or Slavic service book. They are mentioned, however, in the description of the liturgy in the conciliar letter of Paisios of Constantinople,[10] from which the correctors add them to the new edition. After reciting these three troparia, the deacon also says the verse *Otmyi gospodi grekhi...* ("Wash away, O Lord, the sins...") as he wipes the particles from the discos into the chalice. This too comes from the same conciliar letter, which indicates that "many in our church" say this.[11]

Finally, there are a few rubrical changes in the concluding rites of the liturgy. During the final litany after communion, the priest is instructed to fold the antimension, and then to make a sign of the cross over it with the gospel book. This, too, is taken from Paisios' response to Nikon.[12] During the Prayer behind the Ambo, the deacon is instructed to stand before the icon of Christ, holding up his orarion and bowing his head. This rubric comes from the 1620 and 1629 Kievan *Sluzhebniks*. Finally, a rubric is added specifying that the priest himself is to distribute the antidoron during the singing of Ps 33(34). This is taken from the explanation of the liturgy printed in the *Skrizhal'*.

2. The 1657 and 1658 Editions

Four more editions were printed in the last two years of Nikon's rule. The third edition of the Nikonian *Sluzhebnik* appeared on May 5, 1657. This was followed by a fourth on December 10, 1657, a fifth on May 15, 1658, and a sixth on July 1, 1658. The two editions in 1657 are basically reprints of the 1656 text, with only a few insignificant changes in orthography and punctuation. The third edition (May 5, 1657) contains an expanded response by the choir, after the reading of the gospel: *Slava tebe gospodi, slave tebe* (see IX.8.A). The repetition of *slava tebe* is found in no previous Greek edition, but it is indicated in the description of the hierarchal liturgy made for Nikon by Athanasios Patellarios in 1653.[13] In the fifth edition (May 15, 1658), the only significant change is the restoration of the verse *Blagosloven griadyi vo imia gospodne, bog gospod' i iavisia nam* (Ps 117(118):26a, 27a), as a response to the diaconal invitation for the communion of the people (see XXIII.10.B). This is taken from the commentary on the liturgy published in the *Skrizhal'*.[14] Finally, the sixth and final Nikonian edition (July, 1658) contains expanded titles used for the tsar in the litanies, commemorations, and intercessions. We cite an example from the Litany of Peace at the beginning of CHR:

1658 (Moscow) (6th edition)	1655 (Moscow) (1st edition)
[Petition for tsar]	
O Blagochestiveishem, tishaishem, samoderzhavneishem, i bogokhranimom gosudare nashem tsare i velikom kniaze aleksii mikhailoviche...	*O blagochestivom i bogokhranimom gosudare nashem tsare i velikom kniaze, name...*

To the fifth and sixth editions, Nikon also appends the conciliar letter of Paisios of Constantinople, which had already been published in the *Skrizhal'* in 1656.

3. Conclusion

Nikon's opponents were, therefore, correct in stating that the Nikonian editions differed from one another. But these variations were, as we have seen, minor. The Nikonian texts were reviewed at the 1667 Moscow Council, and a new *Sluzhebnik*, containing the acts of this council in an appendix, was published in November 1667. This edition was basically a reprint of the final Nikonian edition of July 1658, which contained all the additions to the 1655 *Sluzhebnik* mentioned above. Another appendix in the 1667 text enumerates the few changes in the Nikonian *Sluzhebnik*, mandated by the council. The only significant ones are as follows:

i) in the prothesis, the names of Anthony and Theodosius of the Caves (in Kiev) are added to the list of holy monks (IV.15.A.vi);

ii) before the gospel reading, the priest is to say *Mir vsem*, and the people respond with *I dukhovi tvoemu* (IX.6.A);[15]

iii) a rubric is added at the second litany of the faithful, indicating that if the priest is celebrating alone, he is not to say all the petitions from the Litany of Peace.[16]

Besides these, there are only insignificant stylistic changes in the liturgy. This edition of the Nikonian *Sluzhebnik* contains the version of the liturgy, in use even day in Slavic practice, with only a few minor changes dating to the 18th century.

NOTES

1. Some of these are cited in chapter one, section 5.
2. DMITRIEVSKII, *OTZYV ORLOVA*, pp. 256-257.
3. On this letter, cited as PAISIOS OF CONSTANTINOPLE, see chapter one, section 6.
4. DMITRIEVSKII, *OTZYV ORLOVA*, pp. 257-258.
5. PAISIOS OF CONSTANTINOPLE, pp. 346-352.
6. *PG* 61:200.
7. A resurrection troparion for Easter. It is sung also, immediately following the gospel at the Sunday resurrectional Matins.
8. The hirmos of the 9th ode of the paschal canon.
9. Troparion from the 9th ode of the paschal canon.
10. PAISIOS OF CONSTANTINOPLE, p. 349.
11. *Ibid.*, pp. 350-351.
12. *Ibid.*, p 563.
13. *DEIANIIA 1666-1667*, pt. 2, f. 50-50v.
14. *Skrizhal'* (Moscow, 1656), pp. 733-735.
15. This change comes from the hierarchal liturgy described by Athanasios Patellarios and printed in *DEIANIIA 1666-1667*, pt. 2, f. 50. This greeting before the gospel is still absent in some non-Muscovite Slavonic recensions of the liturgy, which here, as elsewhere, have preserved older, pre-Nikonian, usages.
16. On the history of this litany, see A. Strittmatter, "Notes on the Byzantine Synapte," *Traditio* 10(1954) 51-108, particularly pp. 65ff.

Conclusion

The prefaces to the Nikonian liturgical books present Nikon's reform as both a "correction," and a "return to the sources." This has been taken at face value in the vast majority of the literature on the subject. Our study has shown the reality of the matter to be quite different, for, in fact, the reform consisted simply in replacing existing Russian practice with 17th century Greek usage. No ancient manuscripts, Greek or Slavonic, were, or could have been, used, for the very simple reason that none of them contained the changes which the Nikonian reformers introduced into the Muscovite books. This, in a nutshell, is a summary of the Nikonian reform.

In the first chapter, we studied the events and chronology of the reform. The "official" account, presented in the preface to the *Sluzhebnik*, is an attempt to justify the reforms by showing:

1) that the Russian Church is required to agree in every detail with the Greek Church;

2) that the reform was sanctioned by the bishops of both the Russian and Greek Churches,

3) who had studied the ancient Slavic and Greek manuscripts brought back by Arsenii Sukhanov,

4) and had concluded, on the basis of these, that the Russian books needed correction;

5) that the correction was then undertaken on the basis of these ancient sources.

We have shown this account to be totally inaccurate.

The Acts of the 1593 Council of Constantinople, cited by Nikon to support the reform, require unity only in matters of faith, and not in rubrical details. This was certainly the way the Greeks understood it, as is evident from the conciliar letter sent by Paisios of Constantinople to Nikon in 1655. However Nikon, who like all Russians identified the most minute liturgical detail with dogma, understood these Acts as requiring liturgical unity.

We saw that the sanction of the Russian bishops was, at best, reluctant. Paul of Kolomna, the one bishop who dared to oppose Nikon on an apparently trivial matter, was removed from his see and disappeared soon after. The other bishops, thoroughly cowed by Nikon's autocratic manner, chose the path of least resistance. The Greek bishops, who frequented Moscow in their search for financial support, agreed with and supported whatever was the current policy of the Russian authorities. The one council held outside Moscow that dealt with the reform was composed exclusively of Greek bishops and, in fact, specifically warned Nikon not to quibble about matters not essential to the faith. This advice went unheeded.

We further saw that the bishops who attended the 1655 Moscow Council did not study, and could not have studied, all the ancient manuscripts brought back from Mt. Athos and the East by Arsenii Sukhanov. First, this council lasted but a week—hardly enough time to examine 498 ancient manuscripts! Second, we know from the research of Belokurov and Fonkich that only three of these manuscripts were, in fact, euchologies, and that none contained the changes introduced in the Nikonian *Sluzhebnik.*

Thus the "correction of the books" could not possibly have been conducted on the basis of these ancient sources. The earliest opponents of the reform were quite right when they said that modern Venetian editions, and not ancient Greek or Slavic books, were used as models for the Nikonian texts. The main source for the reform was, in fact, the 1602 Venice *Euchologion,* as we demonstrate in the third and fourth chapters.

In studying the events of the reform, we saw that it was, in fact, a wholesale adoption of Greek customs. Nikon, encouraged by the tsar and by visiting hierarchs, such as Patriarch Makarios of Antioch, enforced the adoption of Greek usages, including, for example, the three-fingered sign of the Cross and the use of Greek-style vestments. Nikon went so far as to make public declarations of his preference for all things Greek. Acting in despotic fashion, and encouraging the adoption of foreign practices, he alienated the upper classes and provoked strong opposition from the xenophobic Russian populace. It would be easy to see many of the episodes in a humorous vein, were it not for the tragic results which ensued.

In the second chapter, we studied the chief personages in the reform, each of whom had a different background, education, and attitude toward the reform. By understanding the background, motivation, and attitude of its chief promulgators, as well as by analyzing the new liturgical books, we come to an entirely different perception of the reform.

Nikon was the upstart, who rose from a provincial, peasant background, to achieve the second-highest position in Muscovite Russia. As a member of the circle of zealots, he actively participated in the movement to reform all aspects of church life, and to abolish moral and liturgical abuses. An able and intelligent man, he gained the love and respect of the tsar, and this ensured his rapid ascent in the church hierarchy. At first a member of the "provincial" group of zealots, who strongly mistrusted the Greeks, he eventually switched to the grecophile party, which was led by the tsar and his closest advisors. This party had a religious and political ideology, encouraged also by the numerous Greek bishops who constantly traveled to Moscow, which held that Moscow was now the capital of the Orthodox world, that the tsar was the new Orthodox emperor, and heir to the Byzantine throne and tradition. Nikon, a proud man and a lover of power, wholeheartedly adopted this program. Everything he did as patriarch, including the liturgical reform, was intended to manifest this ideal.

Nikon, we saw, also had his personal agenda, which was to establish the supremacy of the church over the state. Already as Metropolitan of Novgorod, Nikon succeeded in being exempted from the provisions of the *Ulozhenie,* a 1649 Code of Law which restricted the power of the Church over its lands. Later, as patriarch, he did everything in his power to aggrandize the Church vis-à-vis the state. As long as he could count on the friendship and support of the tsar, he was able to have his way. But once that support began to fade, Nikon's numerous enemies wasted no opportunity to undermine his position, and his brilliant ecclesiastical career came to an abrupt end.

These facts about Nikon are well-known; but what is not so well understood is the place of the liturgical reforms in his agenda, and his role in carrying them out. We showed that Nikon was not the initiator of the book reform, which had begun already under his predecessor, at the instigation of the tsar and the tsar's close advisors. Moreover, Nikon's personal role in the reform was generally limited to externals, to such things as the manner of making the sign of the Cross, the number of prostrations at the Prayer of St Ephrem, and the style of vestments. He did not know or understand the work that his correctors were doing in the Printing Office, and apparently believed that the new books were being published on the basis of ancient sources. Nikon's own interest was in making the ritual look Greek, and he cared little for the substance of the reform. His real passion lay elsewhere, as in the building of Greek-style monasteries, and in presiding over splendid ceremonies, and in increasing the wealth and glory of the Moscow Patriarchate. Like many Russians, Nikon focused primarily on externals. He would stand at services for hours on end wearing vestments weighing hundreds of pounds; he fasted rigorously and led a strict prayer life. In public, he conducted ornate services, built splendid monasteries and churches, and acquired all the titles and trappings of power. All this was, for him, visible proof that Moscow was indeed the Third Rome.

The real impetus for the reform of the liturgical books, as we have shown, came from the tsar. Nikon was but the person selected by the tsar to implement his program. The patriarch lost interest in the reform even before he abandoned his throne, and it was only due to the continued strong support of Alexis that the book reform continued unimpeded, despite mounting opposition. The tsar's will was expressed at the 1667 Moscow Council, attended by Greek patriarchs, which deposed Nikon, but upheld the new books in no uncertain terms.

Alexis, very pious himself, sincerely sought to forge a new Byzantine empire, with the Russian tsar at its helm. In order to accomplish this, he believed it was necessary somehow to change the prevalent Russian view that the Greeks had lost the true faith, after the Council of Florence and the subsequent fall of Constantinople. One of the chief issues constantly brought up by Russians, as evidence for the heresy of the Greeks, was the difference in liturgical practices. The Russians, we have seen, equated liturgical practice with dogma. Differences in ritual could only be explained as errors on one side or the other. Thus it was evident, for the

Russians, that the Greeks, with their different liturgical practices, were heretics.

Like all peoples, Russians were strongly attached to their customs, but there was more to it than that. When the Russians received Christianity from the Greeks, what they in fact acquired was a set of liturgical practices, through which the faith was mediated. But the Russians did not succeed in absorbing a more essential aspect of this received Christianity: the rich theological synthesis of the Byzantine Church, which underlay the Byzantine liturgical tradition. Not understanding its underlying meaning, they identified the externals—rites and rubrics—with the very essence of the faith.[1] Hence, for them, any change in the external, or the merely accidental, meant a betrayal of the truth, which had to be unchangeable. Since the Russians had no conception of liturgical evolution, or rather rejected its very possibility, they could explain differences in practice only as heresies. The adoption of Greek models was, for them, a condemnation of the Russian past—a rejection, rather than an affirmation, of the Moscow-Third Rome ideology.

Alexis, who wanted to unify the Greeks and the Russians, and to forge the new Byzantium, thus launched a program to unify Russian and Greek liturgical practice. For this purpose, beginning already in 1649, he dispatched the monk Arsenii Sukhanov on several journeys to the Greek lands, to observe Greek liturgical rites, and to collect Greek books and manuscripts. Arsenii faithfully fulfilled his orders: but the books he brought back consisted chiefly of classical and patristic works, and not liturgical sources! The reason for this is obvious. The planned liturgical reform was intended not as a return to ancient practice, but as an alignment of Russian with contemporary Greek practice. For this, the ancient books were not needed. It was only because Russians identified rubrics with dogma that the authorities had to present the reform as a return to the ancient sources: for in ancient times, the Russians believed, Greek and Slavic practice did not diverge. In the same year that he first dispatched Sukhanov to the East, the tsar requested that Kievan scholars, competent in translating books, be sent to Moscow. So the reform was already under way, well before Nikon's ascendancy to the patriarchate.

We saw how ruthless Nikon was in imposing the new books. Alexis took a different approach. He remained in contact with the leading opponents of the reform, including Avvakum, right up until the 1666-1667 Moscow Councils. He sought repeatedly to persuade them to cease their condemnation of the new books as heretical, and was willing to allow them to continue using the old books. This, I believe, indicates the real purpose behind the reform: Alexis simply wanted to change the prevalent Russian attitude which rejected the full orthodoxy of the Greeks. Only after he had failed in repeated attempts to bring this about, did he finally convene a council which anathematized the Old-Believers and condemned previous Russian liturgical practice.

We took a brief look also at the two chief implementers of the reform: Arsenios the Greek and Epifanii Slavinetskii. These two, both highly educated men for the period, did much of the translation and editorial work necessary to publish the new liturgical books. In translating liturgical, patristic, or theological works, both followed a standard method: first, they worked exclusively on the basis of published texts; second, they slavishly followed the original, often keeping the same word-order and even creating calques, in an attempt to be absolutely faithful to the original. These were not liturgical scholars, able to work with and compare ancient manuscripts, or to make critical evaluations of texts. They were chosen for the task simply because they knew Greek. Not surprisingly, the result of their labors—the 1655 *Sluzhebnik* which we examine in the second half of our study—is a slavish copy of the Greek euchology which served as the original.

Arsenios the Greek, we saw, was an unprincipled adventurer, who changed his beliefs whenever the need arose. He was the very personification, for the Russians, of the decadence of the Greek Church. Plucked from a monastery in northern Russia, where he had been imprisoned, Arsenios was put to work by Nikon at the Printing Office. In Russian eyes, the presence of this Greek, a known heretic, was enough in itself to discredit the reform. How could such a person possibly produce "unspoiled" liturgical books? Here again, the typically Russian focus on externals, on Arsenios' past behavior, made it impossible for them even to consider the reform on its own merit.

In the first part of our study, therefore, we examined the history of the reform, based on the plethora of primary and secondary materials published in the context of the centuries-old polemics with the Old-Believers.

Our knowledge of the actual intent of the reform—to align Russian practice with current Greek usage—led us to a reevaluation of these materials from a different perspective. In this new context, we believe, the actions of the ecclesiastical and civil authorities, as well as the reactions of the Old-Believers, are more understandable.

In the second part of our work, we studied the new *Sluzhebnik* published under Nikon. A detailed comparison of this book with the contemporary Greek euchology confirmed the fact that the reform consisted, precisely, in an alignment of Russian and contemporary Greek usage. A line-by-line comparison of CHR, in the Nikonian edition, with the text of the 1602 Venice *Euchologion* demonstrated the complete dependence of the former on the latter. Texts "missing" from earlier Moscow editions were added, and rubrics were modified to agree exactly with the Greek edition. Nikon's correctors sought to preserve even the word order from the Venetian edition. Subsequent Moscow editions under Nikon contain further revisions based chiefly on additional materials made available by the Greeks: the commentaries on the liturgy by John Nathaniel, and the conciliar letter of Paisios of Constantinople, both published in Nikon's *Skrizhal'*, and the description of the hierarchal liturgy by Patriarch Athanasios Patellarios. In a few cases, materials were also borrowed from Striatin and Kievan editions, which also had been published largely on the basis of Greek Venetian editions during the first half of the 17th century.

Thus Nikon's reform can in no way be considered a "correction." The only significant correction is in the text of the eighth article of the Creed. Other changes, far from being corrections, are, in fact, innovations in the text. Obvious examples are the interpolation, into the formulary of both CHR and BAS, of the Troparion of the Third Hour at the epiclesis,[2] and of the words from CHR, "changing [them] by your Holy Spirit," into the epiclesis of BAS. Inconsistent rubrics in the Venetian editions are kept unchanged in the Moscow *Sluzhebnik*. The reform, therefore, was nothing but the uncritical transposition of current Greek practice onto Russian soil. But this, we have seen, was its very intent!

In the present study, we dealt only with CHR and, to a limited extent, with BAS. This was sufficient to indicate the nature of the reform. But other services, PRES, Matins, and Vespers underwent much the same scrutiny, and were similarly "corrected" to make them conform to contemporary Greek practice. A study of these materials will be made available in a series of upcoming articles.

The consequences of the reform are well-known. A large portion of the Russian Church refused to accept the new books, and the resulting schism endures to the present. Russian liturgical practice, aligned with 17th century Greek usage, reached its present formulation, since very few additional changes were made in the next three centuries. Alexis' and Nikon's grandiose schemes of recreating a Byzantine empire never came to fruition, and Greek influence in Russia declined quickly, and disappeared entirely by the end of the century.

On the theological plane, the reform had little significance. Much has been said about Latin influence on the Nikonian books, but our study has shown that this influence was, in fact, minimal. A few latinized rubrics, such as the blessings at the Words of Institution in BAS, did indeed creep in; but these were isolated cases, and they were taken not from the Latins, or even from the latinized editions of Peter Moghila, but from the Greeks. The period of significant Latin influence in Muscovite Russia was to come two decades after Nikon's first *Sluzhebnik* appeared, and it had no direct connection to the liturgical reform. Indeed, Nikon's reform marked the final influx of Byzantine influence in Russia. Unfortunately, this influence manifested itself only on the visible, the external. The substance of the Nikonian reform, we have seen, consisted chiefly in rubrical changes, and in the expansion of secondary rites and formulae. The broadest changes were made in the entrance prayers before the liturgy, in the commemorations at the prothesis and the Great Entrance, and in the formulae of deposition of the gifts on the altar, after the Great Entrance.

It would be tempting and easy simply to condemn the entire reform. From a strictly liturgical perspective, there was certainly no pressing need to bring Russian practice in line with the Greek, as the Greeks themselves tried to persuade Nikon in the 1655 conciliar letter from Constantinople. The draconian measures employed to impose the new practices could well have been tempered. The reform might have been more successful had it been accompanied by a program of education, such as that instituted by Peter Moghila in Kiev only a decade earlier.

The real issue, however, was not liturgical, but ecclesiological. The

"Moscow-Third Rome" ideology held by the majority of Russians in the 17th century was, in fact, a form of narrow, triumphalistic nationalism. Muscovites identified the universal church with the Russian church and suspected the orthodoxy of all others. The Greeks, they believed, had lost the true faith, and this was proved by the fact that Greek liturgical practices differed from the Russian. Tsar Alexis, brought up in grecophile circles, sincerely desired the unification of the Greek and Russian churches. Not having a nationalistic conception of the Church himself, he sought to correct this attitude among the Russians. The way to do this, the tsar believed, was to unify Greek and Russian liturgical practice, for he was well aware that his countrymen identified the faith with liturgical minutiae. In the historical context, his actions make perfect sense.

To accomplish this project, Alexis and his advisors selected Nikon, who had shown himself an able and popular administrator as Metropolitan of Novgorod. But then the project went awry. Nikon alienated many, particularly in the upper classes, by his despotism. Worse yet was the presence at the Printing Office of a man such as Arsenios the Greek, who was totally discredited in Russian eyes. Arsenios' presence aroused the hostility, particularly, of the "provincial" circle of zealots, who distrusted Greeks anyway; these men, Avvakum, Loggin, and others, became the leaders of the Old-Believer movement. The tsar tried to pacify the opposition with repeated attempts at compromise, but by then it was too late. Thus, while the reform succeeded in its primary aim of aligning Greek and Russian practice, it failed to achieve its underlying goal.

NOTES

1. This situation is not peculiar to Russia. The conversion of the "barbarians" in northern Europe had similar disabilities, as recent French historiography has shown. See, for example, the study by Jean Delumeau, *Catholicism between Luther and Voltaire* (Philadelphia: Westminster Press, 1977). On the role of the liturgy in the life of the Russian Church, see also my article entitled "Reflections on Russian Liturgy: A Retrospective on the Occasion of the Millenium," *SVTQ* 33 (1989) 21-34.

2. The troparion existed in the pre-Nikonian editions, but was recited only at the option of the priest.

Index